T0301257

Religion and Finance

Religion and Finance

Comparing the Approaches of Judaism, Christianity and Islam

Mervyn K. Lewis

Emeritus Professor, University of South Australia, Adelaide and Emeritus Fellow, Academy of the Social Sciences in Australia

Ahmad Kaleem

School of Business and Law, Central Queensland University, Melbourne Campus, Australia

Edward **Elgar**
PUBLISHING

Cheltenham, UK • Northampton, MA, USA

Published by
Edward Elgar Publishing Limited
The Lypiatts
15 Lansdown Road
Cheltenham
Glos GL50 2JA
UK

Edward Elgar Publishing, Inc.
William Pratt House
9 Dewey Court
Northampton
Massachusetts 01060
USA

A catalogue record for this book
is available from the British Library

Library of Congress Control Number: 2018958451

This book is available electronically in the **Elgar**online
Economics subject collection
DOI 10.4337/9780857939036

ISBN 978 0 85793 902 9 (cased)
ISBN 978 0 85793 903 6 (eBook)

Typeset by Servis Filmsetting Ltd, Stockport, Cheshire
Printed and bound in Great Britain by TJ International Ltd, Padstow

Contents

Figures

Tables

Boxes

Preface

When a joint work is published, there is always the question of why the particular topic was chosen, and how the authors came to work together. In this case, the sequence was reversed. Dr Kaleem had obtained funding for a sabbatical spent at the University of South Australia, and he suggested to Professor Lewis that, in comparison with interest (usury, *riba*), non-interest financing was a relatively neglected topic, especially when it related to all three Abrahamic religions (Judaism, Christianity and Islam). This initial interaction resulted in a conference paper, 'Non-Interest Financing Arrangements in three Abrahamic Religions', published in 2014 (Kaleem and Lewis, 2014).

The idea was to follow up this research rapidly with a book, but for one reason or another the volume was delayed until 2018. By then, Mervyn Lewis had retired and he took on the major role of writing up the final draft, filling in some of the gaps in the original paper, and broadening the emphasis. As a consequence (and at Dr Kaleem's insistence) the authorship was reversed. Nevertheless, we wish to emphasize that both authors have contributed significantly to the final manuscript.

Overall, we would want representatives and adherents of all three religions to feel that they have been given due emphasis and 'a fair crack of the whip'. Nevertheless, where it is felt that criticisms and questionings are warranted, we have endeavoured not to shy away from doing so. All in all, it has, for us, been a joy (albeit burdensome at times) to prepare the volume, and we hope that our original objective of explaining the emphasis given to non-interest financing techniques has been realized. In general, our aim has been to provide readers with an understanding of the past, an examination of the present, and a look into the future.

Our wives are thanked for tolerating the time that has gone into the book. As in usual in books in which Mervyn Lewis is involved, Kay Lewis has been a faithful scribe and has, once again, kept the large numbers of references under control.

Glossary

Abd Allah: 'servant of God' in Arabic.

Adl: is an Arabic word meaning justice.

Ahl-al-kitab: is an Arabic term used for the People of the Book, e.g. Jews and Christians.

Allah: an Arabic word for God. Other frequent names are Al-Rahman (the Merciful) and Al-Rahim (the Compassionate).

Amanah: means fulfilling or upholding trusts, honesty.

Amin: term used for trustee in Islam.

Ariyah: a contract in which one party loans another the use of some item for an indefinite period of time.

Avak ribbit: the dust of interest. A term used in Jewish literature.

Bai or *bay*: sales in Arabic.

Bai' al-wafa' or *bai' al-'uhda*: sale of property under the condition to buy back after a certain time.

Bai bi-thamin ajil: alternate term used for deferred sale payment agreements mainly in East Asian countries.

Bai'muajjal: is deferred-payment sale.

Bai'salam: prepaid purchase. The term is mostly used in agriculture business.

Batil: is an Arabic word meaning falsehood, null and void.

Bayt al-Mal: state treasury department under Islamic governments in earlier times.

Brahmin: Brahmin is a *varna* (class or caste) in Hinduism specializing as priests, teachers and protectors of sacred learning across generations.

Bukhl: miserliness in Arabic.

Canon: an authoritative decree by an ecumenical council.

Carati: initial form of limited liability shares during the thirteenth century.

Cardo: Christian ethics drawing upon ancient understanding or moral wisdom, especially the cardinal virtues, where cardinal comes from the Latin *cardo*.

Caveat emptor: let the purchaser beware (i.e., he buys at his own risk).

Cocchi-Compagni: amount donated to the Church as a gift and mentioned in a will.

Collateralized debt obligation (CDO): is a type of structured asset-backed security (ABS), originally developed for the corporate debt markets.

Commenda: a form of partnership used during the Middle Ages.

Compagnia: term used for shipping companies or corporations during the medieval period.

Contractus trinus: triple contact devised during medieval years to avoid usury charges from the Church.

Damna et interesse: compensation paid for the non-fulfilment of a commercial contract.

Damnum emergens: represents the actual reduction in the economic situation of the person who has suffered damage and the loss of profits (*lucrum cessans*).

Decalogue: The Ten Commandments.

Dhimmas: is a historical term referring to non-Muslims living in an Islamic state with legal protection. The word literally means protected person.

Eudaimonia: Greek word used for happiness or welfare.

Fard kefaya: is an Islamic term that denotes a religious duty commanded by Allah (God).

Fardh: responsibility or duty.

Fasid: this is an Islamic religious concept which means corruption, defective or voidable.

Fiqh: Islamic jurisprudence.

Fondaco: European trading houses or overseas colonies.

Fuqaha: Islamic jurists, scholars, lawyers.

Gemara: Aramaic for completion or tradition, a rabbinical commentary on the Mishnah, forming the second part of the Talmud.

Geneivat da'at: Jewish term which means creating a false impression.

Gharar: Arabic term for uncertainty, hazard, chance or risk.

Gospel: the teaching or revelation of Jesus.

Hadith: the authentic tradition or sayings of Prophet Muhammad.

Hajj: Muslim pilgrimage to Mecca.

Halacha (*halakha, halakhah, halachah*): Hebrew, 'to go'; Jewish law and jurisprudence, based on the Talmud.

Halal: activities or goods which are allowed under Muslim law.

Hanafi school: it is one of the four religious Sunni Islamic schools of jurisprudence (*fiqh*).

Haram: goods or activities which are prohibited in Islam.

Hetter iska: this is a form of partnership agreement allowed under Jewish law.

Hiba: means gift in Arabic.

Hirs: this is an Arabic word for greed.

Hisba: Arabic term for supervision or monitoring.

Hiyal: Islamic terminology used to avoid straightforward observance of Islamic law in difficult situations while still obeying the letter of the law.

Hobbesian: relating to or characteristic of the ideas of English philosopher Thomas Hobbes, known as the father of social contract theory.

Ihsan: term used in the Qur'an for goodness, kindness, benevolence.

Ijara: term used for leasing under Islamic finance.

Ijara wa iqtina: Islamic finance term for hire purchase or lease purchase.

Ijma: the collective judgments of learned Muslim scholars.

Ijtihad: effort, physical or mental, expended in a particular activity, is an Islamic legal term referring to independent reasoning or the thorough exertion of a jurist's mental faculty in finding a solution to a legal question.

Ikhtiy'ar: free will or free consent.

Iktinaz: hoarding of wealth in Arabic.

Infaq: spending to meet social obligations.

Insan-i-kamil: means the person who has reached perfection; literally, the complete person.

Interesse: denotes the compensation made by a debtor to a creditor for damages caused.

Iqra: recite in Arabic.

Iqtisad: Arabic word for moderation.

Iron flock: it was a partnership cum debt agreement among the Jewish community.

Iska: an investment agreement or joint venture partnership under Jewish law.

Israf: extravagance in Arabic.

Istislah: public interest, or a method employed by Muslim jurists to solve problems that find no clear answer in sacred religious texts.

Istisnaa: Islamic finance term for prepaid purchase in the manufacturing sector.

Jubilee: a year of emancipation and restoration under ancient Hebrew law to be observed every 50 years.

Kadis: term used for judges and judicial magistrates in Islamic countries.

Khilafah (Caliph): representative of God on Earth. The term used in the Islamic world for a position similar to Pope in Christianity.

Khums: an Islamic tax levied on income generated from mining.

Kosher: food prepared according to the requirements of Jewish law.

Kshatriyas: Hindu caste, which means warriors.

La ilaha illa llah, Muhammadu rasulu llah: in its alternative translation, 'There is no God but the God and Muhammad is his Prophet'.

Lifnei ivver: term used for ill-suited advice under Jewish law.

Lucrum cessans: the interest or damages awarded for loss of reasonably expected profits or for loss of use of property.

Mafasid: Arabic term for social disutilities, corruption, rottenness.

Masalih: social utilities.

Maysir: Arabic word for gambling.

Meezan: Arabic term for balance or scale.

Messer Domineddio: literally means 'Mr God-Our-Lord'. Setting aside certain money under the name of God during fourteenth-century Florence.

Mishnah: The oral tradition of Jewish law.

Mitzvot: Religious precepts under Jewish law.

Mora: intentionally delaying the repayment of outstanding loans.

Mortgage-backed security (MBS): this is a type of asset-backed security that is secured by mortgages.

Mozaraah: Arabic term for joint cultivation.

Mudaraba: Islamic profit and loss sharing partnership where investors usually act as sleeping partners.

Mudarib: the term used for an entrepreneur in Islamic partnership.

Mufawada: meaning an unlimited, unrestricted and equal partnership.

Murabaha: is resale with a stated profit; for example, the bank purchases a certain asset and sells it to the client on the basis of a cost plus mark-up profit principle.

Musharaka: joint venture profit and loss sharing in Islamic finance.

Muslim: is one who professes the faith of Islam or is born into a Muslim family.

Mutuum: a term used for usury or profit during the thirteenth century.

Neshekh: term used for interest in Hebrew Bible, which means bite.

New Testament: the second part of Christian Bible.

Old Testament: first part of Christian Bible.

PBUH: peace be upon him.

Pentateuch: Greek word meaning five books: Genesis, Exodus, Leviticus, Numbers, Deuteronomy.

Prestanza: this is a first permanent debt fund established in Italy in 1164.

Qard hasan: Islamic interest-free loan without any specific repayment date.

Qist: term used in the Qur'an for equity or fairness.

Qiyas: analogy from established law.

Rabbinical: Jewish law or rulings expounded by a qualified rabbi.

Rentes: annuity-based contracts established in the early fifteenth century in Europe.

Riba: literally excess or increase, and covers both interest and usury.

Riba al-buyu: it relates to usury involving trade.

Riba al-fadl: it is an exchange of unequal qualities or quantities of the same commodity simultaneously.

Riba al-nisa: involves the non-simultaneous exchange of equal qualities and quantities of the same commodity.

Riba al-qard: it constitutes any excess amount paid for extension of a loan's maturity date.

Ribbit: in Judaism a construct of *tarbit* (increase), prohibited for the lender to charge and for the debtor to agree to make (i.e., interest payments).

Sabr: patience in Arabic.

Sadaqat: optional charity under Islamic law.

Sadaq-e-jaria: term used for an endowment fund under Islamic law.

Sahib al-mal or *rabb al-mal*: term used for investor in Islamic finance.

Salam: tranquillity, inner peace or to remain whole.

Salat: Muslim prayer.

Saracen: term for an Arab or Muslim, especially at the time of the Crusades.

Sawm: Muslim fasting.

Sea loan: A type of commercial loan during the twelfth century where repayment was subject to the safe arrival of the ship.

Shahada: literally means witness of faith. This is one of the Five Pillars of Islam.

Shari'ah or shari'a: Islamic religious law derived from the Holy Qur'an and *sunna*.

Sharikah (or *sharika, shirkah*): is a society or parnership.

Sharikah al aamal: this partnership is created when partners jointly provide some specific services to their customers against services charges.

Sharikah al aqd: contractual or commercial partnership.

Sharikah al-inan: Islamic partnership agreement in which the partners may have equal equity but unequal rights to profit, unequal equity with equal rights to profit, or unequal equity and unequal rights to profit.

Sharikah al milk: property or proprietary partnership.

Sharikah al-wujah: here two or more entrepreneurs establish a credit partnership under joint liability. This arrangement is also known as partnership of the penniless (*sharikah al mafalis*).

Shetar iska: deed to create a partnership under Jewish law.

Shia: is a Shi'ite Muslim, whose members comprise about 10 per cent of the world population of Muslims.

Shi'ite: comes from the religio-political party championing the claims of 'Ali ibn abi Talib and his heirs to the rightful leadership of the community and to their status as Imams. Since the beginning of the sixteenth century, Shi'ism has been the official state religion of Iran and most of its followers live there, although there are communities spread across the Middle East.

Shura: Arabic term for mutual consultation or joint decision-making process.

Societas: a partnership agreement used during the medieval period in Europe where all partners are responsible for the profit and loss generated through business.

Sopracorpo: a type of financial instrument used by European business houses to raise additional capital during the fourteen and fifteen centuries.

Special purpose vehicle (SPV): it is a subsidiary of a company established to meet specific, predefined objectives (i.e., protected even if the parent organization goes bankrupt). The actions of an SPV are usually very tightly controlled and they are only allowed to finance, buy and sell assets.

Structured investment vehicle (SIV): a pool of investment assets that attempts to profit from credit spreads between short-term debt and long-term debt.

Sukuk: interest-free bonds issued under Islamic law.

Sukuk al-ijara: Islamic bonds issued with the backing of leased assets.

Sunna or *sunnah*: portion of Muslim laws based upon the sayings of the Prophet Muhammad.

Sunni: are orthodox Muslims and constitute the majority form of Islam, those who follow the *sunnah* (thus being called the *ahl al-sunnah*), and who do not recognize the authority of the *Shi'ite* Imams.

Sura (pl. *surat*): word used for chapter or portion of the Qur'an.

Talmud: the body of Jewish civil and ceremonial law.

Tarbit or marbit: meaning increase, it is a Jewish term for the recovery of interest by the creditor.

Tawakkal: trust in one God.

Tawarruq: this is an Islamic financial product which allows clients to raise money quickly and easily, in theory without breaking Muslim bans on interest. A customer buys an easily saleable asset from an Islamic bank at a marked-up price, to be paid at a later date, and quickly sells the asset to raise cash.

Tawhid: means unification or unity of God in Arabic.

Torah: (from the Hebrew, to teach), it is the Hebrew name of the Law of Moses or the Pentateuch, the first five books of the Old Testament.

Tosefta: Aramaic for additional or supplementary, a companion volume to the Mishnah.

Trinity: the three persons of the Christian Godhead: Father, Son and Holy Spirit.

Tzedakah: is used for both charity and righteousness, meaning that a person cannot become righteous without charity.

Tzniyut: term used for modesty in Judaism.

Ulama: Islamic religious scholars.

Umma: the whole community of Muslims bound together by ties of religion.

Usher: a term used of an Islamic tax on agricultural income.

Usura: it means enjoyment, denoted money paid for the use of money, and under canonical law meant the intention of the lender to obtain more in return from a loan than the principal amount due.

Wadia: means safe custody or deposit.

Wahhada: which means to unite, promise, unify or consolidate.

Waqf: Islamic laws to establish a trust or charitable organization.

YHVH: name of God in the Tanakh (canon of the Hebrew Bible). There are also titles in the Torah that ascribe to God names such as Elohim (god, or authority), El (mighty one), Shaddai (almighty), Adonai (master), Elyon (most high), Avinu (our father), etc.

Zakat: charity under Islamic law. Derived from Arabic *zakah*, meaning pure, it is one of the Five Pillars of Islam.

Zulm: injustice or the antonym of *adl* (justice). It is also used interchangeably for cruelty or unjust acts of exploitation, oppression, and wrongdoing, whereby a person either deprives others of their rights or does not fulfil his obligations.

1. Defining the issues in religion and finance

THE CHANGED GLOBAL ENVIRONMENT

At the time of writing (September 2018), it is ten years since the onset of the global financial crisis in September 2008. Ex-Chairman of the Board of Governors of the Federal Reserve System, Alan Greenspan, commenting in December 2008, stated: 'in the wake of the Lehman Brothers default on September 15th, 2008, the system cracked' (Greenspan, 2010). In fact, many, including ourselves, trace the beginnings of the crisis to much earlier, ranging from February 2007 to August 2007.[1] But whatever was the starting date, there is no question that the decade since has been dominated by the aftermath and its economic and financial consequences; moreover, in ways that were not foreseen at the time.

Three examples suffice to illustrate the point. First, there appears to be an increasing acceptance, albeit reluctantly, that the world economy since 2008 may have slipped into what former United States Treasury Secretary Larry Summers calls 'The Age of Secular Stagnation', a description that borrows from the concept of secular stagnation first put forward by the American economist Alvin Hansen in the 1930s. The failure of economies fully to recover from the 2008 financial crisis has left a legacy of weak economic growth, low or negative interest rates, rising asset prices, low wage growth, greater inequality and weak investment. In the particular case of interest rates, Jaime Caruana, former General Manager of the Bank for International Settlements, wrote in 2018:

> From a historical perspective, the protracted period of low nominal interest rates that we are currently experiencing is unprecedented. Since 1870, nominal rates in the core advanced economies have never been so low for so long, not even in the wake of the Great Depression of the 1930s. (Caruana, 2018, p. 1)

In an article published in *Foreign Affairs*, Summers (2016) considered that there is a risk that the current slowdown may prove to be enduring rather than cyclical, and that the world might still be only part way through a slow-growth era 'shaped by previously unthinkable and far-fetched policies' such as ultra-low interest rates, noting that at least two dozen countries have central bank policy rates just above or below the zero level, a position considered inconceivable even a few years ago. So as to bring about and sustain such low rates in their own countries, central banks in the G-7 collectively expanded their balance sheets since the onset of the financial crisis by a staggering $5 trillion. This figure is roughly twice as large as the gross domestic product (GDP) of the United Kingdom, and just less than one-third of the GDP of the United States (US). And this position has to be unwound without jeopardizing growth prospects.

On the same point, in an address in Frankfurt in April 2016, International Monetary Fund (IMF) Managing Director Christine Lagarde also expressed concern that the risks had increased of economies becoming trapped in what she called a 'new mediocre' of growth, the danger being that low growth can be self-reinforcing through 'negative effects' that are hard to reverse. In her words, 'the good news is that the recovery continues; we have growth; we are not in a crisis.' However, 'the not-so-good news is that the recovery remains too slow, too fragile, and risks to its durability are increasing' (Lagarde, 2016) – still the case in 2018.

Christine Lagarde's solution is to invest more in infrastructure. The policy mix that has driven monetary policy to such experimental, unprecedented extremes needs to change. 'While [monetary] accommodation should continue in most advanced economies, it is clear that monetary policy can no longer be the alpha and omega to recovery.' Rather, according to Lagarde, investing in badly needed infrastructure is an 'obvious area' of potential, boosting global aggregate demand today while laying the building blocks for future growth – how badly needed is illustrated dramatically by the collapse of the Polcevera river bridge in Genoa in August 2018.

Yet, and this is the second example, the advanced countries have not heeded the call. Only China keeps on building infrastructure seemingly without limits, and its experience is instructive, albeit controversial. No country has invested as much so quickly in infrastructure as has China over the past two or three decades. Moreover, it is encouraging other countries in Asia to follow its path via the Asian Infrastructure Investment Bank, which Larry Summers (2016) thinks is 'a valuable step forward, that should be strongly supported by the global community' (p. 8). Earlier in July 2014, China set up the Shanghai-headquartered BRICS New Development Bank, together with the other four members of the BRICS club: Brazil, Russia, India and South Africa (*The Economist*, 2014b). With these two new banks, along with the Silk Road Fund (a government body which takes minority equity stakes in infrastructure projects), China is seeking to export its infrastructure-led development model to the rest of the world under the 'One Belt, One Road' strategy (now 'Belt and Road') of President Xi Jinping, whereby the Chinese economy is bolstered by building physical infrastructure not just with its immediate and near neighbours (for example, the port facilities and motorways built in Sri Lanka), but in places as far afield as Europe, Africa and the Middle East (Wong, 2016).

When the market reforms began in 1979, China was predominantly agrarian, and the urban population was 19 per cent of the total (and only 10.6 per cent when Mao Zedung and the Communist Party came to power in 1949). By contrast, as of 2016, 779 million of China's 1.4 billion people (or 56 per cent of the population) lived in cities (Salt, 2016), and the 50 per cent watershed for defining an urbanized country was crossed in 2010. China now has seven cities with more than 10 million residents, 37 with at least 3 million, and no less than 170 cities with a population of at least 1 million (Wall Street Journal Custom Studio, 2016). Trillions of dollars spent on infrastructure ($300 billion alone on high-speed rail) has transformed China into an exemplar of modern urban transit, with a platform of expansive highways (such as the 65 000 km National Expressway Network), intercity rail networks and efficient ocean ports (Grimsey and Lewis, 2017).

Much of the differences reflect the reordering of the world economy, as the Chinese (and many East Asian economies) have forged ahead, while the West has been stunted by the overhang of the global financial crisis. In purchasing power parity (PPP) terms,[2] China is already the largest economy, while in 2030, China's GDP in PPP measures is forecast to be 16 per cent larger (ABS Treasury, 2017). Even in US dollar terms (that is, using market exchange rates rather than PPP adjusted rates), China seems likely to pass the United States between 2025 and 2030 (Iley and Lewis, 2013). Again, these data projections reinforce how dramatically the advanced world (Australia exempted) has been held back by the slow recovery from the financial crisis.

Third, a lot of the blame for the financial crisis is attributed to regulatory failures. Regulation is seen as being not only too lax, with authorities catering to private markets in order to reduce costly adherence to rules, but also poorly designed and inconsistent across countries, institutions and market segments (Kodres and Narain, 2012). Others point to 'systems failures', especially in the credit transfer process by which subprime and other low-quality mortgages were packaged into 'toxic' securities and the risks distributed across the globe, infecting banks in many countries (Weber, 2008). In response, there have been massive changes in most countries' bank regulation. A valuable summary, on a global basis, is provided by Six Shadow Financial Regulatory Committees from around the world in Litan (2011). In fact, the international dimension was immediately apparent as

Religion and finance

widespread failures occurred in risk management systems when evaluating the threats posed by the global chains of counterparties underlying derivatives, notably credit default swaps (CDSs) and securities such as synthetic collateralized debt obligations (CDOs) built on them (Das, 2011). Nor have the extra layers of regulation added recently stopped banks from behaving badly. For example, some large international banks appear to have been attempting to 'game' the system by manipulating interbank market rates such as the London Interbank Offered Rate (LIBOR).

It is on this basis that Gordon Brown, former Chancellor of the Exchequer and British Prime Minister, described the global financial crisis as 'the first crisis of globalization' (Brown, 2010). This is an important point, for as Iley and Lewis (2013) document, the US subprime crisis was most certainly not solely a US phenomenon and European (and other overseas banks) poured massive amounts into the mortgage market, and generated much of the excess liquidity that fuelled the crisis.

As Figure 1.1 illustrates schematically, most of the money flowed to the US banking sector via the 'shadow banking system', with the international linkages completed by the wholesale (interbank) funding markets. The shadow banking system was the creation of banks such as Citigroup, UBS and Goldman Sachs. They established specific-purpose highly geared investment vehicles (conduits, structured investment vehicles – SIVs) off-balance sheet, and these subsidiaries or funds invested in assets with a high

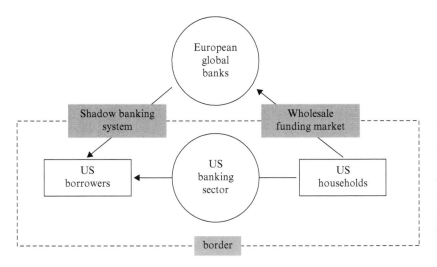

Source: Shin (2011).

Figure 1.1   European banks in the US shadow banking system

return and long duration (for example, structured finance products) and financed themselves by issuing asset-backed commercial paper, typically highly leveraged, 15–20 times the equity capital (Nyberg et al., 2008).

In fact, the whole purpose of this shadow system was one of deception. Employing off balance sheet vehicles in order to avoid regulatory capital meant that in practice the core banks were more highly leveraged than they appeared. SIVs set up by banks to pool loans into asset-backed securities borrowed short-term commercial paper and conduits for constructing mortgage-backed securities (MBSs), in effect enabling banks to develop extensive assets off balance sheet. While investors were presumably aware that these vehicles were autonomous legal entities with little or no formal recourse to the parent, when it came to the crunch the banks were unwilling to abandon the investment companies because of reputation risk. In any case, overlapping shareholders and officeholders, and the stream of management fees paid to the parents, complicated the legal standing of the bank-owned subsidiaries.

According to one observer: 'Few outside the banks themselves knew about the growth and extent of the grey, or shadow, banking system in the guise of conduits, SIVs etc., and since a main rationale for this shadowy sub-system was regulatory arbitrage, the banks were not loudly advertising such activities' (Goodhart, 2008, p. 3). 'Regulatory arbitrage' is a polite way of saying that the banks were again gaming the system by means of highly dubious financial practices; in short, misbehaviour. Banks which used to be seen as paragons of financial virtue have seemingly lost their way.

AN ALTERNATIVE PERSPECTIVE

Undoubtedly, the international, cross-border linkages described above demonstrate that globalization indeed was an integral part of the story. But to put the blame on globalization is to miss the point. There is an alternative interpretation, operating at a more fundamental level, that gets us closer to the heart of the matter, namely the role of greed and a faulty moral compass. From the viewpoint of the Holy religions a very different perspective emerges, and the crisis is the first of a very different kind. Aaron Levine, editor of the *Oxford Handbook of Judaism and Economics* (Levine, 2010a) calls it 'the first post-World War II recession that has its roots in widespread moral failure' (Van Biema, 2008). This is a position, as we shall see, with which Christianity and Islam are most definitely in agreement with Judaism. The starting point, according to all three religions, is that economic and financial activities cannot be divorced from ethics and morality. In this respect, the financial crisis stemmed from a lack of morality and a failure of conscience or sense of self-restraint on the part of those involved.

This alternative vantage point effectively defines our agenda. This book is not concerned with the global financial crisis as such. Nor is it focused on the global reordering of the world economy, or the policy responses that have ensued, except from the moral dimension. Rather, it examines ethical perspectives on such matters from the viewpoint of the three major religions in the Abrahamic tradition, namely Judaism, Christianity and Islam. Ethics can be considered to consist of general principles which help to determine rules of conduct. Any economic system requires a set of rules, a belief system to guide them, and a conscience in the individual which makes them carry them out. Rules can be based on natural law; they can also derive from religious laws, such as those which shape the business ethics for Jews, Christians and Muslims.

According to these religious laws, economic activities ought not to be separated from ethics and morality. In this respect, events in the last decade can be seen as having their roots in moral failure and a lack of conscience or sense of personal responsibility, for the history of morals is a movement from an almost unquestioned uniformity of conduct to an ever-increasing reliance on personal responsibility. Viewed in this light, the crisis can be seen to have had its origins in greed, deception, misleading contracts, excessive speculation, inappropriate incentives and bonuses, a lack of leadership and governance, usurious behaviour, and what has become known as 'financialization'. These faults have been compounded by monetary policy responses over the past decade (for example, ultra-low interest rates) that arguably do not pass the fairness test.

In view of the strong disapproval by the religions of the banks' behaviour, it is more than a little ironic – although not surprising – that the welfare and charitable services offered by the churches have been called upon and put under heavy demand by the hundreds of thousands, perhaps millions, of citizens in the Western world who have been forced into mortgage default and indebtedness by the actions of the banks. For example, in Australia the Brotherhood of St Laurence, the Salvation Army and the Protestant Uniting Churches have offered financial counselling services to distressed borrowers. Indeed, the Brotherhood of St Laurence has even provided small loans to low-income households to prevent them having to resort to the often exorbitant rates charged by the 'payday' lenders (Abraham, 2011).

OUR AIMS

The main objectives of this book are to:

1. explain the teachings of the Abrahamic religions, especially towards various social and moral values which are relevant to financial issues;
2. compare the religious attitudes of Judaism, Christianity and Islam with regard to the prohibition of usury and the role of interest;
3. explain possible reasons behind the institutional shift in Europe and Islamic countries from anti-usury laws towards usury-supportive contracts;
4. explore various partnership-based instruments, sale-based debt instruments and benevolent loans allowed and previously used in Judaism, Christianity and Islam; and
5. revive/develop some old/new concepts in finance which would be equally beneficial for all the stakeholders.

In order to explore these matters, the book is organized along the following lines.

Chapter 2 provides a detailed account of the three religions, in terms of history, denominational composition and fundamental beliefs. While the religions are examined separately, the links between them are outlined. Next, Chapter 3 examines why interest financing, and usurious behaviour generally, was so disfavoured by all three religions, and how they grappled with the problem in what appear to be very different ways (although the end result seems not so very different). Chapter 4 then sets out the social policy recommended by the Holy religions in terms of aspects such as brotherhood, justice, business ethics, private ownership, benevolence and charity, and so on.

Following on from this analysis, Chapter 5 outlines the recommended economic framework, and covers the principles and the practices of the three religions towards various sources of income and expenditure, to which is added the comments and views of various researchers. This chapter ends by comparing the economic teachings of each religion to highlight similarities and differences.

As intimated earlier in this chapter by the assessment of Aaron Levine (2010a), Judaism, Christianity and Islam differ markedly from conventional 'technical' and 'regulatory' explanations of the causes of financial crisis. There is, of course, a rich history of financial manias and crashes, but we do not need to move far beyond the events of the 'great recession' starting in 2006–2008 to illustrate most of the characteristics that typify a crisis. However, the Holy religions take a distinctive view of the basic causes in terms of human fallibility and what either was, or verged upon, immoral behaviour. This is the topic of Chapter 6, which also assesses post-crisis policies from an ethical standpoint.

An evaluation of non-interest financing arrangements forms a core subject matter of this study,[3] and to this end we consider various partnerships and equity-based financial instruments and their acceptability by religions. Chapter 7 provides a detailed discussion analysing and exploring similarities and differences in the equity-type financial instruments used in the Jewish, Christian and Islamic worlds.

Chapter 8 is developed on similar lines to the previous chapter, except that it analyses the various sales-based debt instruments permitted in the Holy religions. This chapter is further extended to the issue of public debt financing, and the debt instruments used by Islamic and Christian governments to finance their budget deficits and other spending policies. It ends by taking up the earlier brief analysis of Chapter 5 of what religious aspects and financial arrangements may have contributed to Muslim countries falling behind the West in recent centuries, an issue raised by Kuran (2011) and Rubin (2014) amongst others.

Chapter 9 attempts to pull some of the threads of this volume together in order to analyse the future of interest-free financing. It asks, first, why the ban on usury has been such an uphill battle for all three religions. The key question under examination here is why interest-based finance has been so seductive and difficult to resist. Then, because Islamic finance is the last bastion of the prohibition of usury, it seeks to establish the question marks that continue to hang over the authenticity of Islamic investment funds, the legitimacy of Islamic sales-based financing modes, and the *shari'ah* acceptability of most *sukuk* (Islamic bonds). Additionally, the chapter traces the evolution of modern Islamic financing from its beginnings to the present day, and asks whether current practices are pushing the system closer to or away from, the 'ideal'.

Finally, Chapter 10 takes all three religions to task for failing to deal effectively with what is, for them, the core issue of the abolition of interest/ usury/*riba*. Judaism takes advantage of what can only be called a double standard, and legitimized pseudo-interest arrangements. Christianity owns up to abandoning the prohibition, but in doing so the Christian West has, in effect, thrown the baby out with the bathwater by divorcing financial behaviour from ethical concerns. Islam, for its part, uses a variety of Islamic instruments to support the ban on usury. The reality is that Islamic banking appears to have chosen appearance over substance. Of course, the religions stand for much more than the prohibition of interest. But on this one point of comparison, none of them can really hold their heads high with any conviction.

NOTES

1. There is no doubt that 15 September 2008 was a seminal date. On the very next day, 16 September 2008, the Federal Reserve (virtually concurrently with the Lehman Brothers collapse) had to provide massive financial support to the insurance giant American International Group (AIG). In the words of Takeo Hoshi (2011), 'the government's decision to let Lehman Brothers fail in September 2008 led to the collapse of the entire financial system' (p. 124). More blunt is Charles Goodhart's (2011) observation that 'what was hideously expensive to all of us was the botched failure to rescue Lehman Bros, which instigated the panic and downturn' (p. 119). Notwithstanding the significance of September 2008, others such as Maurice Obstfeld (2011) have opted for August 2007 as the 'kick-off' date of the global crisis. Similarly, William Cline (2010, p. 261) argues that:

   > Two events marked the onset of the crisis. In July 2007, the investment bank Bear Stearns closed two MBS funds, and in August, the French bank BNP Paribas temporarily suspended withdrawals from three investment funds on grounds that the seizing up in the MBS market in the United States made it impossible to determine a fair valuation for withdrawals.

   While not denying that these events came as a considerable shock to investors, the obvious question to ask of Cline's dating is why, as he said, the mortgage-backed securities market had seized up. For this reason we are persuaded by Ian King of *The Times* that an earlier, seemingly inauspicious event 'lit the fuse of the financial crisis' (King, 2009). Just before midnight on 7 February 2007, HSBC issued the first profit warning in its 142-year history. Its statement admitted that slowing house prices had led to higher delinquency rates among American mortgage customers and that bad debts in the business would be 20 per cent worse than expected. As King notes, 'from there, the red ink started to flow'. Within days, shares in New Century Financial, Fremont General and Nova Star Financial, all specialist subprime lenders, went into freefall, as the true impact of problems in the subprime mortgage market started to become clear. On 2 April 2007, New Century Financial filed for bankruptcy when its 'warehouse' lenders ceased to provide new funding and margins calls by them could not be met (Frankel, 2009). By May 2007, UBS had closed its hedge fund division because of subprime-related losses, and a month later in June 2007 there was speculation that Bear Stearns was struggling due to its exposure to mortgage-backed bonds. Thus we see a strong case for February 2007 as the start of the crisis.

2. The main methods currently used to convert a country's national income in local currency to internationally comparable measures are the exchange rate and purchasing power parity (PPP) approaches. The exchange rate approach simply converts an economy's GDP into foreign currency (usually US dollars) at the official exchange rate. The PPP approach uses converters to adjust money incomes better to reflect the ability of a unit of local currency to purchase goods and services in its country of issue. It converts GDP in national currency to a PPP measure applying international prices for a standard basket of goods and services in the countries involved. In low-income countries, PPP measures of income per capita are usually higher than the official exchange rate measures and more accurately reflect actual living standards, as they adjust for the undervaluation – essentially because wages are low – of non-tradables (goods and services not traded internationally) in these countries (Iley and Lewis, 2013).

3. In this respect, this volume is a continuation of research originally commenced and initially reported in Kaleem and Lewis (2014).

2. The three Abrahamic religions

LINKS BETWEEN JUDAISM, CHRISTIANITY AND ISLAM

Judaism, Christianity and Islam are invariably described in all their forms as the three great monotheistic religions. For Judaism, there are Ultra-Orthodox, Modern Orthodox, Conservative and Reform denominations. In the case of Christianity, a greater diversity exists encompassing Catholicism, Eastern Orthodoxy, Russian Orthodox, mainstream Protestantism (Lutheranism, Calvinism, Church of England (Anglican), Baptist, Methodist, Congregational, Presbyterian, Unitarian) along with a wide, almost bewildering, range of Pentecostal, Evangelical and Charismatic groupings, and also other churches, such as Christadelphians, Seventh Day Adventists and Mormons. Islam divides principally into Sunni and Shia, but there is also Islamic mysticism, Sufism. All groups claim belief in the One (same) Divine Being, respectively Yahweh, God and Allah.

Yet, for many non-Christians, especially Muslims, the Christian belief in the Trinity (Latin = threefoldness), comprising God, Jesus and the Holy Spirit, in which Jesus is truly God and truly human, poses a stumbling block in terms of monotheism. One of the earliest Western creeds, the Apostles' Creed, dating from the end of the fifth century, illustrates the difficulty (see Box 2.1). It begins with God the Father, recounts the story of Jesus Christ, and ends with the Holy Spirit, the Church and the hope of Resurrection, so encompassing the major strands of the Christian belief system. As such, it offers both a coherent 'salvation history and an embryonic version of the Christian doctrine of the Trinity according to which God is both one (monotheism) and three (Trinitarianism)' (Woodhead, 2014, p. 22).

Nevertheless, there is a more embracing feature that unites the three religions. Judaism, Christianity and Islam are often referred to as the Abrahamic religions because of their genetic and spiritual links with Abraham. Abraham was the great father of a multitude of nations (quoting Genesis 17:4), with whom God made a covenant to multiply his descendants and to give them an inheritance: the Promised Land. Abraham

---

BOX 2.1   THE APOSTLES' CREED

I believe in God, the Father almighty,
creator of heaven and earth,
I believe in Jesus Christ, God's only Son, our Lord,
who was conceived by the Holy Spirit,
born of the Virgin Mary,
suffered under Pontius Pilate,
was crucified, died, and was buried;
He descended into hell,
On the third day he rose again;
He ascended into heaven,
He is seated at the right hand of the Father,
and he will come to judge the living and the dead.
I believe in the Holy Spirit,
the holy Catholic Church,
the communion of saints,
the forgiveness of sins,
the resurrection of the body,
And the life everlasting. Amen.

---

is the principal character in Genesis 12–25, along with his wives Sarah and Hagar. Through his son Isaac, his grandson Jacob and his nephew Lot, Abraham was the ancestor of the Israelites, and thus of the Jewish people.

Jesus was a Jew, and his genealogy links him directly with Abraham. For Christians Abraham also serves as a model of faith, a kind of spiritual ancestor. Abraham's oldest son was Ishmael, and from him other peoples were descended, including those we now call Arabs, one of whom was the Prophet Muhammad (pbuh),[1] the human selected as the 'Messenger of God' and the founder of Islam. Consequently, like Christianity, Islam has a genealogical link with Abraham; and for Muslims, too, Abraham is a model, especially in his surrender to God (which is what Islam means).

Coogan (2008) goes on to point out that Abraham's importance for all three religions is also clear in their scriptures. He is mentioned more than five dozen times each in the Old Testament after the narrative of his death in Genesis 25, in the New Testament and also in the Holy Qur'an.

The religions are further unified by their treatment of Jerusalem as the holy city. David, the second King of Israel and scion of a dynasty that lasted more than four centuries, at an early stage in his reign moved his capital from Hebron, the traditional site of the burial of Abraham and his family, to the non-Israelite city of Jerusalem, which then became known as the City of David. Then, to provide divine legitimation for his rule, he brought the ark of the covenant to Jerusalem, so that the city of David also became the city of God.

David's son, Solomon, built the First Temple there, so Jerusalem became the religious centre of ancient Israel and thus the geographical focus of Judaism. According to Coogan (2008), the prayer 'Next year in Jerusalem' near the conclusion of the Passover meal or Seder testifies to this centrality, as does the late biblical identification of the site of the Temple as the mountain where Abraham was to sacrifice Isaac (2 Chronicles 3:1).

As a practising Jew, Jesus went to Jerusalem to celebrate the Passover, and there, we are informed by the Gospels, he was arrested, executed, buried and, according to Christian belief, raised from the dead. Because these events took place in Jerusalem, it became the holy city for Christians.

Muslims accept as essentially valid the earlier revelations found in the Bible, and so for them Jerusalem is also sacred because of its associations with David, Solomon and Jesus. Originally, before Muhammad fell out with the Jews, Muslims prayed to Jerusalem rather than Mecca. Jerusalem's status for Muslims is further enhanced because, according to Muslim belief, the Prophet Muhammad himself was miraculously transported from Mecca to Jerusalem, from which place he was taken to heaven to converse with God.

Jerusalem's continuing importance as holy city for Jews, Christians and Muslims – and hence as focus of conflict in the Middle East – can be traced back to King David having made it his capital more than 3000 years ago.

Finally, the three religions are linked by the chain of prophets. The Greek word from which 'prophet' is derived means someone who speaks for someone else, and more specifically is an interpreter of a divinely given message from God. The Decalogue (Ten Commandments) delivered to Moses at Mount Sinai is the clearest example of prophethood, at least in the biblical sense of intermediaries between God and humanity (rather than those also called prophets who foretell the future). Christianity worships all of the Old Testament prophets, to which is added of course Jesus in his distinctive role as Man-God, although he is unrecognized in Judaism but seen as a prophet in Islam (albeit a special one, since he greets Muslim and other believers on the Day of Judgment).

The beliefs of Islam are those of simple, uncompromising monotheism, building on the Judaeo-Christian tradition but rejecting anything in it that could be interpreted as tending towards polytheism, such as the divinity of Christ or the doctrine of the Trinity. Christ is accepted as prophet, and is, throughout the Holy Qur'an, referred to as 'Jesus, son of Mary'. For Muslims, Jesus, revered as a messenger of God, was neither his son, nor a God himself.

In fact, Islam is the only non-Christian religion that makes it an article of faith to believe in Jesus as a prophet. The Holy Qur'an simply disapproves of the worship of Jesus and Mary besides Allah, which is seen as conflicting with true monotheism, and also exonerates Jesus from having so advised his followers. But a Muslim is not a Muslim unless they believe in Jesus and all the prophets of Allah. Thus Muslims also revere the Old Testament prophets, Abraham (Ibrahim in Arabic), Moses (Musa), Jacob (Yacub), Joseph (Yusuf), David (Dawud), Solomon (Sulaiman), and so on.

Having considered some of the similar beliefs and shared genealogical links between Judaism, Christianity and Islam, we now turn to examine the religions themselves, and some of the major differences that contribute to shaping their views on finance.

JUDAISM

How Old is Judaism?

This may seem a strange question to pose. Judaism is generally regarded as the oldest of the three religions. Christianity builds on the Old Testament and the more than 3000 years of Jewish history. As we noted above, Muslims also recognize the prophets of the Land of Israel and view the messages of Moses and Abraham as precursors of the teaching of the Prophet Muhammad.

Notably, neither the message of the Holy Qur'an nor that of Jesus envisaged the creation of a new religion. The Holy Qur'an teaches that God sent a series of messengers and prophets, merely claiming the Prophet Muhammad to complete their message and being the last of the prophets. Many of the familiar stories and names of the Bible are to be found in the Holy Qur'an. Twenty-eight prophets are recorded in the Holy Qur'an and all of them, except the Prophet Muhammad, are written about in the Jewish and Christian scriptures, although differences exist in the narrations and in the details. In this respect, the Holy Qur'an proclaims no originality in the sense of presenting a new religion. Rather, it revives and fulfils the same message which it maintains God has given to all the prophets throughout the ages and to every people, from Adam through to Jesus, and the Prophet Muhammad.

For a considerable time, perhaps until in the middle of the first century – that is, the generation after Jesus – there was no dividing line between Judaism and Christianity. Jesus, indeed, never thought of himself as preaching a religion other than Judaism, or Torah. Not only did Jesus as a Jew draw his spiritual nourishment from the Old Testament, he conceived his ministry and death in terms of it. He saw himself as its 'fulfilment' in the broadest possible sense of that word: 'Do not think I have come to abolish the Law or the Prophets; I have come not to abolish but to fulfil' (Matthew 5:17). Had Jesus or any of his disciples been asked what religion they were, they would have replied, 'Jewish'.

Doubtless the attitude of Christ himself permeated the way in which the early Christian Church regarded the Old Testament. However, in addition, it must be remembered that there was not then a New Testament. Early Christian writers accepted the Jewish scriptures as authoritative, as they were still writing the New Testament. In the words of Reverend Dr Abba (in whose house in Swansea, Wales, the first-named author stayed in 1973):

> The Old Testament was the first Christian Bible. It was not merely a part of the sacred Canon as it is today; it was the only Bible the early Church had. The Scriptures which were read when the first Christians assembled to break bread were the Old Testament Scriptures. The texts from which the apostolic sermons were preached were Old Testament texts. And when in course of time the New Testament Canon took shape, it did not displace or supersede the Old Testament Scriptures but was added as an appendix to them. (Abba, 1958, p. 49)

Solomon (2014) says that two 'stories' are told about how the two religions of Judaism and Christianity came to split apart and become separate, even while remaining intimately related, at least theologically. According to the traditional Jewish story, Judaism is an ancient religion communicated by Moses at Mount Sinai and preserved by the Jewish people unchanged ever since. At some time in the first century, Jesus followed by St Paul set up a new religion, borrowing important bits from Judaism, abandoning the commandments, and mixing in some strange and incorrect ideas such as the notion that Jesus was the promised Messiah or even the incarnation of God.

By contrast, the Christian interpretation diverges when Jesus enters the scene. Naturally, of course, the traditional Christian story also accepts that Judaism is an ancient religion, received by Moses at Mount Sinai and carefully maintained by the Jews ever since. At some time in the first century, Jesus came and 'perfected' this religion, bringing it to its fulfilment. Unfortunately, the Jewish people did not appreciate what had happened, and continued with the old form of the religion, now rendered incomplete. Nevertheless, on these accounts, there would seem to be agreement that Judaism is the 'mother' religion, and Christianity the 'daughter', if (at least in the Jewish view) an errant one.

Yet, Judaism is not as old as is generally assumed to be the case. Judaism, as we know it today, means much more than these historical roots (and it is perhaps worth observing that, according to Coogan, 2008,

p. 31, 'not a single person or event known from the books of Genesis through to 2 Samuel is mentioned in a contemporaneous nonbiblical text').[2] Our understanding of Judaism today is that of rabbinic Judaism, the way of life formulated by the rabbis from about the second century onwards, and rooted in the Bible. This rabbinic Judaism is the foundation of all the forms of Judaism that exist nowadays. For both Reform and Orthodox Jews, rabbinic Judaism is the reference point for their own beliefs and practices.

While it runs counter to conventional thinking, and as strange as it may seem, the Talmud and other founding texts of rabbinic Judaism were actually written later than the Gospels, which were the founding texts of Christianity. As Solomon (2014, p. 22) wryly observes, when Pope John Paul II referred to Jews as the 'elder brother' of Christians he in fact got it wrong. Both are, naturally enough, children of the Hebrew scriptures, but in terms of the religions' defining texts (New Testament or Talmud) it is Christians who appear in reality to be the 'elder brother'. On this basis, it seems incumbent upon us to examine how Judaism developed.

The Development of Judaism

Judaism is the religion of the Jews. But who are the Jews, and what is the meaning of the term 'Jew'?

> The word 'Jew' is simply an Anglicization, through Greek and Latin, of the Hebrew Yehuda (Judah), the name of one of the Twelve Tribes of ancient Israel. Judah was the main surviving tribe following the Babylonian Exile of 586 BCE, and came to be synonymous with Israel as a whole. (Solomon, 2014, p. 7)

As to who is a Jew, Table 2.1 sets out the main articles of faith and the various definitions of Jewishness. For Orthodox Jews, the answer and solution is simple and ancient (*The Economist*, 2012, 2014a): you are a Jew if your mother is Jewish, or if your conversion to Judaism accorded with the *halacha*, a conversion ceremony, which for a woman involves immersion in a ritual bath and a solemn commitment 'to accept the yoke of *mitzvot* (religious precepts)'. Followers of Christianity and Islam may be surprised to know that for Jews by birth this traditional test makes no reference to faith or behaviour.

However, there is another answer to the question of who is a Jew, for Jews were a 'special people', as it says in the Bible. The Jew was made conscious of belonging to a chosen people, of being a member of a nation which was in some way unique. In one sense, of course, the Jew was right. God, it was argued, had indeed chosen the Hebrew people out of all the

Table 2.1 Jewish denominations and articles of faith

	Source of the Torah*	Authority of religious law	Ritual and practice	Zionism and Israel	Definition of Jewishness
Ultra-Orthodox (*haredi*)	Dictated by God to Moses	All God-inspired and thus immutable	Minutely regulated by *halacha* and therefore unchanging, though emphasis may shift	Originally opposed to Zionism but most now accept Israel; significant immigration to Israel	Jewish mother, or converted by ritual immersion, circumcision (males), accepting the *mitzvot***
Modern-Orthodox	Dictated by God to Moses	As above, but interpreted more flexibly	As above, but some scholars are pushing for change, especially regarding women	See Zionism as a divine manifestation and Israel as religiously significant; substantial immigration	As above, but accepting the *mitzvot* interpreted more flexibly
Conservative	Inspired by God but interpreted by humans	Binding but being continuously developed by rabbis	*Halacha* significantly modernized; women and gay rabbis; ritual non-discriminatory	Support Zionism and Israel; not much immigration	As above, but *mitzvot* commitment interpreted much more flexibly
Reform	Inspired by God but interpreted by humans	No longer binding, except for its ethical aspects	Early radical changes but recent restoration of some rituals and practices	Originally opposed to Zionism; reversed position in mid-twentieth century; not much immigration	Jewish mother or father; for converts, some rabbis require immersion and circumcisions but not *mitzvot* acceptance

Notes:
* First five books of the Old Testament.
** Religious precepts.

Source: *The Economist* (2012).

nations of the earth to be the medium of his revelation to men. He had endowed them with special susceptibilities. He had spoken through their prophets and wrought mighty acts in their midst. They had been the vehicle through which he had revealed his will.

But this sense of vocation of destiny, which the Hebrew had in his very bones, could be wrongly interpreted by him in terms of political domination. He might even come to regard himself as belonging to a Herrenvolk – a superior race (Abba, 1958, p. 209). Indeed, 'Jehovah, they believed, would vindicate His people by making them the lords of the earth' (ibid., p. 210). It would be fanciful not to discern some echoes of this line of thinking in Israel today. Yet voices are raised against such views. As Abba points out: 'The Books of Jonah and Ruth are protests against this narrow nationalism, Israel's vocation, her people are reminded, is not to dominate but to serve; she is called to be missionary nation, to spread the knowledge of the true God throughout the earth' (ibid., p. 210).

Scriptual Sources

Certain key words feature in the Jewish scriptures, namely:

- the sacred writings (the Torah, the Prophets, the Writings);
- Pentateuch;
- Covenant;
- Decalogue (Ten Commandments);
- Talmud;
- Mishnah;
- Gemara.

We now examine how these form the Hebrew Bible and the development of rabbinic Judaism.

Hebrew Bible

By 'sacred writings' is meant the Jewish scriptures which had three parts: the Law, the Prophets and the Writings. These sources begin with the Pentateuch (from the Greek word meaning 'five books') which according to Orthodox Jewish tradition was revealed by God to Moses at Mount Sinai circa 1312 BCE (Levine, 2010b). This compilation comprises the first five books of the Bible: Genesis, Exodus, Leviticus, Numbers and Deuteronomy. It was called by the Hebrew name Torah, which is usually translated as 'The Law', but which really has the wider meaning of 'teaching' or 'instruction'. It was a series of books which instructed those who read them in the ways of God and his requirements for man. Here, then, was the nucleus of a sacred canon of scripture, and it is to these five books of the Torah that the Jews have always ascribed the highest authority.

The teaching of the great prophets has come down to us in the books which bear their names. It was not long before these prophetic works were placed alongside the Torah as sacred books. Before this was actually done, however, they were carefully studied and re-edited, and with them were placed the historical books of Joshua, Judges, 1 and 2 Samuel, and 1 and 2 Kings (the 'Former Prophets'). These books, which incorporate extracts from many ancient sources, were written for the purpose of interpreting the history of Israel in the light of the prophetic teaching and were therefore included with it in this second section of the Hebrew Bible which was called 'The Prophets'. The 'Latter Prophets' are the three major prophets Isaiah, Jeremiah and Ezekial, and the 12 minor prophets, the books of Hosea through to Malachi. A more lengthy selection process took place to define the limits of Old Testament canon, and was not complete until the first century after Christ.[3]

It resulted finally in a third compilation of books called the Writings being added to the existing scriptures of the Law and the Prophets. There was, however, some disagreement regarding what should be included in this third section and what should be left out. The Hebrew-speaking Jews in Palestine limited the number of books to Psalms, Proverbs, Job, Song of Solomon, Ruth, Lamentations, Ecclesiastes, Esther, Daniel, Ezra, Nehemiah, and 1 and 2 Chronicles, leaving out the books which comprise the Apocrypha, which were included by Greek-speaking Jews outside Palestine. Generally, Christians too have felt that the books of the Apocrypha are on a lower spiritual level than are those included in the Hebrew canon.

Consequently, by the end of the first century CE, these three components – the Torah, the Prophets and the Writings – had become the Bible of ancient Judaism, its 'sacred scriptures', that is, writings believed to be divinely inspired and thus having a special authority. For Jews today, they are simply the Bible. As Coogan (2008) points out, modern scholars often use the term 'Hebrew Bible' to distinguish those books from the Christian Bible, which includes the New Testament as well, and also because the designation of Old Testament, which was not used until the late second century CE, might be seen as pejorative, implying that the Jewish scriptures that comprise the 'Old' Testament have apparently been superseded by the later writings that form the 'New' Testament.

Note that the term 'Hebrew Bible' itself is something of a misnomer, since a number of chapters of these scriptures are not in Hebrew, but instead in the closely related Semitic language of Aramaic (the language of

Jesus). There were disagreements between the various Jewish communities about which books belonged to the category of sacred scripture. The Torah was fixed, as were the Prophets, but the Writings were more fluid, being an anthology of poetry, reflections on the human condition and historical narratives.

Covenant and the Decalogue

The book of Exodus records that, following their escape from Egypt, the Israelites headed toward Mount Sinai, where they arrived after a two-month journey. There Yahweh appeared to them with all the manifestations of the storm god – 'thunder and lightning, as well as a thick cloud' (Exodus 19:160) – and in a series of speeches to Moses gave the Israelites their laws. As well as 'instruction' or 'teaching', one of the meanings of the word Torah is 'law', and much of the Torah, the first five books of the Bible, consists of divinely given laws; according to early Jewish scholars, 613 in all.[4]

Most of these laws – called codes – are found in three main collections, these being the Covenant Code in Exodus 20:22–23:19, the Holiness Code in Leviticus 17–26, and the Deuteronomic Code in Deuteronomy 12–24.

Covenant in the biblical tradition is essentially a legal concept meaning 'contract', to describe the relationship between Yahweh and Israel. God made covenants with several individuals and groups in the Bible, including those with Noah and his offspring, Abraham and his offspring and, later, with King David and his dynasty. The most important, however, is the covenant between God and Israel at Mount Sinai.

Unquestionably, the text of this contract or covenant is the most famous of the several ancient particular Israelite law codes or collections: the Ten Commandments or the Decalogue, the latter being seen by Coogan (2008) as a more accurate translation of what the Hebrew Bible calls the 'ten words'. Box 2.2 sets out an abbreviated version of the Decalogue.

Until the seventeenth century, the prevailing view of the Old Testament among both Jews and Christians was relatively simple: it was the word of God. Its human authors were in effect scribes or secretaries, writing down what God dictated to them. God revealed the entire contents of the Torah to Moses, who wrote it down. The ultimate authority therefore was divine, and Moses was the supreme human authority. That tradition was also accepted by the writers of the New Testament (many of whom were Jewish themselves).

With the development of modern philosophy and modern science, however, that prevailing view changed irrevocably, as previously unquestioned

---

BOX 2.2   TEN COMMANDMENTS (ABBREVIATED)

I am the Lord your God, who brought you out of the land of Egypt, out of the house of slavery; you shall have no other gods before me

You shall not make for yourself a statue, or any image of what is in heaven above, or on the early beneath, or in the water under the earth. You shall not bow down to them or worship them; for I the Lord your God am a jealous God . . .

You shall not make wrongful use of the name of the Lord your God, for the Lord will not acquit anyone who misuses his name

Remember the Sabbath day, and keep it holy. Six days you shall labour and do all your work. But the seventh day is a sabbath to the Lord your God; you should not do any work . . .

Honour your father and your mother, so that your days may be long in the land that the Lord your God is giving you

You shall not murder

You shall not commit adultery

You shall not kidnap

You shall not bear false witness against your neighbour

You shall not covet your neighbour's house; you shall not covet your neighbour's wife, or his male or female slave, or his ox, or his donkey, or anything that belongs to your neighbour.

Source: Exodus 20:2–17.

---

dogmas were challenged from a variety of perspectives. In the study of the Old Testament, the first issue addressed was the authorship of the Torah, the first five books of the Bible. For example, did Moses really write the Torah? Another inconsistency was the different names used for God. There were also differences – it must be said, mostly minor – between the version of the Decalogue in Exodus, and that in both Deuteronomy and Exodus 334:11–26, with a very different set of 'ten words'.

Putting aside some of these differences, the Decalogue divides into two sections. The first part requires the worship of Yahweh alone, underlining monotheism. The second part of the Decalogue details the obligations of Hebrews toward their fellow Israelites, that is, their neighbours. The consensus is that all commandments were divinely given, and the tablets were written with the finger of God (Exodus 31:18).

Rabbinic Judaism

The teachings transmitted by the rabbis in the centuries following the destruction of the Second Temple formed the core of what has come to be known as rabbinic Judaism, which still provides the framework for the various types of Judaism practised today. Some describe rabbinic Judaism as the religion of the 'dual Torah', for as well as a written Torah (the Hebrew scriptures) it recognizes an 'oral Torah', or tradition, by which the written is interpreted and supplemented. It is not unusual to come across the terms 'written law' and 'oral law', but 'law' is not a fully accurate translation of Torah, which also means 'way' or 'instruction'.

According to Orthodox Jewish tradition, when God revealed the Pentateuch to Moses at Sinai, he concomitantly revealed to him the oral Torah, which provided a detailed interpretation of the commandments found in the Pentateuch. For many centuries, the oral Torah was not committed to writing, but instead it was kept alive by oral transmission from one generation to the next. Out of fear that the oral tradition would be forgotten, the oral Torah was eventually reduced to writing. This process occurred in two stages: the codification of the Mishnah in the Land of Israel and later the codification of the Talmud in both Israel and Babylonia.

The most widely studied of these rabbinic teachings are known collectively as the Talmud, which has two parts: Mishnah and Gemara. Solomon (2014) provides an invaluable summary for non-Jews (like the present authors) reproduced in Box 2.3. It is clear, as we noted earlier, that both post-date the New Testament Gospels. Given the much earlier Pentateuch and Decalogue, it is perhaps unfair to ask which religion is the elder, but the issue remains. The expression 'Talmud' is often used now for the Mishnah and Gemara together. In this sense, the Talmud is really the heart of present-day Judaism, and after the Bible (Old Testament or Old Covenant) is the work most studied by Jews.

BOX 2.3 TALMUD DEFINED

Talmud = Mishnah + Gemara

There are two Talmudim:

- The Talmud of the Land of Israel (also known as the Palestinian Talmud, or Yerushalmi, i.e. Talmud of Jerusalem), completed about 450 CE
- The Babylonian Talmud, completed about 550 CE. This is larger than the Yerushalmi, and considered to have greater authority.

Source: Solomon (2014, p. 35).

Mishnah

The Mishnah is the earlier work, compiled from the teachings of sages living at the end of the Second Temple period and in the century following the destruction of the Temple. Being a study book of laws and value statements that express the classical rabbis' vision of Judaism, the Mishnah's preoccupation is promotion of a religious and legal tradition both continuous with the past and practical for life in the post-destruction Diaspora. The Mishnah contains multiple opinions on many laws and does not often suggest which is the most authoritative. The plurality of Jewish practice is preserved in the text.

Gemara

Sages in both Babylonia (modern-day Iraq) and the Land of Israel continued to study traditional teachings, including the Mishnah, describing the teachings as having been passed down from Moses at Sinai (either literally or figuratively). The oral discussions were preserved, by either memory or notation, and later edited together in a manner that places generations of sages in conversation with one another. These teachers were interested in bringing greater harmonization between biblical and rabbinic traditions, largely by providing proof-texts for known laws and explaining differences between the biblical and rabbinic versions of laws. This is the origin of the Gemara (= 'learning', 'completion'), a vast Aramaic text that takes the form of a commentary on the Mishnah.

Babylonian vs. Palestinian

There are actually two works known as Gemara: the Babylonian Gemara (referred to as Bavli in Hebrew) and the Palestinian (or Jerusalem) Gemara (referred to as Yerushalmi). The term 'Gemara' itself comes from the Aramaic, giving it the meaning 'teaching'. The laws of the Mishnah are mostly presented in the form of factual cases rather than through simple statements of the legal principles in abstract form, whereas the basic structure of the Babylonian Talmud and the Jerusalem Talmud is a commentary on the Mishnah. Both Talmuds, however, go considerably beyond this description. In that respect, both Talmuds include and discuss sources that were not incorporated in the Mishnah.

The Role of History

Before the spread of Islam, toward the end of the seventh century, many of the tribes of North Africa had been converted to Judaism or Christianity. In what is now south-west Algeria, a powerful Berber tribe, the Jarawa, had become Jewish, led by Kahina, a powerful and, by reputation, fearsome Berber princess. With Kahina at their head the Jerawa defeated the Arab army of Hasan ibn al Nu'man, holding up the Arab invasion of Africa and preventing its further progress into Spain. Kahina, however, was betrayed and killed in battle around the year 700. Whatever she may have achieved for Judaism, the reality of her defeat left two constantly warring big powers, Christendom and Islam, with Jews reduced to subservience throughout both domains (Solomon, 2014, p. 37). This imbalance remains today, with Jews at 13.6 million in 2010, vis-à-vis 2 billion Christians and 1.5 billion Muslims. It is upon these two big religious powers of Christianity and Islam that we now focus.

CHRISTIANITY

Is It in Decline?

Growing secularism in Europe – the traditional heartland of Western Christianity – and the concomitant expansion of Islam there, means that today there may be as many practising Muslims in England as there are practising Anglicans. This juxtaposition has led some commentators to predict that Islam will displace Christianity as the most populist religion perhaps by 2050. Many Muslims believe that one day, due to its innate doctrinal superiority, Islam may become the religion of all mankind. Equally, some Christians consider that one day Christianity will be acknowledged by all and thus will come to dominate the world (Fuller, 2010).

In fact, Table 2.2 suggests neither prediction seems likely. Christianity

Table 2.2 Growth in the number of believers, 2000–2050

Religion	2000	2050
Christianity	1.99 billion	2.616 billion
Islam	1.188 billion	1.784 billion
Hinduism	811 million	1.1 billion
Judaism	14 million	16 million

Source: *Weekend Australian Magazine* (19–20 February 2011, p. 6).

may well remain the most populist, and there is also fast-growing Hinduism which remains in the mix. Judaism continues to be small, at least in terms of population. By way of contrast to the view that Christianity is being undermined by modernity, the period from the late eighteenth to the twenty-first centuries has witnessed its growth and extension to become the world's largest religion. Admittedly, it suffered in the twentieth century at the hands of communist regimes, but more importantly it benefited in the nineteenth and twentieth centuries from being the majority religion of two modern superpowers, first the United Kingdom, then the United States of America. And when Western imperialism waned in the course of the twentieth century, Christianity entered a new phase of revival and growth in Latin America, Africa and parts of Asia, shifting its numerical centre of gravity south, where previously its battles had been in the north between Western and Eastern Orthodoxy.

Christianity's revival has been aided by a number of factors. First, Kaufman (2010) demonstrates that more than 90 per cent of the world's population growth is happening in religious countries, particularly in Africa. Second, there are the missionary activities financed from the United States. Muslims prefer to read the Holy Qur'an in original Arabic, yet only 20 per cent of Muslims speak Arabic as their first language. Memorizing the Qur'an may be valuable (if only to expand Muslims' memory banks), but how many understand what they are memorizing? There are similarities here with Catholicism, which continued until the second half of the twentieth century to conduct church services in Latin (understood by few in the congregation and poorly even by some priests). Thomas Nelson publishes 60 different editions of the Bible every year. Because the Holy Qur'an, dictated by the Angel Gabriel, 'is not about the truth, it is the truth', Muslims are uncomfortable about translations (*The Economist*, 2007). Here Christianity's marketing skills come to the fore, financed by the world's richest and most powerful country, home to 80 million Evangelicals.

The Eastern Orthodox Church

Christianity is often seen as a Western religion because of the dominant role of Rome in the history of Christianity today, and over hundreds of years. But this view is to turn a blind eye to the significance of the Eastern Orthodox Church. In the words of Woodhead (2014, pp. 43–4):

> Despite Christianity's growth in Rome, it was in the eastern rather than the western part of the Roman Empire that its success would be greatest in the period of late antiquity. To view Christianity as a Western religion is to read later history back into early Christianity. In fact its greatest expansion and

BOX 2.4   EXTRACT FROM THE CREED OF NICAEA FROM
THE COUNCIL OF NICAEA IN 325 CE

We believe in One god, the Father, Almighty . . .
And in One Lord Jesus Christ, the Son of God, begotten of the Father, Only-
begotten, that is, from the substance of the Father
God from God, Light from Light, Very God from Very God . . .
And those who say 'There was when he was not' . . . The Catholic and Apostolic
church anathematizes.

Source: Woodhead (2014, p. 45).

most important centres were first established in the Greek-speaking East, not
the Latin-speaking West. This was reinforced by Constantine's transfer of the
imperial capital from Rome to Constantinople (previously called Byzantium,
today called Istanbul) between 324 and 330 AD, and by the gradual transformation of the classical Roman empire into the Christian Byzantine empire, which
survived until 1453.

With Rome 'already reeling under constant barbarian siege' (Fuller,
2010, p. 65), Byzantium – now Constantinople, which the Roman Emperor
Constantine named after himself – was seen as a more secure second capital of the widespread Roman Empire. And so it proved to be. Two distinct
centres of the Roman Empire were born – Western and Eastern – with
doctrinal differences to be resolved. However, the centre of gravity had
shifted to the East. When Emperor Constantine I convened an influential
Council in 325 CE to hammer out the basic principles of Christian theology, it was held in the East in Nicaea. In the form of the Nicene Creed,
it confirmed that Jesus shared the very essence of divinity (see Box 2.4).
Nevertheless, this Creed was not the last word, and more Councils had to
be held. The Nicene Creed was not the definitive statement on Christian
faith for all time, as had been intended.

Following the final collapse of the Roman emperor under the weight
of Germanic invasions in 476 CE, the Western wing came to an end.
Constantinople now inherited the full mantle of the Roman Empire, in control of vast swathes of the Balkans, Anatolia, the Eastern Mediterranean
and North Africa. One of the sources of legitimacy of the Eastern Church
was language. The remnants of the Western Church used Latin. Greek
was the lingua franca of the Eastern Mediterranean, and Greek culture
ruled. Christianity's New Testament was written in Greek, not Latin.
Interestingly, as Fuller (2010) points out, no emperor would ever again rule
over both Rome and Constantinople.

Yet, Constantinople's power could not last forever, despite what Fuller (2010) called its 'magnificent run of another thousand years' after the sacking of the Western Roman Empire. Hemmed in by the rise of Islam, limiting Eastern expansion, Constantinople and Byzantine lands, and thus the last segments of the Greek Empire, fell irrevocably to the Ottoman Turks in 1453.

While the Eastern empire fell, the Eastern Church was far from at an end. It sent missionaries to establish new linguistically based churches in Bulgaria, Serbia, Macedonia, Albania and Romania. Even Russia chose Eastern Orthodoxy; a choice that did little for improving the welfare and lot of the peasantry, a point emphasized by Jonathan Dimbleby in his book *Russia* (2008), where he observes:

> in *Russia under the Old Regime* the historian Richard Pipes has written a masterly analysis of the trajectory of Russian Orthodoxy. 'No branch of Christianity has shown such callous indifference to social and political injustice,' he writes, adding 'The ultimate result of the policies of the Russian Orthodox church was not only to discredit it in the eyes of those who cared for social and political justice, but to create a spiritual vacuum. This vacuum was filled by secular ideologies which sought to realize on this earth the paradise that Christianity had promised to provide in the next.' No one could put it better. (p. 94)

The East–West Divide

The result can be seen readily in Europe today. Serbs, Bulgarians, Romanians, Russians, and the southern half of Albania were converted to Eastern Orthodoxy. Rome converted the Poles, Czechs, Slovaks, Croats, Slovenians and Hungarians, who chose Catholicism. A sharp Latin–Orthodox 'fault-line' runs from the Baltic Sea through to the Aegean Sea, 'casting the die for the entire future political and cultural orientation of those countries that lasts until today' (Fuller, 2010, p. 71).

The fault-line also defines religious adherence. The Eastern Orthodox Christian Church remains the second-largest single Christian community in Christianity after Catholicism. Moreover, Russia constituted a huge geopolitical prize for Orthodoxy continuing to this day. Russia is the single largest Orthodox community in the world, and the only religious connection that the Orthodox Church possesses to a major world power. Yet, although the Orthodox Church in Russia remains a major force, Russia also contains the largest population of Muslims of any 'Western' country: some 20 million, or nearly 15 per cent of the overall population (Fuller, 2010, p. 163).

Although Orthodox communities are counted in the ranks of Christians alongside Catholics, marked differences exist between the two (although seemingly not as poisonous as that between Sunni and Shia Muslims if we judge that division in terms of the Middle East today). One was the 'Great Schism' in the Christian Church between Rome and Constantinople that broke out in 1054 CE, over what Fuller describes as an 'unbelievably arcane debate' (Fuller, 2010, p. 73). Constantinople insisted that the Holy Spirit proceeds directly from the Father, whereas Rome maintained that the Holy Spirit emanates from the Father and Son together. This division has yet to be reconciled. Also, Orthodoxy rejected the Roman Church's doctrine of the Immaculate Conception of Mary and the existence of purgatory; matters that had been adopted by Rome for many hundreds of years. Geopolitical rivalry undoubtedly played its part, and increasingly strained relations between the Eastern and Western Churches broke down completely in the thirteenth century when invading Western crusaders entered Constantinople. To this day, Latin-speaking Catholicism and Greek (and Balkan and Muscovy)-speaking Orthodoxy remain separate churches and religious cultures.

Most certainly the religious cultures differ considerably. Orthodoxy views religion as being about spirituality, and the liturgy (along with incense, splendid iconography, richness of garments) is designed to stir the heart and move the soul with the mystery of God. From their perspective, adherents to Orthodoxy consider that such spiritual qualities are diminished by the more secular environment in which Catholic and Protestant Churches operate in the West, along with their social concerns and political activities (matters which, to Western eyes, are sorely missing from the more aloof Eastern Orthodox tradition).

The Reformation

Christendom, it would seem, is particularly prone to schism. Once it is accepted – and this is the basic message of Protestantism – that each individual has the right to interpret God's word for himself or herself, it becomes much harder to maintain unity of the sort that marks Catholicism and Eastern Orthodoxy. The Reformation, that began with Lutheranism, Calvinism, Anglicanism (Episcopalian), and was followed by Methodists, Congregationalists, Presbyterians, Baptists, Quakers, then Mennonites, Amish[5] and Mormons, has ballooned out to a bewildering range of evangelical, charismatic and other denominations.

The (Protestant) *Dictionary of Christianity* (Barrett, 1990) estimates that 20 800 different Protestant denominations are in existence today. The *World Christian Encylopedia* (Barrett et al., 2001) places the total at an astonishing 33 820. While the precise figure can be questioned, these numbers undeniably reflect the fruits of the seeds sown by the Reformation. Fuller (2010) considers that such proliferation validates fully Catholic fears about the consequences of loosened centralized control over church doctrine and hierarchy. On the other hand, it can be argued that an advantage that the Christian West enjoys is religious freedom (for example, as guaranteed by the US constitution). The United States, as we have noted, has 80 million Evangelicals. (Fitzgerald, 2017, describes Evangelicalism as a religion of the heart, as opposed to the head.) Free entry and open competition in product and service markets is the basis of free market economics, and it would seem to be a boon to growing religion as well. Or, to put it another way, 'American Evangelism has flourished precisely because America has no official church' (*The Economist*, 2007, p. 77).

Christian Beliefs

This diversity of Christianity makes it difficult to summarize the essence of Christianity in a few words. Rather than attempting to do so, we refer readers to Woodhead's (2014) Oxford volume and additionally draw upon two studies, both cited in Wilson's (1997) valuable survey. The first is by Wogman (1986), in which six features of Christianity are singled out, two relating to beliefs and four to ethics and behaviour. The central beliefs are the physical existence of God's creation and the priority of grace over works. The latter has crucial implications for the economic principles of production and distribution, as Wogman makes very clear:

> If justice, ultimately, is only the proper rewarding of economic behaviour, then we have a clear paradigm for economic organisation. People should simply get what they 'deserve', nothing more and nothing less. But on the other hand if justice is patterned in accordance with the priority of grace, then economic goods should be produced and distributed in such a way as to enhance human well-being and self acceptance and communal fellow feelings without asking first whether people have deserved what they receive. (Ibid., p. 35)

The four issues relating to Christian behaviour follow from these beliefs, these being respect for both physical well-being and social relationships, a sense of vocation (and utilization of 'talents'), the responsibility of stewardship of resources, and the realistic recognition of original sin with its implication that economic behaviour may be corrupted by self-centredness.[6]

The second study is by Novak (1982), who emphasizes six theological doctrines of Christianity: the Trinity, the incarnation, competition (as seen above), original sin, the separation of realms, and the compassion and sacrificial love of God. We have already considered five of these earlier in this chapter, the addition being the separation of the realms, namely to render unto Caesar what is Caesar's and to God what is God's (Matthew 22:21). While not all Christians would agree, it does bring out the message that Christianity is not theocratic and is, by nature, relatively tolerant; or at least is now (overlooking in the past the behaviour of the Crusaders, the ejecting of Muslims from France and Spain, the Inquisition, and the harsh treatment of usurers).

ISLAM

Introduction

Much like Judaism is based around 'the law', so too is Islam based around Islamic law or the *shari'ah* (formally *shari'ah Islami'iah* but generally abbreviated to *shari'ah* or *shari'a*). The literal meaning of the Arabic word *shari'ah* is 'the way to the source of life', and in a technical sense it is now used to refer to a legal system in keeping with the code of behaviour called for by the Holy Qur'an and the *hadith* (the authentic tradition). Muslims cannot, in good faith, compartmentalize their behaviour into religious and secular dimensions, and their actions are always bound by *shari'ah*. Islamic law thus embodies an encompassing set of duties and practices including worship, prayer, manners and morals, marriage, inheritance, crime and commercial transactions: that is, it embraces many aspects that would not necessarily be considered as law elsewhere. It is thus entirely religious, and as sacred law contains the core of Islamic faith itself.

Growth of Islam

Islam, numerically the second-largest religion (see Table 2.2), was promulgated by the Prophet Muhammad in Arabia early in the seventh century CE. The religion spread rapidly and barely a century after the Prophet's death in 632 CE had travelled across the whole northern coast of Africa and into Spain; in the East it crossed Persia and reached the Indus. A second wave of conquest by the Ottoman dynasty from the 1300s established the dominance of Islam in South East Europe. Nevertheless, the Eastern Christian Church's Patriarch of Constantinople retained considerable authority even after the Muslim Ottoman Empire took over Byzantium (Woodhead, 2014).

In Asia, Pakistan was established in the twentieth century as a Muslim state. India was ruled mainly by Muslims (the Mughals, with their brilliant architecture) for more than 700 years, and Muslims still comprise around

14 per cent of the Indian population. The non-Chinese inhabitants of Malaysia are predominantly Muslim; Indonesia is 90 per cent Muslim; and Muslims constitute 12 per cent of the population of Thailand and the Philippines. China itself has a large Muslim population, mainly Turkic-speaking Uighurs, Kazakhs and Kirgiz; so do the adjoining 'stans' of the Old Silk Road. Islam holds sway in the Nile Valley, in most of what used to be called French West Africa; along with Northern Nigeria and Somalia, Tanzania and Kenya on the East Coast. In all, Muslims form a majority of the population in more than 40 countries. There are sizable, and growing, numbers of Muslims in the West (Pew Research Center, 2016). In 2010, 44 million Muslims were living in Europe (6 per cent of the population), of which 19 million were in the European Union (3.8 per cent). In 2016, 3.3 million Muslims were living in the United States (1 per cent of the population). All Muslims are bound by a common faith. Yet Muslim individuals, like all persons, carry multiple identities of family, clan, region, ethnicity, nationality, religious adherence, gender, language, class, income and profession.

Muhammad and the Meaning of Islam

Islam follows Judaism and Christianity as the third and last of the great monotheistic religions. One who professes the faith of Islam is a Muslim. The origins of the word *Islam* are in the root *s-l-m* which means 'tranquillity', 'inner peace' (*salam*) or 'to remain whole'. The term *aslama* means 'to submit oneself with complete peace of mind' or 'to give oneself up to God', and it is from this that the word *Muslim* derives. Frequently *Islam* is defined simply as 'submission to God' or 'surrender to God'. Those who 'submit to' this path form the *umma*, the community of Muslims.

Belief in the sovereignty of God is at the centre of the Islamic faith, in that it is focused around the worship of God (in Arabic, *Allah*) and divine revelations as given in the Holy Qur'an, revealed between 610 and 632 CE to the Prophet Muhammad ibn 'Abd Allah. Muhammad, at the age of 40, reported a remarkable experience in 610 during a sojourn in the mountains, when visited by the Angel Gabriel. The Prophet Muhammad was torn from sleep in his spiritual retreat on Mount Hira close to Mecca, felt himself overwhelmed by a devastating divine presence, and received the command, '*iqra*': 'recite'. So begins the opening passage of Surat al-Alaq (96), and the Word of God had been spoken for the first time in Arabia and in (classical) Arabic. These revelations continued over a period of 23 years for the rest of his life, and constitute the Qur'an: the Recitation. It should be noted that the word 'Allah' for the name of God was known and used before the Holy Qur'an was revealed; for example, the name of the Prophet's father was Abd Allah, or 'servant of God'. Consequently, the Holy Qur'an is for Muslims in a most literal sense the word of God, and Islamic law flows directly from it and is wholly inspired by it. A work roughly the same length as the New Testament, the Holy Qur'an calls on polytheists (believers in many Gods), Jews and Christians alike to commit themselves to God's final revealed message. All injustices of this world are to be redressed in the next. There is to be a Resurrection and a Day of Judgment. Paradise (heaven) awaits those who heed the call, hell for those who ignore it; a position that fits in with the Judaeo-Christian heritage. Interestingly, according to Islam, Jesus did not die on the cross but was taken up to heaven by God. It will be Jesus, not Muhammad, who will return on the Day of Judgment to quell the anti-Christ, punish the enemies of Islam, and bring justice (Fuller, 2010, p. 34). Many may find this recognition of Jesus surprising.

Islam, Judaism and Christianity

At this juncture it seems appropriate to seek to clarify the relationship of Islam with Judaism and Christianity, for this is an area around which much misunderstanding has existed. One misconception has been analogical. Since Jesus Christ is the basis of Christian faith, it was sometimes assumed – quite incorrectly – that the Prophet Muhammad was to Islam as Christ was to Christianity. Hence the old term 'Muhammadanism' wrongly given to Islam in the West until relatively recently. Although for Muslims the Prophet Muhammad is *insan-i-kamil*, the perfect person, he is not divine, and is seen not as the founder of Islam, merely as God's messenger, carrying the message of Islam, of inner peace and tranquility. As the name of Islam is not linked to the founder of the religion (like Buddhism after Buddha), it is also not tied to a geographical area; unlike Hinduism, which derives its name from Hind or the river Indus, or Judaism, which gets its name from the land of Judaea.

Islam, Christianity and Judaism are interlinked because all three are, in reality, worshipping the same One God. Thus the God of Muslims is the same God of the Jews and the Christians, although without what perhaps might be seen as the racial exclusiveness attributed to him by Judaism, or the intricate theology woven around him by Christianity in the form of the Trinity by which God is considered to exist as Father, Son and the Holy Spirit.

Islam and Judaism, as we noted earlier, share a genealogical link as well as a strict monotheistic relationship. In addition, both have a well-defined system of sacred law. Both forbid the eating of pork and other meat which has not been ritually killed (*kosher* to the Jews, and *halal* to the Muslims). Both forbid statues and religious images, and are shocked by Christian art. There are many similarities in ritual and practice. Both insist on the unity of God and reject the Christian creed of the Trinity. Muslims reject the Christian concept of original sin, and the idea that there can be any intercessor between a person and God, since in Islam each person is responsible for their own salvation.

In reviving the message that God sent to all prophets from Adam to Jesus to Muhammad, the Holy Qur'an does not proclaim a new religion, only that the Prophet Muhammad is the last of the line. Moreover, the Holy Qur'an explicitly declares: 'We make no distinction between any of them' (S2:136). For this reason, Muslims cannot understand why Christians do not accept the Prophet Muhammad as a prophet, since they grant that status to Jesus. In the Holy Qur'an, Jews and Christians are called *ahl-al-kitab*, the People of the Book, and were generally allowed to practise their beliefs freely in the Islamic empire, which has played host to Christians and Jews for centuries.

Despite the common roots and common bonds between the three religions, there are, of course, some significant differences. Prophet Muhammad's revelation was the first time God had sent a messenger to the Arabs (the Qureysh) and had revealed a scripture in their own language. Significantly, at one point, the Prophet Muhammad is called 'the seal of the prophets' (S33:40). In some eyes, this may have implied no more than that the revelations confirmed those given to previous prophets, but it has come to mean that the Prophet Muhammad was the final, uniting prophet of the covenant, correcting errors that had crept into previous revelations, and giving the full and most perfect version of God's revelation to humanity.

While God alone is god, and the Prophet Muhammad is not regarded as divine, the Prophet Muhammad is unique in the respect and reverence afforded him by Muslims. His behaviour and words are studied by Muslims, and his life is an example to be followed.

Six Beliefs and Five Duties

The fundamental articles and duties of the Islamic faith are contained in the Six Beliefs and the Five Duties which every Muslim must uphold or perform. These are set out in Figure 2.1. The Six Beliefs entail:

1. a belief in the One God;
2. an acceptance of all Prophets of God (including Moses, Jesus and Muhammad);

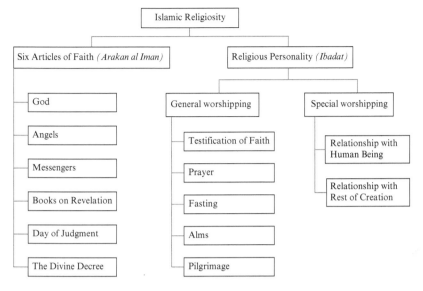

Source: Krauss et al. (2007).

Figure 2.1   Islamic religiosity

3.   a belief in the Angels;
4.   a belief in the key Holy books sent by God, which include the Old and New Testaments and the Qur'an;
5.   a belief in the Day of Judgment and Resurrection; and
6.   belief in destiny or fate and the decree of God.

These theological underpinnings of the new faith system facilitated easy transmission, explanation and acceptance.

   To become[7] a Muslim all that one has to do is to 'testify' by reciting the words, 'I believe that there is no god but Allah, and that Muhammad is the Messenger of Allah'. This is the first of the so-called Five Pillars of Islam, or fundamental observances, which form the basis of the Muslim faith:

1.   Acceptance of the *shahada* or witness of faith which consists of reciting the sentence '*la ilaha illa llah, Muhammadu rasulu llah*' (in its alternative translation, 'There is no God but the God and Muhammad is his Prophet'). Anyone who utters the *shahada* in full faith and with pure heart must be regarded as a Muslim.
2.   Prayer, or *salat*, is prescribed to be performed five times per day (at dawn, around midday, in the afternoon, at sunset, and at night before

going to bed), preceded by self-purification through ritual washing, performed facing in the direction of the Holy Mosque in Mecca, demonstrating 'submission to God's will' by word of mouth and physical gesture.[8]

3. Alms, or *zakat* (a term derived from the Arabic *zakah*, meaning 'pure'). The Holy Qur'an stresses that the giving of alms is one of the chief virtues of the true believer, the generally accepted amount being one-fortieth of a Muslim's accumulated personal or business wealth. Because all such revenue benefits the poor and pays for certain activities within a community, the very act of giving shows the believer's sense of social responsibility, thus leaving acquired wealth free of disrepute.

4. Fasting, or *sawm*. All believers are required to observe the ninth lunar month of the Muslim year, Ramadan, as a period of fasting in which they abstain from eating, drinking, smoking and sexual relations from sunrise to sunset (Holy Qur'an 2:185–6). The purpose is to subjugate the body to the spirit and to fortify the will through mental discipline, thus helping the believer to come nearer to God.

5. Pilgrimage. The *hajj*, or pilgrimage to Mecca, must be performed at least once in the life of every Muslim, health and means permitting (Holy Qur'an 3.97).

Above all, however, the practising Muslim is expected to respect the teachings of the Holy Qur'an in its entirety: the basis of Islamic law.

Islamic Law

The unique validity of Islamic law comes from it being the manifested will of God, who at a certain point in history revealed it to mankind through his Prophet Muhammad; as such it does not rely on the authority of any earthly lawmaker. Its origins in addition to the Holy Qur'an, are to be found in the judgments given by the Prophet himself, reflecting the application of rules, principles and injunctions already enunciated in the Holy Qur'an. However, these rules and injunctions did not delineate all possible problems, and in the century after the Prophet Muhammad they were supplemented by references to the *sunna* or standard practice. This was known from thousands of statements about what the Prophet had said or done and found in the literature of the *hadith*. The *shari'ah* grew out of the attempts made by early Muslims, as they confronted immediate social and political problems, to devise a legal system in keeping with the code of behaviour called for by the Holy Qur'an and the *hadith*.

The study of the *shari'ah* is *fiqh* (jurisprudence), and its practitioners are *fuqaha* (jurists). Another word used is *ulama*, which is properly 'those who know' but is mostly translated 'scholars' or 'scholar-jurists'. This is because in Islam the place of theology is taken by laws and jurisprudence. Those who deal with the intellectual aspects of the religion are jurists and not theologians, and at the centre of higher education is jurisprudence and not theology. *Ijma*, the informed consensus of the community of scholars, was established, not for matters of faith or fundamental observances – which were agreed – but on the application of *shari'ah* to worldly affairs. This source is of importance for Islamic finance because models of Islamic banking are not mentioned in either the Holy Qur'an or in the *hadith*, although the basic principles which govern the system are.

Additional sources of law are *qiyas* (analogy from established law) and *ijtihad* (formulation of law by the individual's struggle for proper understanding). Using reason and judgement to determine a course of action in keeping with the spirit of the Holy Qur'an and *hadith* is called *ijtihad*, and decisions made in this manner are *ijma*, the collective judgments of learned Muslim scholars, the *ulama*. In making decisions, account must be taken of earlier opinions, previous discussions and the reasons for them, and a general sense of justice. *Qiyas* means analogical reasoning, using past analogies with their decisions as precedents in each new situation. Thus the sources of the *shari'ah* are the Holy Qur'an and the *sunna* (the primary sources) and the interpretations and opinions of the learned jurists (the secondary sources).

A GOLDEN AGE OF ISLAM?

All three religions have had 'great moments' that define their faith and shape their 'world-view'. For Jews, one such set of experiences revolved around Moses, the Decalogue and their selection as the Chosen People. More recently, it has been the return to the homeland of Israel, controversial as this remains today. For Christians, the defining aspect was the belief that Jesus was the Son of God, rather than a divinely inspired human, followed by the Resurrection.

For Muslims, one great event was the visitation by the Angel Gabriel, the recitation and the instruction to promulgate the message that God is One and carry it to the corrupt society of pagan and polytheistic Mecca. Another 'great moment' for Muslims, in contrast to Christianity, comes from its historical origins. Gellner (1981, p. 2) observes that Christianity initially flourished among the politically disinherited and did not assume a dominant position for a considerable time. Jesus was a revolutionary, but not a political one, and this potential for political modesty has underpinned the intellectual base of Christianity ever since. In comparison, Islam, unlike Christianity, was not born within an empire. On the contrary, it was born outside the two empires of its time, and created an empire of its own which found legitimization in faith. Seen from a Muslim viewpoint, then, Islam acts as the blueprint as well as the social cement of a civilization (Iqbal and Lewis, 2009). To Muslims, all the good of that civilization can be attributed to motivation by faith, and the bad to a deviation from the model set forth by the Prophet and his immediate successors during what is seen as the 'Golden Age'.

According to Deepak Lal (1999) there is a yearning to purify Islam from all the corruptions that have crept in over the centuries into Muslim lives, and thereby recreate the 'golden era' of Islam. The period of the four rightly guided Caliphs (Abu Bakr, Omar ibn-al-Khattab, Uthman and 'Ali) is generally regarded as an ideal time, when Islam was practised perfectly and, with the dramatic conquests and the expansion of the Islamic state, it appeared that 'God smiled on Muslims' (Lal, 1999, p. 50).

The difficulty with this response is the potential for perpetual disappointment. As Lindholm (1996) observes:

> In the memory of Muslims ever since, this period appears as a divine ordered social formation flowering under the benign regime of the community's duly elected representative – the Caliph . . . Muslim thought is saturated with longing for a return of this idealized era when ordinary men and women are imagined (in the soft glow of collective memory) to have acted together selflessly under the leadership of just and divinely guided Caliphs to realize the will of Allah in the world of human beings – a realization validated concretely through the vast power and wealth acquired by the victorious army of the faithful. (Ibid., p. 80)

Even allowing for 'apocryphal exaggeration' (Atiyah, 1955, p. 36) and some less than ideal circumstances ('three of the four caliphs were assassinated'; Watt, 1996, p. 40), suggesting that 'the early Caliphate was not devoid of worldly struggles over power and glory' (Lindholm, 1996, p. 87), the fact remains that the hold of this period of history over Muslim thinking remains strong, and there are good reasons for this admiration. In the words of one (generally unsympathetic) Western observer: 'Its [Islam's] rise is one of the wonders of world history – a chain reaction of conquest and conversion, an amassment not just of territory but of millions of hearts and minds. The vigour of its ideal of justice allowed for levels of tolerance significantly higher than those of the West' (Amis, 2008, p. 81).

From a Muslim perspective, there was much more. It was a golden period that saw *wahy*, that is, revelation (guidance of God) come to man, Muhammad, after a break of some 600 years, and he interpreted, disseminated and implemented that message in the life of individuals and a community in a way that provided a benchmark and blueprint for all generations. The *Rahidun* caliphs tried their utmost to follow the path that their leader had demonstrated. In terms of governance, the period was marked by good conduct and a responsible attitude to the public purse. It was also a period of small government, and the four rightly guided Caliphs were circumspect in the powers that they exercised.

> For six months, until the community decided to contribute to his sustenance, Abu Bakr was a part-time leader in Medina, continuing his usual work as merchant, and milking his neighbors' sheep for additional income. Later Caliphs were not much more powerful. Abu Bakr's successor, Umar, was obliged to count the camels sent as tribute by himself, with only voluntary help. (Lindholm, 1996, p. 85)

In short, they were free of the trappings and the seductions of empire to which later Muslim dynasties were to succumb.

To what extent the 'golden era' can be reconstructed seems at best an open question, but there is no doubt that the achievements of this period result in a very different world-view from that held by most Christians. As Lindholm goes on to remark:

> Remembering their glorious world-conquering past, Muslims have not pictured the 'City of God' in the Christian manner as beyond ordinary ken, achieved in the radiant future by faith and renunciation. For them, God's mandate was actually realized in historical reality, under the authority of the Prophet himself and the four pious rulers after him. (Ibid., p. 79)

> Recalling their millennial past, the Muslim devout, unlike their Christian cousins, have never inwardly consented to the disjuncture between the religious experience of the community of believers (equal before God, led by the Prophet and his deputies) and the reality of power-seeking secular rulers prone to political intrigue and the use of physical coercion. (Ibid., pp. 80–81)

PRINCIPLES AND PRACTICE IN CHRISTIANITY

The Western Christian world-view draws a sharper distinction between principles and their exemplification. The principles may remain unchanged, but most Westerners would expect that the process of putting these principles into practice would not be unchanging. That is, while the Holy books contain the word of God and embody universal truths, they were given to particular peoples facing particular problems at particular times and cannot be used in their strict literal form for all times. Hence, from this viewpoint, the translation of the essential truths into practice would not stand still in the face of changes in social mores about, for example, the role of women in society.

Nevertheless, the common heritage and commonality on the nature of people leads to some similarities in the profile of conduct required of individuals while dealing with others. On this account, one must regard Christianity as close to Islamic thinking (hardly surprising in view of the origins of the two religions). In fact, this was clearly the case on matters such as the ban on usury when the Catholic Church and canon law was in power. But since the Renaissance and the rise of Protestantism the emphasis has been on the much-quoted answer by Jesus on the question of taxes. Although already mentioned, it is worth citing in full; see Matthew 22:15–21 (Phillips edition):

> The Pharisees went off and discussed how they could trap him in argument. Eventually they sent their disciples with some of the Herod-party to say this, 'Master, we know that you are an honest man who teaches the way of God faithfully and that you are not swayed by men's opinion of you. Obviously you don't care for human approval. Now tell us – Is it right to pay taxes to Caesar or not?'
>
> But Jesus knowing their evil intention said, 'Why try this trick on me, you frauds? Show me the money you pay the tax with.' They handed him a coin, and he said to them, 'Whose face is this and whose name is in the inscription?'
>
> 'Caesar's,' they said.
>
> 'Then give to Caesar,' he replied, 'what belongs to Caesar and to God what belongs to God!'

Focus on this Biblical injunction has encouraged a divergence in the West between the sacred and secular. As Noonan (1993) observes, after the Middle Ages, even the Church's teachings on issues such as usury, marriage and religious freedom have undergone substantial change approaching dominant secular trends of the epoch. Under Islam, however, any separation between the realms of God and Caesar is an anathema. In fact, the Holy Qur'an (5:46–7) goes a step further than that and interprets the mission of Jesus Christ (5:46–7) in no less equal terms. Why have these two civilizations diverged so on the basic ideas of running a society?

Islam would answer that basic truths have been upheld. The Christian Church would argue that the essential aims (for example, preventing exploitation of borrowers by usury) have not changed, but have been reinterpreted in the light of different circumstances (for example, the rise of a modern competitive international financial system replacing a more localized, tribally based system). In fact, as we shall see, in terms of reality rather than rhetoric, Islamic practices on the question of interest or usury are much closer to those in the West than is commonly known. Indeed, we will show that the prohibited practice of *riba* has become the norm in the

Islamic world at the same time as the principle of prohibition continues to be proclaimed by the very bankers who breach it. Such observation underscores the emphasis of this volume, and the search for, and examination of, whether there are genuine non-interest financing arrangements.

NOTES

1. When Muslims mention the Prophet Muhammad in speech or print, they usually follow the name with an expression in Arabic which can be translated as, 'May the peace and blessings of Allah be upon him'; sometimes written as 'pbuh', short for 'peace be upon him'.
2. This is 'not to say that there may not be some authentic historical memory preserved in the narrative of earlier times, but it has been so refracted by the lenses of various sources that we care little about what may actually have happened' (Coogan, 2008, p. 32).
3. The Rabbinic Synod held at Jamnia, circa AD 90, is generally regarded as marking the close of the Old Testament canon (Abba, 1958).
4. In the wake of the Holocaust (or as Jews prefer, the Shoah – the destruction), Emil Packenheim grimly argued that there should be a 614th commandment, to add to the 613 of tradition: to survive as Jews to remember never to despair of God, lest Hitler is handed a posthumous victory (Solomon, 2014, p. 121).
5. For a recent account of Amish life, see Lewis (2015b). As this study demonstrates, the high degree of trust and forgiveness that marks these communities makes them prone to Ponzi schemes.
6. The doctrine of original sin in the context of the 'gift' of free will is examined in Boyce (2014).
7. Muslims believe that at birth all humans are naturally *muslim*, that is, at peace with and submissive to God. It is thus inaccurate to speak of a convert to Islam; rather, one is a revert.
8. Here, and in most of what follows, we refer to Sunni muslims. For example, Shias pray three times per day.

3. Attitudes of Judaism, Christianity and Islam to usury

HISTORICAL CRITIQUES

This chapter is concerned with the opposition of Judaism, Christianity and Islam to usury, that is, the practice of levying interest and other financial charges[1] in excess of the principal amount of a loan. Such opposition led eventually either to a redefinition of usury or to the quest for developing non-interest financial arrangements and techniques, which constitutes much of the subject matter of this book. But an appropriate starting point is to assess what was considered so abhorrent about usury (or interest).[2]

It is worth noting, however, that the three Abrahamic religions are not alone in their objection to usury. Hinduism, Buddhism and Greek and Roman philosophers can be added to the list. In Ancient India laws based on the Veda, the oldest scriptures of Hinduism, condemned usury as a major sin and restricted the operation of interest rates (Gopal, 1935; Rangaswami, 1927).[3] More frequent and detailed references to interest payment are to be found in the later Sutra texts (700–100 BC), as well as the Buddhist Jatakas (600–400 BC). It is during this latter period that the first sentiments of contempt for usury are expressed. For example, Vasishtha, a well-known Hindu lawmaker of that time, made a special law which forbade the higher castes of Brahmins (priests) and Kshatriyas (warriors) from being usurers or lenders at interest. Also, in the Buddhist Jatakas, usury is referred to in a demeaning manner: 'hypocritical ascetics are accused of practising it' (Jain, 1929; Visser and McIntosh, 1998, p. 176).

Among the ancient Western philosophers who condemned usury can be named Plato, Aristotle, the two Catos, Cicero, Seneca and Plutarch (Birnie, 1958). Evidence that these sentiments found their concurrent manifestations in the civil law of that period can be seen, for example, from the Lex Genucia reforms in Republican Rome (340 BC) which outlawed interest altogether. Nevertheless, in practice, ways of evading such legislation were found, and practising usury re-emerged in later republics.

In Judaism, the Torah (the Hebrew name of the Law of Moses or the Pentateuch, the first five books of the Old Testament) prohibited usury amongst the Jews, while at least one authority sees in the Talmud (the oral law which supplements the written scriptures for orthodox Jews) a consistent bias against the appearance of usury or profit (Neusner, 1990b). Under Christianity, prohibitions or severe restrictions upon usury operated for more than 1400 years. Generally, these controls meant that any taking of interest was forbidden, and the same was true of the Islamic ban on usury, for in the Holy Qur'an the prohibition is frequently enunciated – a position which is maintained to this day.

In the case of Christianity, however, gradually under the weight of the Protestant Reform only exorbitant interest came to be considered usurious and this view came to be reflected in 'usury laws'. Yet the Roman Catholic Church only relented in the nineteenth century, although not abandoning the principle itself.

Interestingly, the so-called 'Golden Rule', which guides much of Western Kantian or welfare liberalism or humanist thinking, can be seen, without too much of a stretch, as supportive of an anti-usurious position, since it revolves around reciprocity in actions and behaviour as a basis for personal interaction. The Golden Rule is widely attributed to Jesus, that is, 'Do unto others as you would have them do unto you': Jesus in the Gospels, Matthew 7:12, Luke 6:31, Luke 10:27. However, in reality, the Golden Rule was actually first enunciated by Confucius (*c.* 551–479 BCE): 'Zigong asked: "Is there any single word that could guide one's entire life?" The Master said: "Should it not be reciprocity? What you do not wish for yourself, do not do to others" – Confucius in the Analects 15:24' (Leys, 1997).

JUDAISM AND THE OLD TESTAMENT

Given that Judaism, Christianity and Islam share much the same heritage in terms of the injunctions of the Old Testament prophets, how did they end up at different positions on the question of usury? This question is heightened when it is apparent that all three religions were grappling with the same issues.

For example, there is a strong emphasis in the Old Testament injunctions against interest on the need to protect the poor from the insatiable demands of the lenders:

> If thou lend money to any of my people that is poor by thee thou shalt not be to him as a usurer, neither shall though lay upon him usury. (Exodus 22:25)

> And if thy brother be waxen poor, and fallen in decay with thee; then thou shalt relieve him: *yea, though he be* a stranger, or a sojourner; that he may live with thee.

Take thou no usury of him, or increase: but fear thy God; that thy brother may live with thee.
Thou shalt not give him thy money upon usury, nor lend him thy victuals for increase. (Leviticus 25:35–7)

Lord, who shall abide in thy tabernacle? Who shall dwell in thy holy hill?
He *that* putteth not out his money to usury, nor taketh reward against the innocent. He that doeth these *things* shall never be moved. (Psalm 15:1, 5)

The context in Exodus was a community of poor people, following the arduous experience of the exodus from Egypt, and the extreme state of poverty of the weak party was connected with the prohibition of usury; an emphasis reflected also in Christianity and Islam.

However, all three religions were challenged by the rise of a mercantile society, especially Christianity and Islam, but we begin with Judaism, which came upon a literal but nevertheless straightforward, solution. In Exodus (and Deuteronomy), the biblical (Hebrew) term for interest is *neshekh*, although in Leviticus the term *neshekh* occurs alongside *tarbit* or *marbit*. In the *Encyclopedia Judaica* it is argued that *neshekh*, meaning 'bite', was the term used for the exaction of interest from the point of view of the debtor, and *tarbit* or *marbit*, meaning 'increase', was the term used for the recovery of interest by the creditor (Cohn, 1971, p. 28). But in both meanings, it seems to be the case that the prohibition on interest is not a prohibition on usury in the modern sense of the term – that is, excessive interest – but of all, even minimal, interest. Cohn concludes that there is no difference in law between various rates of interest, as all interest is prohibited. Nowadays, however, the prohibition of taking interest is couched in terms of *ribbit*. As Feldman (2010) explains, although interest is referred to by the Torah as *neshekh* (biting) and *tarbit* (increase), it has been known since Talmudic times as *ribbit* (a construct of *tarbit*).

Three other features of the Mosaic injunctions relating to interest are notable. First, in at least two cases, the ban on usury is connected to poverty and consumption loans (likely the main form of loan at that time). Second, two of the passages extend the ban to any form of loan, not just of money, by including food given for profit. Any time-contingent contract might therefore be regarded as usurious. Third, the emphasis is upon brotherhood and the unacceptability of usury when applied to 'brothers'. In effect, the 'sin' (which is shared not only by lenders, but by anyone involved in the transaction, such as witnesses and scribes), is an 'undermining of the familial relationship amongst members of the Jewish people' (Feldman, 2010, pp. 241–2).

For Jews, the Mosaic injunctions offered an escape clause in terms of what has become known as the 'Deuteronomic double standard'. Consider the injunction in Deuteronomy: 'Thou shalt not lend upon usury to thy brother; usury of money, usury of victuals, usury of any thing that is lent upon usury: Unto a stranger thou mayest lend upon usury; but unto thy brother thou shalt not lend upon usury' (Deuteronomy 23:19–20). This command makes it clear that the prohibition refers to loans to 'brothers' that is, fellow members of the tribe or adherents to the common faith. Charging interest to 'foreigners' was acceptable. In this way, the Jews justified taking interest from Gentiles, and Christians charged interest to Saracens (as Arabs and, by extension, Muslims in general were called in the Middle Ages).

These three qualifications were to prove instrumental to the later removal of the ban under Christianity. Even at the time, the 'Deuteronomic double standard', as Nelson (1949) termed it, was difficult to explain away by Christians, since Jesus had preached the oneness of friend and foe alike. In addition, the idea that usury to any group could be considered religiously sound was contradicted by the passage from the Psalms quoted above. One possible way around this conundrum would have been to follow the lead of Jewish Church leaders who defended the practice of those of their brethren who lent at usury to Gentiles by arguing that the verse from the Psalms can be attributed to David who was Moses' disciple and could not, therefore, place himself in contradiction to his master by altering Mosaic law (Cohn, 1971).

But what of lending to fellow Jews? A solution came in *hetter iska* (permission to form a partnership) which converts a commercial lender– borrower relationship into a silent partnership. This technique established the basis for the Jewish 'legalization' of interest. David Bleich (2010) calls his chapter in *The Oxford Handbook of Judaism and Economics* 'Hetter Iska, the Permissible Venture: A Device to Avoid the Prohibition Against Interest-Bearing Loans'. Cohn (1971) explains that a deed, known as a *shetar iska*, was drawn up and attested by two witnesses, stipulating that the lender would supply a certain sum of money to the borrower for a joint venture: the borrower alone would manage the business and he would guarantee the lender's investment against all loss; he would also guarantee to the lender a fixed amount of minimum profit. The amount of the capital loan plus the guaranteed minimum profit would be recoverable on the deed at the stipulated time it matured.

Although the word 'device' may have negative connotations, Bleich (2010, p. 198) classified them into three distinct categories: (1) those that are inconsistent with the spirit of the law; (2) those considered commend- able and actively encouraged; and (3) those to which there is an attitude of complete neutrality. An unacceptable use of *hetter iska* occurs when a person is not in any way engaged in a business enterprise, so that the arrangement 'appears to be nothing more than a subterfuge' (Bleich, 2010, p. 206). In fact, Cohn (1971) observes that over time this form of legalizing interest became so well established that nowadays all interest transactions are freely carried out, even in compliance with Jewish law, by simply adding to the note or contract concerned the words *al-pi hetter iska* (Cohn, 1971, p. 32). This is explored further in Chapter 7.

Consequently, we concentrate on the Christian and Islamic views on usury in the rest of this chapter. Since Islam is the only religion that still maintains, at least in principle, a prohibition on interest or usury, it makes sense to start with its position.

ISLAM AND USURY

The Prohibition of *Riba*

Islam bans Muslims from taking or giving interest (the Arabic term for which is *riba*), and this prohibition makes an Islamic banking system differ fundamentally from a conventional banking system. Technically, *riba* refers to the addition in the amount of the principal of a loan, according to the time for which it is loaned and the amount of the loan. While earlier there was a debate as to whether *riba* relates to interest or usury, there now appears to be consensus of opinion among Islamic scholars that the term extends to all forms of interest.

Later we explore in more detail the origins of the terms 'interest' and 'usury', and the way in which in Western usage the meanings have been transposed over time, so that the former meaning of usury and the present meaning of interest are practically identical (Divine, 1967). Usury (from the Latin *usura* meaning enjoyment, interest or money paid for the use of money) was a term originally used to describe interest generally, but in modern times in the West has come to mean excessive interest, particularly that in excess of maximum rates fixed by law (Munn et al., 1991). Some Islamic modernist views have contended that *riba* refers to usury practised by petty moneylenders and not to interest charged by modern banks, and that no *riba* is involved when interest is imposed on productive loans. But these arguments have not won general acceptance amongst Muslim writers.

In any case, it is doubtful whether the distinction between interest and usury matters to the orthodox Muslim. The term *riba*, in Islamic law (the *shari'ah*), means an addition, however slight, over and above the principal. According to the Federal Shariat Court of Pakistan, this means that the concept covers both usury and interest; that it is not restricted to doubled and redoubled interest; that it applies to all forms of interest, whether large or small, simple or compound, doubled or redoubled; and that the Islamic injunction is not only against exorbitant or excessive interest, but also against a minimal rate of interest (Hamid, 1992; M.S. Khan and Mirakhor, 1992).

The fundamental sources of Islam are the Holy Qur'an and the *sunna*, a term which in Ancient Arabia meant 'ancestral precedent' or the 'custom of the tribe', but is now synonymous with the teachings and traditions of the Prophet Muhammad as transmitted by the relators of authentic tradition. Both of these sources treat interest as an act of exploitation and injustice and, as such, inconsistent with Islamic notions of fairness and property rights.

The prohibition of *riba* is mentioned in four different verses in the Holy Qur'an, as given below, from the English translation of the Holy Qur'an revised and edited by the Presidency of Islamic Researches, 1413 AH:

That which you give in usury
For increase through the property
Of (other) people, will have
No increase with Allah:
But that which you give
For charity, seeking
The Countenance of Allah. (*Surah al-Rum*, 30:39)

That they took usury,
Though they were forbidden:
And that they devoured
Men's wealth wrongfully; –
We have prepared for those
Among them who reject Faith
A grievous chastisement. (*Surah al-Nisa*, 4:161)

O ye who believe!
Devour not Usury,
Doubled and multiplied;
But fear Allah; that
Ye may (really) prosper. (*Surah al-Imran*, 3:130)

Those who devour usury
Will not stand except
As stands one whom
The Satan by his touch
Hath driven to madness.
That is because they say:
'Trade is like usury,'
But Allah hath permitted trade
And forbidden usury.

Those who after receiving
Admonition from their Lord,
Desist, shall be pardoned
For the past; their case
Is for Allah (to judge);
But those who repeat
(The offence) are Companions
Of the Fire: they will
Abide therein (for ever).

Allah will deprive
Usury of all blessing,
But will give increase
For deeds of charity:
For He loveth not
Any ungrateful Sinner.

O ye who believe!
Fear Allah, and give up
What remains of your demand
For usury, if ye are
Indeed believers. (*Surah al-Baqarah*, 2:275–6, 278)

The first quotation emphasizes that interest deprives wealth of God's blessings. The second condemns it, placing interest in juxtaposition with wrongful appropriation of property belonging to others. The third enjoins Muslims to stay clear of interest for the sake of their own welfare. The fourth establishes a clear distinction between interest and trade, urging Muslims to take only the principal sum, and to forgo even this sum if the borrower is unable to repay. The ban on interest is also cited in unequivocal terms in the *hadith* or *sunna*. In the *hadith*, the Prophet Muhammad condemns the one who takes it, the one who pays it, the one who writes the agreement for it, and the witnesses to the agreement.

The concept of *riba* is not limited to interest. Two forms of *riba* are identified in Islamic law. They are *riba al-qarud* which relates to usury involving loans, and *riba al-buyu* which relates to usury involving trade. The latter can take two forms. *Riba al-fadl* involves an exchange of unequal qualities or quantities of the same commodity simultaneously, whilst *riba al-nisa* involves the non-simultaneous exchange of equal qualities and quantities of the same commodity. The prohibition applies to objects which can be measured or weighed and which, in addition, belong to the same species. Forbidden are both an excess in quantity and a delay in performance.

Riba al-qarud, the usury of loans, involves a charge on a loan arising due to the passage of time, in other words a loan at interest, and is sometimes referred to as *riba al-nasia*, the usury of waiting. It arises where a user of

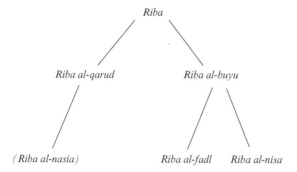

Source: El Diwany (2003).

Figure 3.1   Different forms of riba

another's wealth, in any form, is contracted by the other to pay a specified increase in addition to the principal amount in repayment. If the increase is predetermined as a specified amount at the outset of the transaction, however this increase occurs, then the loan becomes a usurious one. The prohibition has been extended to all loans and debts where an increase accrues to the creditor.

Figure 3.1, based on El Diwany (2003) classifies the forms of *riba* that are defined in Islam. A general principle of Islamic law, based on a number of passages in the Holy Qur'an, is that unjustified enrichment, or 'receiving a monetary advantage without giving a counter-value', is forbidden on ethical grounds. According to Schacht (1964), *riba* is simply a special case of unjustified enrichment or, in the terms of the Holy Qur'an, consuming (that is, appropriating for one's own use) the property of others for no good reason, which is prohibited. *Riba* can be defined formally as 'a monetary advantage without a counter-value which has been stipulated in favour of one of the two contracting parties in an exchange of two monetary values' (Schacht, 1964, p. 145).

Revisionist Views

Nevertheless, despite these clear injunctions the orthodoxy has been challenged. Some scholars have questioned the circumstances surrounding the ban in the Holy Qur'an and have wondered whether the objection to *riba* applies (or ought to apply) with equal force today.[4] Fazlur Rahman (1964), in particular, argues as a dissenting view that there has been a disregard of what *riba* was historically, why the Holy Qur'an banned it so categorically, and the function of bank interest in a modern economy.

The essence of Rahman's position is that *sunna* is not fixed, but dynamic. The prohibition on *riba* clearly does extend back to the Holy Qur'an and the Prophet. But the particular definition given to *riba*, as formalized by earlier generations and enshrined in the *hadith* – namely, that it represents any amount of interest – need not be applied. What is needed instead, according to Rahman, is to study *hadith* in a situational context in order to understand the true meaning and extract the real moral value. Rather than apply *hadith* directly, they should be studied for clues to the spirit of the injunction.

On this basis, it might be argued that the interest prohibition relates only to exorbitant interest rates and not to all forms of interest. The reference cited above in the Holy Qur'an to *riba* 'doubled and multiplied' (S3:130) may reflect that at the rise of Islam the practice of lending money was being exploited so as to reap excessive gains from the interest charged on loans. If borrowers could not meet the due date by which to return the capital borrowed, the lenders would double and then redouble the interest rates, thus reducing the debtor to penury. Such practices were deemed intimidatory, unjust and against social and economic welfare. The Islamic interdiction of *riba* therefore fell into the net of social reform instituted by the Prophet upon pre-Islamic practices. Certainly, the Islamic code urges leniency towards debtors, and the Holy Qur'an specifies no punishment for unpaid debts.

Similarly, the characteristics of Arab society at the time should be recalled: a largely agricultural, partly nomadic, civilization living as settled communities in walled towns (to protect themselves from marauding Bedouins), linked by caravan routes to each other and Asia Minor. In such an environment, the need for borrowing often arose, not from normal commercial expansion, but from misfortune: famine, crop failure, loss of a caravan, and so on. To charge interest to kin, under such circumstances, would violate tribal loyalty. Since crop failure and so on may occur to anyone, through no fault of their own, a system of lending freely without interest could be seen as a sort of mutual-help insurance system.

Drawing on some of these points, modernists have raised a number of issues about the definition of *riba*. Some have claimed that Islam has prohibited 'exploitative' or 'usurious' *riba* rather than interest per se, thereby allowing for a 'fair' return on loanable funds (Rida, 1959). Others like the Syrian Doualibi, would differentiate between 'consumption' loans and 'production' loans on the grounds that the verses in the Holy Qur'an relating to *riba* go hand in hand with injunctions to alleviate the condition of the poor, needy and weaker sections of the community (cited in Abu Zahra, 1970). The view has also been advanced that the prohibition of *riba* covers only individuals, not the giving or taking of interest among corporate entities such as companies, banks or governments. Some such as Tantawi, the Sheikh of al-Azhar in Cairo, even argue that bank interest is a sharing of the bank's commercial profit and, being a profit share, is therefore permissible. This view, like the other modernist views, has been almost unanimously rejected.

Also rejected have been those arguments that see fixed interest rates to be *haram* and variable interest rates *halal*. It is said that if the rate of interest is allowed to vary then this is permissible, since the actual rate of return is not fixed in advance. While it is true that the absolute amount of interest under a floating rate contract is not fixed, the formula is specified (for example, the London Interbank Offered Rate, LIBOR, plus a set spread) and in this sense the payment is predetermined. In effect, both fixed and variable loan contracts require interest to be paid, and only the method of determining the amount of interest differs.

'Zeros' have also been rejected. When first introduced, some commentators argued that the zero-coupon bonds are 'Islamic' because no interest is paid during their lifetime. A bond is a 'zero-coupon bond' if no coupons (that is, interest instalments) are due to the bondholder during the life of that bond. Investors therefore are only prepared to buy zero-coupon bonds at a price that is below face value, so that when the bond matures, the difference between the purchase price and the face value is realized as a gain of waiting. Again, interest is paid; it is just that it is all paid at the maturity date instead of in instalments over the life of the bond.

Thus, despite the modernist views on the meaning of *riba* and how it should justifiably be defined, the dominant position remains intact. One of the most important documents on Islamic banking, the Council of Islamic Ideology (CII) Report (1983) is explicit: 'There is complete unanimity among all schools of thought in Islam that the term *riba* stands for interest in all its types and forms' (p. 7).

Razi's Five Reasons

This leaves the question: why? Razi (1872 [1938]), a Persian-Arab scholar (1209) set forth some of the reasons as to the prohibition of *riba*. First, that *riba* is but the exacting of another's property without any counter-value, while according to the saying of the Prophet a man's property is as unlawful to the other as his blood. It is argued that *riba* should be lawful to the creditor in return for the use of money and the profit which the debtor derives from it. Had this been in the possession of the creditor he would have earned profit by investing it in some business. But it should be noted that profit in business is uncertain, while the excess amount which the creditor gets towards interest is certain. Hence insistence upon a certain sum in return for what is uncertain is but harm done to the debtor.

Second, that *riba* is forbidden because it prevents men from taking part in active professions. The moneyed man, if he gets income through *riba*, depends upon this easy means and abandons the idea of taking pains and earning his livelihood by way of trade or industry which serves to retard the progress and prosperity of the people. Third, that the contract of *riba* leads to a strained relationship between man and man. If it is made illegal there will be no difficulty in lending and getting back what has been lent, but if it is made legal, people, in order to gratify their desires, will borrow even at an exorbitant rate of interest which results in friction and strife and strips society of its goodliness.

Fourth, that the contract of *riba* is a contrivance to enable the rich to take in excess of the principal which is unlawful and against justice and equity. As a consequence of it, the rich grow still richer and the poor still poorer. Fifth, that the illegality of *riba* is proved by the text of the Holy Qur'an and it is not necessary that men should know the reasons for it. We have to discard it as illegal though we are unaware of the reasons (Razi, 1872 [1938], Vol. 2, p. 531).

For most scholars, the last is sufficient. Since the meaning and scope of *riba* and its grave nature have been brought to light in the Holy Qur'an (S2:225), its prohibition cannot be questioned, as the verse 'God permitteth trading and forbideth *riba*' is quite clear. When the text is clear on this point there is no need for further clarification. Because the Holy Qur'an has stated that only the principal should be taken, there is no alternative but to interpret *riba* according to that wording. Therefore, the existence or otherwise of injustice in a loan transaction is irrelevant. Whatever the circumstances are, the lender has no right to receive any increase over and above the principal.

CHRISTIANITY AND USURY

Our aim now is to examine the attitudes of the Christian Church to usury, and to compare Christian doctrine and practice with the Islamic position.[5] Our major focus will be upon the medieval Christian Church. The Middle Ages usually refers to the period in Europe, between the disintegration of the Western Roman Empire in 476 CE and the onset of the Italian Renaissance, and covering an area stretching from Sweden to the Mediterranean. This was the period when the Church had vast secular and religious authority and was a universal and unifying force across Christian countries, much like Islam is today amongst Muslims. The analysis needs to extend to at least the sixteenth century, for the great medieval unity of Christendom – and its views on usury – went largely unchallenged until the Protestant Reformation and the rise of Calvinism.

To medieval Christians, the taking of what we would now call interest was usury, and usury was a sin, condemned in the strongest terms. For Muslims, the prohibition on *riba* in the Holy Qur'an is equally clear-cut. On the face of it, the Islamic position on usury would seem to be little different from the official Christian position in the Middle Ages.

While this parallel is essentially correct, the process of getting there is greatly complicated by the origins of the words themselves. Interest derives from the medieval Latin word *interesse*. Usury comes from the Latin word *usura*. The problem is that theologians and ecclesiastical law treated the two as different in kind. In particular, *interesse* was permitted and *usura* was forbidden (Nelson, 1949, p. 17). *Usura*, meaning enjoyment, denoted money paid for the use of money, and under canonical law meant the intention of the lender to obtain more in return from a loan than the principal amount due. It equates to what we would today call interest, measured by the difference between the amount that a borrower repays and the principal amount that is originally received from the lender (Patinkin, 1968). Both usury and interest also correspond to *riba*, which as we have seen literally means 'increase' or in excess of the original sum.

Medieval canon law thus prohibited payment for the use of a loan, which (following Roman law) it called *usura*. But while a person was prevented from charging money for a loan, he could demand compensation – *damna et interesse* – if he was not repaid on time. *Interesse* referred to the compensation made by a debtor to a creditor for damages caused to the creditor as a result of default or delays in the repayment of the principal, corresponding to any loss incurred or gain foregone on the creditor's part.[6] Because such *interesse* was lawful and conceptually distinct from unlawful *usura*, it is easy to understand why the term 'interest' has come to be universally adopted in post-medieval societies, and also why in the Middle Ages creditors had a strong incentive to seek to disguise usury as *interesse* and accordingly not fall foul of the Church.

What was the authority for the Church's rulings on these matters? It needs to be recalled that the Church was the single most powerful institution of the Middle Ages, and held sway over people's lives by a combination of secular and spiritual power. Its landholdings made it the greatest of the feudal lords, and its estates were the source of much economic production and consumption. In addition, the Church had a doctrinal unity and claimed command over the totality of human relations. Like Islam today, Christianity then was not just a religion, but a way of life governing both conduct on earth and spiritual salvation in the other world.

Christian doctrine derived from three basic sources. First, there were the scriptures, especially the Gospels and the teachings of Jesus. Second, as the Middle Ages progressed and the Church became increasingly institutionalized, the words of Jesus were not sufficient to cover all eventualities and were supplemented, and to a large degree supplanted, by canon law based on the rulings of ecumenical councils and Church courts. Third, schoolmen and theologians laid the foundations of Christian theology, drawing on ethical principles developed by Greek philosophers such as Plato and Aristotle.

Biblical Sources

The Holy Qur'an – a work roughly the same length as the New Testament – contains four clear strictures on the subject of usury (see above). The New Testament has three references to usury, and the Old Testament has four.

Of the three passages on usury in the New Testament, two of them are identical and relate to the Parable of the Talents (Matthew 25:14–30 and Luke 19:12–27). Both, it must be said, are decidedly ambiguous on the question of usury (Gordon, 1982). The servant who returns the talents as he received them is castigated by the nobleman for not having 'put my money to the exchanges, and then at my coming I should have received my own with usury' (Mt. 25:27). If interpreted literally, this verse would appear to condone the taking of usury, yet at the same time the recipient is criticized for 'reaping that thou didst not sow' (Luke 19:21).

However, the other reference in the New Testament is clear: 'But love ye your enemies, and do good, and lend, hoping for nothing again; and your reward shall be great, and ye shall be the children of the Highest' (Luke 6:35).[7] Jesus himself exhibited a distinctly anti-usury attitude when he cast the moneylenders from the temple, while the Sermon on the Mount revealed strongly anti-wealth sentiments as well.

In the case of the Old Testament, three references to usury given earlier in this chapter come from the Pentateuch, the Law of Moses, and from Psalms and attributed to David. However, for Christians the Deuteronomic double standard could not be applied (although some Christians did to Saracens).[8] 'Brothers' had been universalized by the New Testament (Luke 6:35, as quoted above) and there was accordingly no scriptural basis for charging interest to anyone.

Canonical Law

Islamic law – the *shari'ah* – grew out of the attempts made by early Muslims, as they confronted immediate social and political problems, to devise a legal system in keeping with the code of behaviour called for by the Holy Qur'an and the *hadith* ('traditions' or 'sayings' related to the life of Prophet Muhammad). Scholars developed these systems by treating the Holy Qur'an as containing the general principles by which all matters should be regulated, and where the meaning of the Holy Qur'an was imprecise they sought clarification from the *hadith*. Thus the foundations of the *shari'ah* were the clear and unambiguous commands and prohibitions to be found in these sources. With the passage of time, scholars came to agree increasingly on the basic laws and the principle of *ijma*, or consensus of the community of believers, was established.

Much of the same process of evolution took place in the early Christian Church, and canon law was fashioned by the ecumenical councils, the popes and the bishops. The early Church first condemned usury by the 44th of the Apostolic Canons at the Council of Arles, 314, followed by Nicea in 325, and Laodicia in 372. The first canon law ruling against usury was the Papal Encyclia *Nec hoc quoque* of Saint Leo the Great, Pope from 440 to 461. The last Papal Encyclical against usury, *Vix pervenit*, was issued in 1745 by Pope Benedict XIV (although it was not an infallible decree). In between, and beyond that date, the Catholic Church maintained its opposition to the practice, although the emphasis did change over time.

At first, the Church's prohibition on usury did not go beyond the clergy, although more general disapproval was expressed to laity by the first Council of Carthage (345). Roll (1953) argues that a wider prohibition was unnecessary. In the absence of a developed money economy and capital market, with most feudal dues rendered in kind, the Church was not only the largest production unit but also virtually the only recipient of large sums of money. For the Church to charge interest on consumption loans to the needy would rightly be seen as exploitation. Interest-free loans were 'good business' in that they generated enthusiasm amongst the people for religion (Glaeser and Scheinkman, 1998). Also, to allow usury might encourage private profiteering by clerics and perhaps open the door for simony (the buying and selling of any spiritual benefit for a temporal consideration).

As trade and commerce expanded in the later Middle Ages, and the demand for loans increased, to combat 'the insatiable rapacity of usurers' the Church's prohibition was extended to laymen in ever more strident and stringent forms (Divine, 1967). These condemnations came from the great Lateran Councils,[9] Lyon II and Vienne. The Second Lateran Council (1139) condemned usury as 'ignominious'. Lateran III (1179) introduced excommunication (exclusion from the Christian community) for open usurers. Lateran IV (1215) censured Christians who associated with Jewish usurers. Lyon II (1274) extended the condemnations to foreign usurers. Finally, the Council of Vienne (1311) allowed excommunication of princes, legislators and public authorities who either utilized or protected usurers, or who sought to distinguish between allowable interest and usury.[10]

It was thus with good reason that Tawney (1926, p. 58) described this period as the 'high-water mark' of the ecclesiastical attack on usury. It was also at this time that an extra dimension was added to the Church's arguments against usury in the revival of Aristotelian logic and its combination with Roman law by St Thomas Aquinas (1225–74).

Aquinas and Aristotle

The third influence upon the Church's view on usury came from the medieval Schoolmen and in particular the most important of them, Saint Thomas Aquinas, who is generally acknowledged as the greatest of the scholastic philosophers, ranking in status alongside Plato, Aristotle, Kant and Hegel (Bertrand Russell, 1946). St Thomas in *Summa Theologica* succeeded in persuading the Church fathers that Aristotle's views should form the basis of Christian philosophy, and resurrected Aristotle's views on usury. The Greeks themselves (like the Romans later) exhibited no compunction about the taking of interest, but Plato disliked usury and in *The Republic*, his ideal state was opposed to all credit transactions except those undertaken on the basis of friendship and brotherhood, and explicitly prohibited lending at interest.[11] Plato's pupil Aristotle also opposed interest, based on a distinction between natural and unnatural modes of production, the latter including income from moneylending. Interest thus violates natural law; a position with which St Thomas and the Church concurred.

Christian theologians argued that the preferred way of making an investment was not by moneylending, but through partnership, since any contract had to avoid usury, yet give legitimate compensation to the investor (Mews and Walsh, 2011). In *Summa Theologica*, St Thomas observes that in a partnership the person supplying money can legitimately claim his share of the profit, while collecting usury was morally wrong because no risk was shared (Aquinas, 1985, p. 245).

WHY DID CHRISTIANS ABHOR USURY?

Having examined the sources of the Christian doctrine on usury in terms of the Bible, the canon law and the writings of the Fathers and Schoolmen overlaid on Greek philosophy, it is now time to pull the threads together. At least ten justifications could be offered by the medieval Churchmen for the ban on usury.

First, usury contravened the teachings of Jesus. Although the passages in the Gospels can be variously interpreted, the absence of a specific condemnation cannot disguise the fact that on the basis of Jesus's casting out of the moneylenders, and the principle 'actions speak louder than words', the lending out of money at interest was regarded as the very worst form of gain.

Second, Hebrew law prohibited usury unambiguously. The only point at issue was to whom and how widely the ban applied. However, from the very earliest years, Christians at least should have had few illusions on that score. St Jerome (340–420) and St Ambrose (340–97) claimed that 'brothers' in Deuteronomy had been universalized by the prophets and the New Testament ('love thine enemies'), leaving no scriptural warrant for levying usury at all.

Third, the scriptures also severely restricted loan-related activities. Much lending of money occurred against objects held in trust (a pawn or pledge) by the lender. The prohibition of usury also extended to the types of collateral which could be used. The usury restriction in Exodus is immediately followed by the injunction, 'If thou at all take thy neighbour's raiment to pledge, thou shalt deliver it unto him by that the sun goeth down' (Exodus 22:26).

This and other limitations on pledges are given in Deuteronomy 24, and there are restrictions on collateral in the *halacha* (Rabinovich, 1993). These presumably had the intention of reducing the power of the creditor, and preventing the debtor from having to observe usurious contracts (and thus himself commit a sin). Under Talmudic law, it is not only the creditor who takes interest who is violating the biblical prohibition, but also the debtor who agrees to pay interest, the guarantor who guarantees the debt which bears interest, the witnesses who attest the creation of an interest-bearing debt, and even the scribe who writes out the deed (Cohn, 1971).

Fourth, usury was contrary to Aristotle. Once canonists accepted Aristotle's distinction between the natural economy and the unnatural art of money-making, then it followed that the science of economics had to be seen as a body of laws designed to ensure the moral soundness of economic activity. Money, according to Aristotle, arose as a means of facilitating the legitimate exchange of natural goods in order to provide utility to consumers. As such, money was barren. Interest was the unnatural fruit of a barren parent, money:

> The most hated sort [of wealth], and with the greatest reason, is usury, which makes gain out of money itself, and not from the natural object of it. For money was intended to be used in exchange, and not to increase at interest . . . Of all modes of getting wealth, this is the most unnatural. (Aristotle, 2013, *Politics*, 1258)

In fact, usury (which of course meant all lending at interest) was doubly condemned. Through usury, the accumulation of money becomes an end in itself, and the satisfaction of wants is lost from sight. Those doing so are rendered 'deficient in higher qualities' (Aristotle, 2013, *Politics*, 1323).

Fifth, St Thomas Aquinas augmented the Aristotelian view with the doctrine of Roman law which divided commodities into those which are consumed in use (consumptibles) and those which are not (fungibles). Wine is an example of the former (although not a good one to use for Muslims and many Christians). 'If a man wanted to sell wine separately from the use of wine, he would be selling the same thing twice, or he would be selling what does not exist: wherefore he would evidently commit a sin of injustice'. Since 'the proper and principal use of money is its consumption', 'it is by very nature unlawful to take payment for the use of money lent, which payment is known as interest' (Aquinas, 1985, *Summa Theologica*, II 78).

Sixth, closely related was the view that usury violated natural justice. When a loan of money is made, the ownership of the thing that is lent passes to the borrower. Why should the creditor demand payment from a person who is, in effect, merely using what is now his own property? To do so would be to rob from those who make profitable use of the money. Profits should rightly belong to those who make the money profitable.

Seventh, St Thomas also condemned usury because it 'leads to inequality which is contrary to justice'. The Biblical admonitions on usury are surrounded by references to the 'poor', 'widows and orphans', and those in poverty to whom one is encouraged to 'lend freely, hoping for nothing thereby'. Prohibitions on usury were allied to the notion of a 'just price', which featured in Aristotle's *Ethics* (Thomson, 1953). The moral justification for trade, and wealth derived from trade, depended on whether the exchange which was effected is just. A 'proportionate equality' between the parties prior to exchange is essential if justice is to underlie commercial transactions (Thomson, 1953, Book V, Ch. 5, 152). This was unlikely to be the case when money was lent to needy persons for the purposes of consumption. Usury, and the search for gain for its own sake, was the basest aspect of trade, leading men to the desire for limitless accumulation. In this respect, usury laws were 'commands to be lenient, merciful and kind to the needy' (Maimonides, 1956).

Eighth, since interest was regarded as the means by which the wealthy received an 'unearned income' from the unfortunate, it cut across medieval views on work. Work was a positive virtue and supplied the only justification for any kind of economic increment and profit. Consider the scriptures: 'In the sweat of thy face shalt thou eat bread, till thou return unto the ground' (Genesis 3:19). A university professor, for example, who might otherwise be accused of selling knowledge, which belongs only to God and cannot be sold, could at least argue on this basis that he is working and therefore merits a salary (Le Goff, 1979). But this defence did not help the usurer: 'The creditor becomes rich by the sweat of the debtor, and the debtor does not reap the reward of his labour' (Tawney, 1926, p.115). Not only does the usurer not work, but he makes his money work for him. Even in his sleep, the usurer's money is at work and is making a profit. Nor does money observe the Sabbath. Even the peasant lets his oxen rest on Sundays. But the usurer does not let his money respect the day of rest (Baldwin, 1970, Vol. 2, 191).

Ninth, to the canonists, time was an important consideration in the sin of usury. Interest was a payment for the passage of time. Moreover, usury was defined broadly. Under Charlemagne, who first extended the usury laws to the laity, usury was defined in 806 CE as 'where more is asked than is given' (Glaeser and Scheinkman, 1998, p.33), while in the thirteenth century usury or profit on a loan (*mutuum*) was distinct from other contracting arrangements. A usurer, in fact, was anyone who allowed for an element of time in a transaction, such as by asking for a higher price when selling on credit or, because of the lapse of time, goods bought cheaper and sold dearer (Tawney, 1926, pp.59–61).[12] The sin was in exploiting time itself. Time belongs to God, a divine possession. Usurers were selling something that did not belong to them. They were robbers of time, medieval gangsters (Le Goff, 1979, pp.34–5).

Finally, tenth, most damning of all was that interest was fixed and certain. It was a fixed payment stipulated in advance for a loan of money or wares without risk to the lender. It was certain in that whether or not the borrower gained or lost, the usurer took his pound of flesh (Tawney, 1926, p.55). What delineated usury from other commercial transactions was in it being a contract for the repayment of more than the principal amount of the loan 'without risk to the lender' (Jones, 1989, p.4).

It was this last point which created an unbridgeable divide between commercial motives and divine precepts. According to Tawney, medieval opinion, by and large, had no objection as such to rent and profits, provided that they were not unreasonable and exploitive. In addition, the ecumenical authorities had endeavoured to formulate the prohibition upon usury in such a way as not to conflict unnecessarily with legitimate trade and commerce. But no mercy was to be shown to the usurer. In many areas of economic activity, temporally based returns were permitted because they involved the taking of a certain amount of risk. But where no risk was considered to be involved, interest-taking was strictly forbidden. The usurer's crime was in the taking of a payment for money which was fixed and certain; thus the primary test for usury was whether or not the lender

had contracted to lend at interest without assuming a share of the risk
inherent to the transaction. If the lender could collect interest regardless of
the debtor's fortunes, he was a usurer (Jones, 1989, pp. 118–19).

COMPARING ISLAMIC AND CHRISTIAN VIEWS

The Parallels

To those who had forgotten – or perhaps been unaware of – the extent
to which Islam builds on, and sustains and fulfils, the message of its two
monotheist antecedents, the similarities between the views in the previous
section and those of Islam outlined earlier may well be unexpected. In
particular, the attitudes seeing usury as the worst form of gain, as lacking
any scriptural warrant whatsoever, as involving unjustified collateral,
forcing the debtor to sin, as unnatural and barren, as an unwarranted
expropriation of property, as devoid of true work, and fixed, certain and
lacking in risk-sharing, all of these are echoed in (or echo) Islamic views.
This parallel is especially so in the case of the last, in that a loan provides
the lender with a fixed return irrespective of the outcome of the borrower's
venture, whereas the reward to capital should instead be commensurate
with the risk and effort involved and thus be governed by the return on the
individual project for which funds are supplied.

There are other parallels as well. Islam comprises a set of principles
and doctrines that guide and regulate a Muslim's relationship with God
and with society. In this respect, Islam is not only a divine service, but also
incorporates a code of conduct which regulates and organizes mankind
in both spiritual and material life. The Aristotelian idea that ethics should
govern the science of economics would sit comfortably with an adherent,
as would the view that the Church (Muslims would of course substitute
God) has command over the totality of human relations.

Yusuf al-Qaradawi (see Hussain, 1999) gives four reasons for the Islamic
prohibition of interest (*riba*), similar to those quoted earlier of Razi (1872
[1938]):

- Taking interest implies taking another person's property without
  giving him anything in exchange. The lender receives something for
  nothing.
- Dependence on interest discourages people from working to earn
  money. Money lent at interest will not be used in industry, trade
  or commerce, all of which need capital, thus depriving society of
  benefits.

- Permitting the taking of interest discourages people from doing good. If interest is prohibited, people will lend to each other with goodwill, expecting nothing more back than they have loaned.
- The lender is likely to be wealthy and the borrower poor. The poor will be exploited by the wealthy through the charging of interest on loans.

These points are virtually identical to some of the early Christian views. There is also a shared concern about the time element in contracting. Compensation from licit forms of Islamic financing must differ from interest not only by being calculated on a pre-transaction basis but also cannot be explicitly related to the duration of the finance.

The Differences

However, there are differences too. The first, and most obvious, concerns the central scriptural authority. In the case of the Bible, there are enough ambiguities – New versus Old Testament, Mosaic versus later Hebrew law, and a very parabolic parable – to keep an army of scholars employed (as indeed they did); whereas the injunctions in the Holy Qur'an are forthright. Second, while canon law and scholastic philosophy sought to augment scripture, the essential feature of that source was that it could – and did – change in response to the temper of the times and new religious thinking; whereas the Holy Qur'an provided a fixed and certain point of reference. Third, to the extent that Christian doctrine rested on an Aristotelian foundation, it was vulnerable to the charge of being, at heart, anti-trade and commerce. Aristotle adopted the view, later followed by the Physiocrats, that the natural way to get wealth is by skilful management of house and land. Usury was diabolical and clearly the worst way of making money. But there was also something degraded about trading and exchanging things rather than actually making them, as summed up in the medieval saying, '*Homo mercator vix aut numquam Deo placere potest*' – the merchant can scarcely or never be pleasing to God. By contrast, the Holy Qur'an endorsed trade, so long as it was not usurious.

On all three counts, where Christianity was somewhat equivocal in comparison with Islam, its stand on usury was subject to erosion. Perhaps ironically, the one aspect on which it was more forthright than Islam undoubtedly served to reinforce that trend. This was in the area of punishment.

Christian Sanctions on Usurers

A Christian usurer faced five sanctions. First, he had eventually to face his Maker, and the Church left him in no doubt that he faced the fiercest of the fires of hell. In the scale of values, the usurer was linked with the worst evil-doers, the worst occupations, the worst sins and the worst vices. Indeed, the prohibition of usury is even more rigorous than the commandment against murder; murder could be condoned in some circumstances, but nothing could excuse usury. Also, echoing Talmudic law, the sin is shared by all of those who conspire in the acts: public officials who sanction usury, and even the debtors themselves. Debtors who contract to pay usury without explicitly demurring in some way are declared to share the creditor's sin: without the addict, the dealer could not survive.

Second, disclosure meant becoming a social outcast. It has been said that the usurer was 'tolerated on earth but earmarked for hell' (Lopez, 1979, p. 7), but this was not so. Public opinion was that usurers should be exterminated like wolves, and their bodies thrown on the dung heap. They should be condemned to death and hanged, or at the very least banished from the country and their property confiscated.[13] They were fit only to associate with Jews, robbers, rapists and prostitutes, but were worse than all of them. Thirteenth-century society was classified according to two groupings: a classification by sins and vices, and a classification according to social rank and occupation. On both lists, usurers were at the bottom of the heap. They were publicly preached at, shamed, taunted and reviled.

Third, the usurer would be punished by the Church, and by the orders of the Church. The Lateran Councils laid down clear rules for offenders: they were to be refused communion or a Christian burial, their offerings were not to be accepted, and open usurers were to be excommunicated. There could be no absolution for them and their wills were to be invalid. Those who let houses to usurers were themselves to be excommunicated. No usurer could hold public office. Church courts and civil courts fought over the lucrative business of who would levy the fines.

Fourth, the only salvation for the usurer lay in restitution. Restitution had to be made to each and every person from whom interest or increase had been taken, or to their heirs. Were that not possible, the money had to be given to the poor. All property that had been pawned had to be restored, without deduction of interest or charges. And the ecclesiastical authorities could move against the usurers and their accomplices even if the debtors would not.

Fifth, the usurer risked condemning his wife and heirs to penury, for the same penalties were applied to them as to the original offender. They also faced a lifetime of humility and devotion. Certain actions of the living (alms, prayers, masses) could aid in the posthumous redemption of the usurer: the sinful husband might be saved by the faithful wife. By becoming recluses, and engaging in alms, fasts and prayers, the wife and children might move God to favour the usurer's soul.

Islamic Sanctions

In comparison with these punitive measures, the sanctions imposed on the Islamic usurer seem less extreme. That the usurer will not fare well on the Day of Judgment is clear enough. Consider Zamakhsharî on *sura* 2:275/276:

> Those who consume interest (ar-ribä) shall not rise again (on the day of resurrection), except as one arises whom Satan has prostrated by the touch (that is, one who is demon-possessed): that is because they have said: 'Bargaining is just the same as interest', even though God has permitted bargaining but has forbidden interest. Now whoever receives an admonition from his Lord and then desists (from the practice), he shall retain his past gains, and his affair is committed to God. But whoever repeats (the offence) – those are the inhabitants of the fire, therein dwelling forever.[14]

However, no specific penalty was laid down in the Holy Qur'an, and it was left to the jurists to determine the scale of punishment, qualification and legal validity (Schacht, 1964, p. 12).

As for the legal status of *riba* transactions, Islamic law recognizes, first, a scale of religious qualifications; and second, a scale of legal validity. Interest is forbidden (*haram*), but on Schacht's (1964, p. 145) interpretation a contract concluded in contravention of the rules concerning *riba* is defective (*fasid*) or voidable rather than null and void (*batil*). Nevertheless, this distinction between the two is not recognized by all schools of Islamic law, and since *riba* is a special case of 'unjustified enrichment' by which the property of others is consumed (or appropriated for one's own use) for no good reason, the *riba* element cannot be enforced. It is a general principle of Islamic law, based on a number of passages in the Holy Qur'an, that unjustified enrichment, or 'receiving a monetary advantage without giving a countervalue', is forbidden, and he who receives it must give it to the poor as a charitable gift. The latter condition is the practice of Islamic banks when extant transactions are found to have violated the ban on interest, and the earnings are distributed by *Shari'ah* Boards to various *zakat* funds.

THE CHRISTIAN USURY BAN IN PRACTICE

Usury was clearly a sin, but it was one that many Christians found difficult to resist, despite the severe temporal penalties exacted by the ecclesiastical authorities. It was much better for the interest element to be concealed, and many a technique was developed in order to gain while not violating the letter of the law. Of course, it hardly needs to be said that such stratagems are not unknown in Muslim economic life.

Our examination of these arrangements in medieval Christianity is grouped under five headings. First, there are the variations upon *interesse*. Second, there are those transactions which took advantage of the international dimension. Third, interest income could be converted into other permissible forms of income. Fourth, some of the legal fictions that were employed borrowed directly from those being used contemporaneously by the early Muslim community to circumvent the ban on *riba* (as others did from Jewish evasions). However, it is the fifth category which is particularly interesting. Intriguingly, some other practices followed seem to be virtually identical to those which have gained approval today in Islamic financing.

Interesse

A number of techniques rested on the distinction between *usura*, which was unlawful, and *interesse*, compensation for loss, which was lawful. Under the doctrine of *damnum emergens*, the suffering of loss, the lender was entitled to exact a conventional penalty from the borrower if he failed to return the principal at the agreed time, that is, if he defaulted. This provision opened the door to the taking of interest, since the courts assumed that there had been a genuine delay and that a bona fide loss had occurred. By making very short-term loans and simulating delay (*mora*) in repayment, interest could be concealed.

Payment could also be demanded under the doctrine relating to *lucrum cessans*. As well as compensation for damage suffered, the lender could be compensated for the gain that had been sacrificed when money was lent. A creditor with capital invested in a business could claim compensation on this account, and the growing opportunities for trade made it easier to prove that gain had escaped him. A wide range of financial transactions could be legitimized in this way, especially since a special reward could be claimed by the lender because of the risk which had been incurred.

International Transactions

The international dimension could also be utilized, using the 'Deuteronomic double standard', to charge interest to enemies such as the Saracens during the Crusades. But by far the most common activity involved foreign exchange. Lending gave rise to interest, which was contrary to nature and the law, but the sale of one asset for another (including coinage) was legitimate. If the asset was a foreign one, the price at which the sale was concluded could be used to conceal that the transaction was really the combination of a loan with a foreign exchange transaction.

The most typical case was that of the bill of exchange, and special 'foreign exchange fairs' which operated between 1553 and 1763 were held at regular intervals – usually four times a year – largely for the purpose of issuing bills payable there and organizing foreign exchange clearing (Kindleberger, 1984; de Cecco, 1992). A rule endorsed by most scholastic writers exempted from the anti-usury laws the buying and selling of bills issued in terms of a foreign currency and payable in a foreign country; a sort of medieval equivalent of a eurocurrency transaction today. A bill was an ideal vehicle because it involved an extension of credit in one place, used for the export of goods, and payment of the loan in another place, but in a different currency. This feature made it possible to disguise a domestic credit transaction in the form of currency exchange (Einzig, 1962).

Usually a medieval bill of exchange transaction consisted of the sale for local currency of an obligation to pay a specified sum in another currency at a future. It thus involved both an extension of credit and an exchange of currency. A modern-day bank would handle this transaction by converting the foreign into the local currency at the ruling spot rate of exchange, and then charging a rate of discount for the credit extended when paying out cash now for cash later. To do so then would have been usurious, for discounting was not an allowable activity. Consequently, by not separating the two elements involved, the medieval banker bought the bill at a price which incorporated both an element of interest and a charge for his services as an exchange dealer.

Of course, the banker then had an open book which had to be closed by reversing the transaction and buying a bill in the foreign location, and receiving payment in his own currency. In this circumstance, the fluctuation of exchange rates provided a convincing case of risk, since the terms at which the reverse deal could be undertaken would not be guaranteed at the time of the original transaction. It was this risk that reconciled bill dealing with the laws.[15]

Once the bill of exchange became admissable, it was a short step to lend money domestically by means of fictitious exchange transactions involving drafts and redrafts between two places. For example, a merchant needing cash would get it from an Italian banker by drawing a bill on the banker's own correspondent at the fairs of Lyons or Frankfurt. When this bill matured, it would be cancelled by a redraft issued by the correspondent and payable by the borrowing merchant to his creditor, the banker. Thus, the latter would recover the money which he had lent. To confuse the theologian, the real nature of the *cambio con la ricorsa*, as it was called, was clouded in technical jargon and was further obscured by clever manipulations in the books of the banker and of his correspondent. But once these trimmings were stripped away, it was simply discounting taking place under the cover of fictitious currency exchanges (de Roover, 1954, 1963).

Many bankers had a guilty conscience about getting around the usury laws in this way, as reflected by those of their number who included in their wills and testaments a distribution to the Church or to the needy in restitution for their illicit returns (Galassi, 1992). Other bankers institutionalized their attempt to buy 'a passport to heaven': in fourteenth-century Florence, the Bardi and Peruzzi banks regularly set aside part of their annual profits for distribution to the poor, holding the funds in an account under the name of Messer Domineddio, 'Mr God-Our-Lord' (Galassi, 1992, p. 314).

Income Conversions

Converting interest income into permitted sources of earnings lay at the heart of all of the techniques, including those above. Land provided the vehicle for the one form of investment that was widely understood and universally practised, even by the Church itself. This was the rent charge. Those with funds to lend could purchase a contract to pay so much from the rents of certain lands or houses or premises in return for the sum outlaid. For example, around 1500 CE, £10 a year for £100 down was about a normal rate in England. Such an investment was not regarded as usurious, despite being as fixed, certain and safe in medieval conditions as any loan. As in most legal systems, observance of the letter rather than the spirit of the law often took precedence.

THE ISLAMIC PROHIBITION HISTORICALLY

Not surprisingly, the same pressures to follow form over substance in commercial dealings existed in the Islamic countries, and at much the same time. Commercial practice was brought into conformity with the requirements of the *shari'ah* by the *hiyal* or 'legal devices' which were often legal fictions. Schacht (1964) defines the *hiyal* as 'the use of legal means for extra-legal ends, ends that could not, whether they themselves were legal or illegal, be achieved directly with the means provided by the *shari'ah* (p. 78). Frequently, he argues, these were the maximum that custom could concede, and the minimum that the theory demanded.

As in the West, Muslim merchants utilized the potential of the bill of exchange to (and perhaps beyond) the limits of the law. Another device consisted of giving real property as a security for the debt and allowing the creditor to use it, so that its use represented the interest; this transaction was not dissimilar to the rent charge. Closely related to this transaction was the sale of property with the right of redemption (*bai' al-wafa', bai' al-'uhda*).

A popular technique consisted of the double sale (*bai 'atan fi bay'a*). For example, the (prospective) debtor sells to the (prospective) creditor an item for cash, and immediately buys it back from him for a greater amount payable at a future date; this amounts to a loan with the particular item concerned as security, and the difference between the two prices represents the interest. Schacht claims that there were 'hundreds' of such devices used by traders *cum* moneylenders, all with a scrupulous regard for the letter of the law.[16] It goes without saying, of course, that from an Islamic perspective these legal fictions or *hiyal* are strictly prohibited. The mention in the Holy Qur'an of the example of a Jewish community nullifying the Sabbath command leaves no scope for such a subterfuge (S2:65).

It seems quite likely that many of these *hiyal* were conveyed to medieval Europe by Muslim traders presumably through the principles and practice of the triangular international trade and commerce which connected the Islamic countries, Byzantium and (at that stage) the relatively undeveloped West. Such transmission is suggested by the etymological sources of the vocabulary of medieval finance. For instance, we can cite the medieval Latin *mohatra*, from Arabic *mukhatara*, a term for the evasion of the prohibition of interest by means of a double sale; the French term *aval*, from Arabic *hawala*, for the endorsement on a bill of exchange; the term 'cheque', from Arabic *sakk*, 'written document'; and the term *sensalis* (*sensale, Sensal*), from Arabic *simsar*, 'broker'.

Some of the more approved modes of Islamic financing also featured in medieval Europe. Since the legal form of the financing was what ultimately mattered, the owner and the prospective user of funds could, as an alternative to arranging a loan, form a partnership (*nomine societatis palliatum*), with profit and loss divided among them in various ways. What was of crucial importance, theologically, was that the provider of funds had to share in the partner's risk. That proviso rendered the arrangement broadly equivalent to that of the Islamic *musharaka* (used in present-day Islamic finance and discussed later) under which an entrepreneur and investor jointly contribute funds to a venture, and divide up the profits and losses according to a predetermined ratio. Finance-based partnerships involving merchants are mentioned in Islamic sources around 700 CE, but the origins in the West (the *commenda* and the *compagnia*) go back no further than the tenth century (Lopez, 1979).

Of course, it was also possible to use the partnership form as a legal fiction to cloak what was really interest rate lending in all but name. For example, a person might have lent money to a merchant on the condition that he be a partner in the gains, but not in the losses. Another favourite method, used particularly in the City of London, was for the 'partner' providing funds to be a 'sleeping' one to conceal the borrowing and lending of money. Even more complicated devices such as the *contractus trinus* (triple contact), were devised which, while approved by custom and law, caused much theological strife.[17]

Mudaraba Investments

More interesting still was the existence in Middle Ages Europe of *mudaraba*-type arrangements when the medieval banks took in funds from depositors. (*Mudaraba* is one of the partnership-based building blocks of current Islamic finance, as examined later in Chapter 7.) Under these types of account no fixed return was specified, but the depositor was offered a share or participation in the profits of the bank. For example, on 17 November 1190, a servant of the famous Fieschi family entrusted 'capital' of £7 Genoese to the banker Rubeus upon condition that he could withdraw his deposit on 15 days' notice and that he would receive a 'suitable' return on his money (de Roover, 1954, p. 39). Much closer to present-day *mudaraba* were the investment modes offered by the Medici Bank. For example, the famous diplomat and chronicler Philippe de Commines (1447–1511) placed with the Lyons branch of Medici a time deposit which, instead of yielding a fixed percentage, entitled him to participate in the profits 'at the discretion' of the bank (*depositi a discrezione*). As another illustration, the contract between this same bank and Ymbert de Batarnay, Seigneur du Bouchage, concerning a deposit in 1490 of 10 000 *écus* does not mention any fixed percentage but states, on the contrary, that this sum was to be employed in lawful trade and the profits accruing therefrom were to be shared equally between the contracting parties (de Roover, 1948, p. 56).

The historian Raymond de Roover called this 'strange behaviour' and dismissed the practice as merely a legal deception to skirt the usury laws. Viewed from the perspective of Islamic banking nowadays, however, the arrangement seems an entirely appropriate response, valid in its own right.

It would thus be fascinating to know how widespread this type of the contract was (it was obviously in operation for more than 300 years), and why it later fell into disuse.

THE CHRISTIAN RETREAT

With the advent of the mercantile era (*c.* 1500–1700) the practice of the taking of interest, which had been forbidden by the Church, gradually came to be accepted (although cases involving usury were still being heard in England in the reign of Queen Elizabeth I) and eventually sanctioned. Why did the prohibition on usury break down throughout Europe? As in any other area of enquiry, a number of strongly intertwined factors were involved, making it difficult to disentangle cause from effect.

'Deregulation'

Tawney was the first to connect this shift in religious thought with the rise in commerce. He argued that economic growth swelled the channels for profitable investment to such an extent that the divorce between theory and reality had become almost unbridgeable. Greater investment opportunities made the usury laws more costly and tiresome to enforce, while the devices to get around the prohibition had become so numerous that everyone was concerned with the form rather than the substance of transactions. In effect, the ban had become unworkable and the rulings themselves were brought into disrepute.

All of this can be interpreted in terms of the economic theory of regulation. When the bans were introduced in the early Middle Ages, the Church itself was the centre of economic life, and canon law was concerned with ensuring that its own representatives were kept in line. As the outside market grew and commerce expanded, more and more activity moved outside the controlled (that is, non-usury) sector. At first, the Church extended the regulations (that is, the ban on usury) to the non-controlled activities. When the market continued to expand, and the legal devices to circumvent the regulations expanded also, the Church's condemnations became at first more strident and its penalties more severe as it tried to keep a lid on interest transactions. But at some point the tide turned. As the thinly disguised interest economy continued to grow, more and more were willing to seek immediate gains in the present world and take their chances in the hereafter, hoping that a deathbed confession and token restitution would ensure an easier route to salvation. The Church itself was forced to devote more of its energies to examining the accounts of moneylenders and merchants in order to root out the various subterfuges used to conceal usury. In short, the cost of maintaining the regulations increased. Regulatory theory predicts that a stage might be reached when the least-cost solution is to 'deregulate' and remove the irksome controls.

Then the problem, of course, is how to save face and break from the past, particularly when so much intellectual capital and moral fervour has been devoted to the issue. It was necessary to avoid the charge of hypocrisy or moral backsliding. Again, we can explain what happened in terms of the theory of regulation, by borrowing from what is known as the theory of regulatory 'capture'.[18] One strand of that literature concerns what happens if there are a number of competing regulatory agencies (as in United States banking, for example), fighting over common turf and seeking to widen their constituency. Then, 'competition in laxity' may be the result. Something like this may have happened with the Christian Church on usury: competition to the orthodoxy of Catholicism came from the rise of Protestantism associated with the names of Luther and Calvin, and laxity from the relaxation of the usury laws.

Calvin

Luther was rather ambivalent on the topic of usury, but Calvin was not. His denial (in a series of letters beginning in 1547) that the taking of payment for the use of money was in itself sinful has been hailed as a 'turning point in the history of European thought' (Ashley, 1888, 1893 [1913]), as the foundation stone of the 'spirit of capitalism' (Weber, 1904–05 [1930]) and the 'Gospel of the modern era' (Nelson, 1949). Earlier, St Paul had declared that the 'New Convenant' between Jesus and the people had superseded the old covenant of Mosaic law, so that Judaic law was no longer binding on Christian society (Letter to the Romans, Ch. 3). Calvin went further. He argued that neither the old Halachic code nor the rulings of the Gospels were universally applicable and binding for all time, because they were shaped by and designed for conditions that no longer exist. Rather, they should be interpreted in the light of individual conscience, the equity of the 'golden rule' (do unto others as you would have them do unto you), and the needs of society.

Thus under Calvin's reformation the lender is no longer a pariah but a useful part of society. Usury does not conflict with the law of God in all cases and, provided that the interest rate is reasonable, lending at interest is no more unjust than any other economic transaction; for example, it is as reasonable as the payment of rent for land. Although Calvin repudiated the Aristotelian doctrine that money was infertile, he nonetheless identified instances in which the taking of interest would be an act of sinful usury, as in the case of needy borrowers oppressed by circumstances and faced with exorbitant interest rates. But these are problems inherent in the social relations of a Christian community, to be solved in the light of existing circumstances and the dictates of natural law and the will of God, not by blanket prohibition.

Redefining Usury

Calvin's doctrine has become the language of modern Protestant Christianity, but the practical reality of the time was that everyone who sought a more liberal approach to usury turned to Calvin for support. Throughout Protestant Europe, governments embraced his views to abolish the legal prohibition of interest. Earlier, after Henry VIII's break with Rome, a statute was enacted in England in 1545 legalizing interest but limiting it to a legal maximum of 10 per cent, and legislation laying down a maximum rate in place of a prohibition of interest was made permanent by law in 1571 (although the 10 per cent legal ceiling was gradually lowered to 5 per cent per annum by the time of Adam Smith). Such 'usury laws' became the norm thereafter in Protestant Europe.

Two important consequences then followed. First, a wedge was thereby driven between the meanings of 'interest' and 'usury'. Interest could be seen as admissable compensation to a lender, fully in line with the spirit and letter of the law. Usury, by contrast, according to Jeremy Bentham's (1787 [1818]) description, was 'the taking of greater interest than the law allows' (as cited in Mews and Walsh, 2011, p. 212). For example, Adam Smith (1776 [1937]) distinguished between interest as legitimate compensation to a lender, and usury, which was always illegitimate since it involved a lender demanding money over and above any reasonable compensation for the loan purely for the sake of profit (Kerridge, 2002, p. 5).

A second consequence was that the 'usury laws' theselves came under attack, notably by Jeremy Bentham (1787 [1818]) in his volume *Defence of Usury*, on three grounds. First, Bentham saw the laws as driving the poor and needy into the arms of black-market moneylenders where they would face far more disadvantageous terms. Second, he argued that, while excess profits from usury could be used for 'wasteful consumption', there are many other ways and sources of income that can support 'prodigality', so why single out usury? Third, Bentham worried that the usury laws may have 'nipped in the bud', 'destroyed outright' and put impediments in the path of entrepreneurs and inventive industry. Mews and Walsh (2011, p. 211) consider that Bentham's tract had a 'huge impact' on trivializing the notion of usury, leading to the eventual abolition of the usury laws in Britain in 1854. A byproduct of these moves, they contend, was 'to promote a tendency in the West to divorce financial behaviour from ethical concerns' (ibid.). True indeed, as demonstrated far too often over the last decade.

Meanwhile, the retreat of Catholic canon law was in general slower and involved the concession of exceptions while clinging to the principle. Nevertheless, in the nineteenth century, the Roman Catholic authorities also relented by the issuance of some 14 decisions of the Congregations of the Holy Office, the Penitentiary, and the Propaganda stating that the faithful who lend money at moderate rates of interest are 'not to be disturbed', provided that they are willing to abide by any future decisions of the Holy See. Nonetheless, the Church still provides in the Code of Canon Law (*c.* 2354) severe penalties for those convicted of usury in the modern sense, that is, excessive interest (Nelson, 1949; Divine, 1967).

Consequently, theologically speaking, the great achievement of Calvin and his followers was, in effect, to have turned Deuteronomy on its head. Finding a solution to the troublesome 'Deuteronomic double standard' had long worried Christian theologians imbued with ideas of universal fraternity. Amongst the early Church, the distasteful implication that usury was lawful when levied upon some ('foreigners'), but unlawful and sinful when applied to others ('brothers'), was initially resolved by not charging interest to anyone. Following Calvin, the resolution came about instead by charging usury to all, but at a rate deemed not to be injurious.

Other factors may have featured in the erosion of the usury prohibition that we shall mention briefly. One was a shifting allegiance involving borrowers and lenders. In the Middle Ages, Church property was almost entirely in land, and landowners have always been borrowers rather than lenders. But when Protestantism arose, its support came chiefly from the middle class, who were lenders rather than borrowers. With this changing 'constituency' first Calvin, then other Protestants, and finally the Catholic Church sanctioned usury. Related to this argument is the distinction between consumption loans and production loans, which we have seen also features in some revisionist Islamic literature on *riba* (Shah, 1967; Rahman, 1964). In the early Middle Ages most loans would have been consumption loans, for which the potential for exploitation is presumably greater than for production loans. By the time of Calvin the position had reversed, and protection from exploitation could be achieved by proscribed maxima in excess of the 'natural' commercial rate. In terms of Max Weber's (1904–05 [1930]) *The Protestant Ethic and the Spirit of Capitalism*, 'Calvin developed a theology with an affinity to capitalism' (Abraham, 2011, p. 242).

CONCLUDING REMARKS: SOME QUESTIONS FOR ISLAM TODAY

One question concerns interest rate lending. Why was this so attractive and seductive to Christians? Why did lenders and borrowers strive to engage in this form of financing? The Church regarded usury as diabolical and, at base, exploitative. But it would be facile to see extortion as the only, or even major, reason for its popularity with lenders. The modern theory of financial intermediation considers interest rate loans as 'optimal' incentive-compatible forms of contracting in the face of certain types of information asymmetries and moral hazard. If so, a question-mark has to be raised over the universal applicability of some Islamic financing techniques, such as *mudaraba* and *musharaka*, and the Islamic banks have in fact been circumspect in their use. This issue is taken up in Chapter 9.

A more difficult question is posed by the historical interpretations of Tawney and Weber. Both of these authors trace the birth of capitalism to the rise of Protestantism and the relaxation of the ban on usury. To them, the abolition of the restrictions on usury was a necessary, if not sufficient, precondition for the development of an enterprise economy. They argued that prohibition against usury had its roots in a peasant society, close to subsistence levels, in which the ethical problem is relatively simple. When a crop fails and a family goes hungry, a non-interest loan will often be a duty: fraternal brotherhood offers a charitable hand, not a self-seeking one. But it is an entirely different matter to extend this type of ethical kinship to the realms of a national, indeed international capital market, in which the contracting is between relatively anonymous commercial lenders and borrowers. Such an attempt, it was said, risked either deception or failure, or both.

Exactly how important the relaxation of the usury laws was to the achievement of economic growth remains a contentious issue, since the alterations to the usury laws likely responded to the rise of commerce as well as perhaps influencing it (Iannaccone, 1998). It has been argued, on the one hand, that the prohibition of usury impeded the development of capitalism by restricting the supply of loanable funds and keeping interest rates high, since the laws undermined the enforcement of contracts (the authority of any civil law permitting interest was consistently denied by the Church, which ruled such contracts to be null and void). On the other hand, some contend that the operation of the prohibition during the formative years of capitalism in the late Middle Ages may well have had the important effect of diverting funds, which might otherwise have been loaned out at interest, into equity-type investments which nurtured a spirit of enterprise and contributed to development in these formative years (Spiegel, 1992).

Nevertheless, it is the case that the Christian Church maintained a prohibition on usury (interest) for more than 1400 years, and once the terminological difficulties are sorted out and the doctrinal sources examined, it is apparent that the official Christian objection to usury was almost identical to the Islamic position.

There were differences too. In fact, the divergences between the two religions on their stance about usury go a long way to explaining why Christianity relaxed and eventually retreated from the ban on usury, while Islam has not. One factor was the lack in Christian creed of an overriding injunction on the subject like that in the Holy Qur'an. That deficiency, along with ambiguities on related issues such as the acceptability of trade, opened up Catholicism to the inroads of Protestant revisionist interpretations on usury and what we have called 'competition in laxity'.

Another difference came from the severity of the temporal penalities applied to usurers by the Christian ecclesiastical courts. These inhibited much legitimate trade and at the same time raised the incentive to evade the prohibition in the form of taking advantage of various legal loopholes, which brought the institution itself into disrepute because of the transparency of some of the devices. There is, of course, an obvious lesson here, which has not gone unheard in Islamic circles (e.g., Gafoor, 1995).

At the same time, however, it can also be claimed with considerable justification that in medieval Christendom too much time was devoted to evasion, and by the Church to condemning and rooting out the evaders, than to finding acceptable non-interest alternatives to usury. In Islam, compliance has been left as a matter for the individual (and his Maker), but the Islamic community and the Islamic bankers have spent much effort examining the legitimacy of particular transactions and formalizing procedures which have enabled everyday banking, finance and commerce to be conducted on a *halal* basis. But to what extent are the methods employed genuinely legitimate, in the sense of meeting the spirit as well as the letter of the law? These are some of the issues considered in later chapters.

NOTES

1. Traditionally, the concern was about the interest rate in excess of the principal amount. Nowadays all financiers, but especially providers of payday loans, charge 'establishment fees' and 'late payment fees' that constitute usurious-type charges, and can inflate the 'real' repayment costs (that is, effective interest) to as much as 780 per cent per annum for short-term loans (see Lewis, 2015b).
2. Except where explicitly identifying and interpretative difference, 'usury' and 'interest' are to a considerable degree used interchangeably in the following discussion, recognizing

the points made in the previous note. However, once usury laws came to be enacted, a distinction can be made between legitimate compensation to a lender (interest) and usury or excessive or unreasonable demands (Mews and Walsh, 2011).

3. The Veda is the literature of the Aryans who invaded North India about 1500 BCE. Vedic law operated until about 500 BCE.

4. Modernist views are outlined in Rahman (1958, 1964), Rippin (1993), Rayner (1991) and Saeed (1996).

5. Based on Lewis (1999a) and later writings on this topic by this author.

6. The compensation originated from *id quod interest* of Roman law, which was the payment for damages due to non-fulfillment of a contractual obligation (*Encyclopedia Britannica*, 1947 edn).

7. This and other passages below come from the Authorised Version or King James Version of 1611 prepared by scholars in England.

8. This practice was often rationalized as an instrument of warfare. Pope Alexander III in 1159 argued that 'Saracens and heretics' whom it had not been possible to conquer by force of arms would be compelled under the weight of usury to yield to the Church (Nelson, 1949, p. 15).

9. Named after the old Lateran palace in Rome, the scene of five ecumenical councils.

10. The Church's position is outlined in Jones (1989), Le Goff (1979, 1984), Nelson (1949) and Noonan (1957).

11. Platonic and Greek economic thought is explained by Trever (1916) and Langholm (1984).

12. There is similarity here with the Rabbinic rulings in the Mishnah, the collection of legal interpretations of Exodus, Leviticus, Numbers and Deuteronomy. Loans of goods and speculative trading in wheat are ruled as morally equivalent to usury (Baba Mesia 5:1) (Levine, 1987).

13. All of these actions were recommended in Thomas Wilson's *Discourse upon Usury* (1572) quoted in Nelson (1949).

14. From the commentary of the Persian-Arab scholar Abu l-Qasim Mahmud ibn Uma az-Zamakhshari completed in 1134 CE, as reported in Gätje (1997).

15. Due to the slowness of communications at that time, even a sight draft was a credit instrument, since time elapsed while it was travelling from the place where it was issued to the place where it was payable. The theologians insisted upon the observance of the *distantia loci* (difference in place), but they tended to downplay the fact that the difference in place necessarily incorporated a difference in time (*dilatio temporis*). As the jurist Raphael de Turri, or Raffaele della Torre (*c.* 1578–1666), put it succinctly: '*distantia localis in cambio involvit temporis dilationem*' (distance in space also involves distance in time). Although he could not deny that a *cambium* (exchange) contract was a loan mixed with other elements, he wrote a treatise full of references to Aristotle, Aquinas, and a host of scholastic doctors in order to establish that exchange dealings were not tainted with any usury. In other words, the exchange transaction was used to justify profit on a credit transaction (de Roover, 1967).

16. The first and simplest *hiyal* were probably thought out by the interested parties who felt the need for them, the merchants in particular, but it was quite beyond them to invent and apply the more complicated ones. They would likely have had to have recourse to specialists with knowledge of the *shari'ah*. The early development of Islamic law is examined by Lindholm (1996).

17. The kind of loan which the Church condemned – a loan in which the creditor claimed interest from the beginning of the loan and stipulated the return of his principal, whether the enterprise was successful or not – could be considered a combination of three separate contracts. The components were a *commenda* in the form of a sleeping partnership, an insurance contract against the loss of the principal, and an insurance contract against fluctuations in the rate of profit. What clearly was legal was that A could enter into partnership with B; he could further insure the principal against loss with C; and contract with D against loss caused by fluctuations in profits. The essence

of the triple contract was that it combined three separate contracts which were legal when struck in isolation between different parties, but when combined and made between just two parties had the effect of contracting for an advance of money at a fixed rate of interest. If it was lawful for A to make these three contracts separately with B, C and D, why was it not possible for A to make all three of them with B? This was the dilemma posed by the triple contract. Pope Sixtus V denounced the triple contract in 1585 in response to Luther's offensive against the Church's position in his tract *On Trade and Usury* (Luther, 1524 [1915]). Nevertheless, it led to a religious quandary and perhaps even hastened along the removal of the ban on usury (Nelson, 1949; Anwar, 1987; Taylor and Evans, 1987).

18. The 'capture' theory of regulation is associated especially with Downs (1961), Stigler (1964 [1975], 1971) and Stigler and Friedland (1962 [1975]). Stigler argued that regulation increases the well-being of the soliciting groups in the regulated industry, while Downs argued that the political process is geared up to supply those vested interests.

4. Social policy in the Abrahamic religions

INTRODUCTION

Religion is a set of beliefs which shapes a person's life, ranging from spirituality to ethics in daily life, including financial matters. There has been consideration among academic researchers as to how religion (beliefs, norms and values) affects the economic decisions of individuals, groups and society at large (Iannaccone and Finke, 1996). In the words of Rae (1997, p.6), 'we are seeking from Scripture general principles or norms that govern economic life and can be applied to different economic arrangements'.

Judaism and Islam view wealth as a blessing of God and the appointment of man only as custodian upon its rightful use. Christianity saw wealth as a test from God, and charity and good deeds as the only solutions. All three religions either prohibit, or have prohibited, usury or interest. Alternatively, a concept of brotherhood is promoted to bring equality among communities. Further, mandatory or optional charity, benevolent loans, sabbatical from loans, and even trade in Islam, are declared among alternatives to usury.

Religious financing is a latest addition in finance which only recently caught the attention of Western academics after some significant developments in Islamic banking in Muslim countries. According to Tinker (2004), religious[1] financing starts from interpreting the sacred scriptures to answer modern-day economic requirements. This is followed by empirical studies to compare the religious principles and empirical realities. Subsequently, policy proposals are developed that endeavour to apply the Holy intentions to reality.

The central theme of this chapter is to explore the social policy framework approved and promoted in Judaism, Christianity and Islam. But first we consider religion and the role of ethics in society and, by extension, economic life.

RELIGION AND THE SOCIAL ETHIC

The economist Joan Robinson (1962) in her iconic book *Economic Philosophy*[2] argued that society cannot work unless there is some agreed standard of morality so that members of the society 'have common feelings about what is the proper way of conducting its affairs' (p. 9). Fortunately, as she notes, there are certain basic ethical feelings that we all, or at least most of us, share. 'We prefer kindness to cruelty and harmony to strife; we admire courage and respect justice' (p. 18).

Nevertheless, self-interest is a powerful force, and 'social life is impossible unless the pursuit of self-interest is mitigated by respect and compassion for others' (ibid., p. 10). For this objective to be achieved there needs to be a set of rules to reconcile contrary and conflicting tendencies. That is, 'there must be some mechanism to make an individual keep the rules when they conflict with the immediate advantage' (p. 10).

Use of force or the threat of punishment is one possibility, albeit expensive and time-consuming. It is also ineffective because there are many situations (for example, submission of tax returns) where external constraints are weak, and honesty and self-restraint is needed. It is simply not possible to provide enough law enforcement officers, accountants and inspectors to verify more than a small portion of all transactions that take place in an economy, so that societies require that most transactions be based on voluntary compliance. In such a context, ethical norms are paramount, and society's attitudes to morality can give further force to them or cause them to be weakened.

Joan Robinson considers that the mechanism by which the feelings and claims of others are imposed upon us is 'the moral sense or conscience of the individual' (ibid., p. 11). But from where do our ethical feelings arise? Are they, as she suggests, simply a separate part of our make-up, like our ability to learn to talk?

In the past, morality has flowed from religion. Joan Robinson is dismissive of the role of religion, and is particularly scornful of Dostoevsky's statement 'If God is dead, everything is permitted', yet she accepts that 'religion is a useful way both of strengthening the desire of the individual to do whatever he thinks right and of improving a particular view of what is right'. However, in her view, 'morality is desired and respected for its own sake; religion is being recommended to us because it supports morality, not morality because it derives from religion' (ibid., p. 15).

Modern philosophers, or at least most of them, reject the significance of religion for ethics and morality (Blackburn, 2001, pp. 9–17). Indeed, there is even a lack of agreement on a fully satisfactory definition of what is moral (Iqbal and Lewis, 2009). According to writers such as Veatch (1971), the problem is that mainstream Western philosophy does not distinguish between values (in which there is a 'right' and 'wrong') and tastes (in which there is no 'right' or 'wrong'). In contrast to the Platonic concept of the Good and the Kantian focus on the Ought and its justification, modern analytic philosophy has sought to develop against the backdrop of a value-neutral world. In the words of Joas (2000): 'In analytic philosophy, substantive clarifications of ethical questions were temporarily replaced by the attempt to construct a neutral metaethics, that is to say, a discipline that sets itself the goal of clarifying ethical statements, but is itself at the same time governed by the norm of value-freedom' (p. 125).

Yet, not all agree with this value-free emphasis. One of the most significant exceptions in recent decades to the neglect in Western philosophy of the question of the genesis of values is Charles Taylor (1989), for whom moral feelings necessarily reveal our value standards and would simply not be moral feelings if they were not related to our conception of the 'good'. He argues that an individual's moral and religious experience can call for an interpretation rooted in the cultural repertoire of interpretative patterns in which God, in the sense of the traditional faith of a particular culture, is indispensable. Thus, for him, a return to something like a metaphysical theory of the good is conceivable, even though he accepts that it is not possible for a philosophy which seemingly now has little interest in the realm of values, and which endeavours to find a neutral meta-position when dealing with ethical matters.

Reinforcing this concern with ethical standards, there has been some revision among some philosophers (e.g., Goodin, 1992) about what a concern with ethics can be expected to achieve. Morality in economic and social life is not simply a matter of counteracting and curbing the self-interest of others. It has long been recognized that ethical standards can make one 'good', irrespective of whether they are a matter of inner virtue (Aristotle) or external duty (Kant) (see Thomson, 1953; Kant, 1940). But modern social science points to other ways in which ethics can be good and can do one good. Obviously, in a Hobbesian sense, ethics are pragmatically sound in allowing one to benefit from the constraints that ethics imposes on others. That much is known and is familiar territory. But it is not just the case that, net of the costs to oneself, one benefits from the fact that others are bound by ethical considerations.

Moreover, according to some scientific thinking, moral judgements about what feels fair or not, or good or not, draw importantly on the social nature of moral intuition. Thus at a 2009 discussion on ethics sponsored by the Templeton Foundation, the view was expressed that we do not just care about our individual rights, or even the rights of other individuals. We also care about loyalty, respect, traditions and, significantly, religions.

People link themselves together into communities and networks of mutual influence and seek goodness, not as a means, but as an end in itself (*International Herald Tribune*, 10 April 2009, p. 7).

As a consequence, the suggestion is that ethics can be empowering as well as constraining. Ethical norms, and the institutions underwriting them and giving force to them, can widen horizons and choices, enabling individuals to do more things than would have been possible in their absence. Trust and certainty in the integrity of market exchanges and interpersonal dealings is an important social lubricant, as Arrow (1974) observed many years ago. In this respect, ethics might be thought of as a pure 'public good' in an economic sense. In this context, we have Joan Robinson's criteria for a workable economy: 'any economic system requires a set of rules, an ideology to justify them (for example, a market economy or a command economy), and a conscience in the individual, which makes him strive to carry them out' (Robinson, 1962, p. 18).

The corollary of this line of thought about ethics is that the behaviour of those abusing the system is corrosive not only because it enables some in society to secure an unfair advantage over others; those engaging in it are harming us all by eroding norms and institutions which benefit us all. Declining morality in society can set in train a cycle of decline. An insistence upon the maintenance of high standards in all facets of life – private and public – rightfully becomes a cornerstone of a successful society.

Without metaphysics, the very essence and narrative of our being – for example, the purpose of life and successively unfolding accountability within and beyond it – might be in danger of being sent to the realm of doubt and oblivion. Hence the context within which 'right' and 'wrong', 'good' and 'evil', 'virtues' and 'vices', attain their meaning is diminished, potentially opening the way for the promotion of social arrangements that are based on selfish egoistical conceptions of justice.

ETHICAL FOUNDATIONS

All of the Abrahamic religions have strong ethical foundations, outlined below. Not only have these foundations had a legacy in shaping modern-day culture, laws and societal norms, but the religions have also imparted a considerable influence through the number of adherents: 2 billion Christians, 1.2 billion Muslims and 14 million Jews, as noted earlier. In his book, *Shall the Religious Inherit the Earth? Demography and Politics in the Twenty-First Century*, Eric Kaufman (2010) documents that more than 90 per cent of world population growth is happening in religious countries, especially Africa, eclipsing developments in a now more secular Western Europe. Add to these trends the strength of religion in the United States with its global outreach, along with the rebirth of Orthodoxy in Russia and other previously communist countries, and it would seem that secularization is on the wane around the globe. These developments would seem to be contrary to the so-called 'secularization model', in which it is hypothesized that 'economic development reduces individual participation in formal religious services and personal prayer decreases religious beliefs and diminishes the influence of organized religion on politics and government' (McCleary and Barro, 2006, p. 49).

THE JUDAIC HERITAGE

Although Judaism is small in numbers, it provides the starting point for the other two religions. Indeed, following the scriptures, a long line can be traced from the call of Abraham and Sara, and their mission to establish the 'Kingdom of God' coming on earth, and the subsequent creation of the Jewish people who were to receive certain sacred possessions, by which God would bless all nations (Long, 2010). These possessions include the gift of the Divine name, the Torah (encompassing the Ten Commandments) and the tabernacle or temple as the place where heaven and earth meet, the meeting place of God on earth. According to the Holy Bible, the Christian Church continues the Abrahamic mission, which extends to the Redemption brought by Jesus, whose whole life and suffering, as an example to humanity, maintain the lineage. While Christianity builds directly on the Jewish historical tradition of spirituality and moral law, it is not a big step from Judaism and Christianity to Islam. Muslims recognize the Old Testament prophets of Israel and take the teachings of Moses and Abraham as precursors for the message of the Prophet Muhammad. As noted in Chapter 2, Muslims worship Jesus Christ as a prophet. In fact, as we said, Islam is the only non-Christian religion that makes it an article of faith to accept Jesus as a prophet, and a Muslim is not a Muslim unless they believe in Jesus and all the prophets of God.

The core of Jewish law, by which adherents to Judaism are expected to conduct their daily lives, is contained in the divine revelation in the Torah, or the Pentateuch – comprising the books of Genesis, Exodus, Leviticus, Numbers and Deuteronomy – along with how these have been interpreted by rabbinical scholars, as explained in Chapter 2. As Rodney Wilson (1997) observes, the issue of how to engage with Gentiles is as old as Judaism itself, and explicit guidance is provided on this matter. Seven commandments were given to all the children of Noah – that is, all of humanity – to be found in the Mishnah, the written works from the oral tradition in rabbinical Judaism, and represent what ought to be observed. Long (2010) states that these commandments were interpreted as what should be expected from a righteous Gentile living in the Holy Land, as well as the basic morality one should expect from any human being. 'They are the basic Jewish ethic for Gentiles. They should establish courts of justice, avoid idolatry, blasphemy, sexual promiscuity, murder, stealing, while observing certain food laws' (Long, 2010, p. 26). Thus not only has Judaism shaped Christianity, but it also laid down basic ethical rules for Gentiles.

CHRISTIAN ETHICS[3]

Christian ethics distances itself from both the Aristotelian tradition and modern ethics. The purpose of Christian ethics is to help us to live well, to offer moral guidance on our everyday activities, and in so doing make God's name holy (Long, 2010, p. 106). By contrast, ethics is most usually understood as a thoroughly human endeavour, and we are ethical through our own resources. This was the position taken by Aristotle. He taught that everything possesses a natural end to which it gravitates. People have a natural end, too, ethically speaking, to which they are directed, which is to achieve a good life and attain happiness. Likewise, much of modern ethics sees the autonomy of human nature – and reason – as the basis of ethics.

To Christianity, this falls short of the mark. To many Christians the idea that the good can be achieved through our own resources borders on a heresy. In particular, this view denies that we need grace and spiritual virtues in order to realize our ends. While the Christian faith agrees with Aristotle that there is a good end for which we were created, it disputes that we have in our make-up all of the characteristics needed to naturally attain it. In the Christian view something more is called for, namely 'grace' or the 'gift' of the Holy Spirit, in order to reach this goodness. As Long (2010, p. 3) puts it, 'the common Catholic expression "grace presupposes and perfects nature" captures this insight well'.

Christian ethics drew upon ancient understanding or moral wisdom, especially the cardinal virtues, where 'cardinal' comes from the Latin *cardo*, meaning 'hinge' or 'axis', the implication being that the cardinal virtues, which are justice, wisdom, courage and temperance, create the hinge for a moral life. For example, the Roman orator and philosopher Cicero (Marcus Tullius Cicero, 106–43 BC) stated that everything morally right derives from one of four sources:

1. the full perception and intelligent development of the true (wisdom or prudence);
2. rendering to every man his due, and with the faithful discharge of obligations assumed (justice);
3. the greatness and strength of a noble and invincible spirit (courage);
4. the orderliness and moderation of everything that is said and done wherein consists temperance and self-control (temperance). (Long, 2010, p. 16)

In what ways do Christian ethics relate to ancient traditions? Ethics is about pursuing what is good and eschewing what is regarded as evil. Aristotle in his *Nicomachean Ethics* (Thomson, 1953) considered that people's actions were directed to one thing more than any other, and that was happiness (*eudaimonia* in Greek). That was the over-riding good shaping moral actions. Christians thought that they had found the true happiness desired by the Greeks in the figure of Jesus and the way of life he called 'blessed'. Long (2010) ventures the opinion that 'the eudaimonistic ethics of the ancient Greeks was fulfilled in the beatitudes Jesus announced in his Sermon on the Mount', 'blessed are they for theirs is the Kingdom of heaven' (Matthew 5:7) and 'you are the light of the world, a city built on a hill' (Matthew 5:14).

St Augustine (AD 354–430) defined seven virtues. Four of them are temperance, fortitude, justice and prudence. These ancient virtues are transformed and completed with the 'theological' or 'infused' virtues found in scripture, namely faith, hope and love. Combining them gives rise to the seven virtues as depicted in Christian art and embedded by St Thomas Aquinas (1225–74) into a foundation and basis of Christian doctrine.

At the same time, nevertheless, to be avoided are the seven deadly vices, paraded by the Church to help people identify sin: pride, covetousness, lust, gluttony, sloth, anger and envy. Pride elevates one's own achievements at the expense of those of neighbours, friends and enemies. Covetousness is the undue worship of temporal things. Lust is the excessive appetite for sexual pleasure for self-gratification. Gluttony and drunkenness is the overindulgence in food and drink. Sloth is the lack of willingness to fulfil one's obligations. Anger reflects a desire for revenge and lack of self-control. Envy is a feeling of discontent induced by the success or goodness of others. Nowadays, in relation to riches and wealth, it has given rise to the expression, 'the politics of envy'. Although the seven deadly sins featured in almanacs and 'hell and damnation' sermons, it needs to be emphasized that the mere avoidance of them is most certainly not the purpose of Christian ethics.

Here, then, we have the building blocks of Christian ethics; the pursuit of God's goodness by those on the way to a city of God. Faith, hope and love sustain those on the way. The beatitudes are the city's perfections, and the gifts and fruits of the Holy Spirit make possible its achievement (Long, 2010, p. 47). The beatitudes are: poverty of spirit, meekness, mournfulness, righteousness, mercifulness, purity of heart and peaceableness. These are the 'acts' or 'works' of the virtues and gifts. The gifts order reason and the will or desire, of which four perfect reason – wisdom, knowledge, understanding and counsel – while the other three are fortitude, piety and fear.

Christian ethics, as Long (2010) explains it:

> is not a precise science but the cultivation of practical wisdom that comes from diverse sources. It draws on all that is good in God's creation and among the nations. But it also acknowledges that creatures cannot attain their true end without the gift of God's own goodness . . . God's divine goodness extends to the Redemption brought by Jesus, whose life, teachings, death, resurrection and ascension perfectly perform that goodness. He then shares it with us through his body, the Church, making possible a communication of his life through Sacraments, God's Word and the infused virtues, gifts and beatitudes they bring. (p. 121)

Of course, there are many Churches that make up Christianity, and one can speak of Catholic ethics, Orthodox ethics, Lutheran ethics, Anglican ethics, Reformed ethics and Evangelical ethics, in which there are different emphases. Yet, if we consider the Orthodox Churches of the East and the Catholic Church of the West, both draw upon the sacraments, virtues, gifts and beatitudes as central to Christian life and acts. In the case of the Protestant and Catholic positions, the 'Joint Declaration' affirmed on 31 October 1999 (Lutheran World Federation and the Catholic Church, 1999) claims that the Protestant and Catholic positions can be reconciled: 'Together we confess: By grace alone, in faith in Christ's saving work and not because of any merit on our part, we are accepted by God and receive the Holy Spirit, who renews our hearts while equipping and calling us to good works' (para. 15). Moreover, there is little doubt that Jesus's teachings and the New Testament have 'the capacity to stir human hearts, transform human freedom, and stimulate human service to humanity' (Johnson, 2010, p. 125).

ETHICAL PRINCIPLES IN ISLAM[4]

Why are we here, and what kind of life ought one to live? For adherents to Islam the answer is clear. The revelation given to Muhammad in the form of the Holy Qur'an, the sacred book of Muslims, responds to such questions by taking the position that everything in the universe is part of a meticulous plan being executed by Allah, the Arabic word for God. His will reigns supreme and has created humankind not in vain but to serve as his viceroy on the earth. In this capacity, people are required to act as agents and trustees of God in managing the resources of the earth such that all benefit equitably and the original balance in creation is maintained.

To this end, trustees are bound by a covenant with God, given limited free will, monitored on a continuous basis, and made accountable for all actions. Personal responsibility is the cornerstone of such accountability. Thus, 'no bearer of burdens can bear the burden of another' (17:15). This holistic approach to conduct does not differentiate temporal from the spiritual and requires people to surrender their limited free will voluntarily to the revealed will of God (51:56–7). Nothing in life thus remains 'profane'. Each and every act undertaken with the intention of fulfilling the covenant with God becomes an act of worship (51:56–7).

Embedded in the notion of trusteeship is a call for conduct based on a code of personal ethics and a blueprint of justice. Together these canons establish rights and obligations across a network of relationships – familial, social, economic, political and environmental – and regulate community affairs. There are certain fundamental beliefs and actions to which Muslims individually must adhere. These are the fundamental articles and duties of the Islamic faith as contained in the Six Beliefs (in God, the angels, the prophets, the Holy books, the Day of Judgment and the decree of God) and the Five Duties (testimony or affirmation of God and Muhammad, prayer, almsgiving, fasting and pilgrimage) which every Muslim must uphold or perform (see Chapter 2). At another level, Islam has permitted the retention of existing indigenous institutions and cultural and administrative practices in local communities, within the basic principles of Islam, although these are sometimes very elastic and controversial. There is no world body and no unified authority for the religion. Instead, emphasis is laid on facilitating peaceful interaction among a large number of communities, internally organized around their own sets of beliefs and ways of life, different in at least some respects from one another.

Islam views justice as the precondition for preserving peace, equilibrium and harmony on earth, characteristics which are essential in their own right as well as to enable people to understand the demands of their position as the trustees of God on earth. Justice must be understood as a set of pairs of individual freedoms and limits, rights and obligations, and *masalih* and *mafasid* (social utilities and disutilities) elucidated by God (16:116) through his prophets (7:157) so that human beings honour the rights of their fellow beings and do not exploit them. Justice also has to be complemented with benevolence, so that in the words of Maududi (1994), the former removes conflict and bitterness from a society, while the latter imparts grace and excellence to it by filling it with 'pleasant' harmony and 'sweet' accord.

In general, the Holy Qur'an brings three terms – *adl* (justice), *qist* (equity or fairness), and *meezan* (balance or scale) to signify justice and equity. Such is the centrality of justice that, on Normani and Rahnema's (1995) count, 'justice' or synonymous terms appear more than 1000 times in the Holy Qur'an. Among the meanings of these words are: to straighten, setting in order, and fixing in the right place; to balance, counterbalance or establish equilibrium; to be equal or equivalent or to match; fairness, impartiality, absence of discrimination; and honesty, straightforwardness, uprightness, righteousness and correctness. The antonym of *adl* is *zulm*, which is used in the Holy Qur'an (2:124; 4:148) to mean indulgence in wrong, evil, iniquity, injustice, oppression, and unfairness that eventuates in corruption and disruption of peace. It also means darkness that beclouds and overshadows the truth.

The Holy Qur'an and *sunna* (see Chapter 2) elucidate all these different dimensions of *adl*, *qist* and *meezan* with reference to the divine attributes, the standards of conduct required of individuals, and the characteristics of systems of governance put in place to rule a people. As al-Ghazali (translated by Bagley, 1964, p. 55) illustrates, the paramount duty of government in Islam has been historically understood as to bring development and prosperity to the world through justice and equitable rule. The idea is to provide persons with the necessary security and patronage so that they can develop their full potential as free individuals, and procure the needs and demands of their body and soul without violating the liberty of others. To this end, the Islamic economic and business philosophy accepts the profit motive, protects lawfully gained private property, prohibits intervention in real supply-and-demand-driven market prices, and admits the market economy in general.

Against this larger setting, earning one's livelihood and engaging in economic activity is considered obligatory and next only to devotional worship. Work is equated with seeking the bounties of Allah (16:14). Through it, human beings can test their potentialities, suffice their earthly requirements, and fulfil their obligations. Asceticism is discouraged and begging is frowned upon unless one is desperate (57:27). Income through one's own labour is considered a means to befriending God, and trading within the Islamic ethical framework earns the Almighty's choicest blessings.

PUTTING ISLAMIC PRINCIPLES INTO PRACTICE

A large number of Islamic concepts and values define the extent and nature of everyday life and business activity (Rahman, 1994). There are many positive values such as *iqtisad* (moderation), *adl* (justice), *ihsan* (kindness par excellence), *amanah* (honesty), *infaq* (spending to meet social obligations), *sabr* (patience) and *istislah* (public interest). Similarly, there are a number of values which are negative, and thus to be avoided: *zulm* (tyranny), *bukhl* (miserliness), *hirs* (greed), *iktinaz* (hoarding of wealth) and *israf* (extravagance). Activity within the positive parameters is *halal* (allowed and praiseworthy), and within the negative parameters *haram* (prohibited and blameworthy), which has to be moderated. Production and distribution which are regulated by the *halal–haram* code must adhere to the notion of *adl* (justice). Collectively, these values and concepts, along with the main injunctions of the Holy Qur'an, provide a framework for a just business and commercial system (Lewis, 2007, 2011a). A brief summary is given here.

Trade and Commerce

Many verses in the Holy Qur'an condone trade and commerce, and the attitude of Islam is that there should be no impediment to honest and legitimate trade and business, so that people earn a living, support their families and give charity to those less fortunate. Nevertheless, Muslims should not allow their business activities to dominate so that making money becomes a first priority and they neglect religious duties.

Work and Production

Islam requires every individual to work and to produce. Prophet Muhammad teaches: 'Never be lazy and helpless' (Rahman, 1994, p. 9). There is no good in an individual who does not want to produce and earn money. To Muslims, the unproductive hand is an unclean impure hand. According to Islam, work and investment are the only legitimate means of acquiring property rights (Askari and Taghavi, 2005). Thus, the route to economic achievement is hard work and the assumption of risk. It is not through entitlement and inheritance. Useful work is that which benefits others and society. Subsequently, those who work hard are acknowledged and are rewarded.

Poverty and Riches

Pursuing economic activities and achieving economic progress via work and investment must, however, be rooted in moral and legitimate foundations. Islam preaches moderation and a balanced pattern of consumption. Luxury and overconsumption are condemned, as is poverty. Every being has a minimum requirement to be able to live in dignity. The system is balanced out through the act of *zakat* (almsgiving as an essential part of the system and faith), supplemented if necessary by temporary tax on the rich and affluent to balance the budget as a religious duty (*fard kefaya*).

Communal Obligations

Individuals are expected to feel socially responsible for others in the community. One cannot enjoy life while others cannot. In general, the aim of the Islamic economic system is to allow people to earn their living in a fair and profitable way without exploitation of others, so that the whole society may benefit. Islam also emphasizes the welfare of the community over individual rights.

Stewardship of Resources

Mankind has been appointed God's vice-regent on earth and given the sacred duty of the stewardship of all natural and created resources. Ownership of property is therefore a trust (*amanah*) to be enjoyed conditionally so long as man follows the *shari'ah* and remains worthy of the trust. People have the right to use natural and other resources for the benefit of mankind. But earth is a trust from God and should be looked after by those who have charge of it and who will ultimately be accountable to God for their actions.

Ethical Standards

Under Islam, the paramount rule in business is honesty and fair dealing (Hussain, 1999). A Muslim business person should therefore be a person of high moral values who would not set out to deceive or exploit others. Those engaging in trade and commerce should behave equitably. Vendors of goods should not hide any defects in them, nor lie about the weight or quality of the goods. Dealing in stolen goods is prohibited. Hoarding is forbidden when the intention is to force up the price in times of scarcity and so profit at the expense of others.

Commercial Obligations

The general principle is contained in the Qur'anic verse: 'O you who believe! Fulfil (all) obligations' (S5:1). While generally cited as the basis of Islamic contract law, Yusuf Ali (1938) suggests that these obligations are multifaceted, covering divine obligations, mutual obligations of commercial contracts and social relationships, treaty-based obligations as members of civil communities, and general obligations and allegiances as a citizen of the state. Islamic law provides freedom of contract, so long as the terms do not conflict with *shari'ah*. In particular, it permits any arrangement based on the consent of the parties involved, so long as the shares of each are contingent upon uncertain gain and are a function of productive transformation of resources. These conditions apply to the four root transactions of sales (*bai*), hire (*ijarah*), gift (*hiba*) and loan (*ariyah*), the first two of which feature prominently in Islamic financing.

ISLAMIC ETHICS: A SUMMING UP

Muslims are expected to conduct their activities in accordance with the requirement of their religion to be fair, honest and just toward others. Business activity, in consequence, must be broadly inspired and guided by the concepts of *tawhid* (oneness and unity of God), *ihsan* (goodness) and *tawakkal* (trust in God), while regulated within those boundaries by a legal framework committed to values such as justice and the ban on *riba* (interest) and the prohibition of *ihtikaar* (hoarding) and other malpractices.

Of course, the desire to achieve justice in exchange or 'fair trade' is not confined to Muslims. However, there are some differences between the Islamic and some alternative visions (Iqbal and Lewis, 2009). First, whereas the modern-day welfare liberal might appeal to humanist principles or documents such as the Universal Declaration of Human Rights, the Islamic position is rooted in the metaphysical and the responsibilities of adherents as the trustees of God on earth. The nature of these responsibilities means that the challenge lies not in freeing oneself for what Aristotle calls the pursuit of the highest good – contemplation of unchanging truths per se – but rather in using such self-examination and soul-searching as a means to internalizing universal moral truths so as to undermine inhibitions within people (for example, pride, greed) that compel them to indulge in injustice and miserliness. The idea is that, with a reformed frame of mind, justice and benevolence flow naturally, and so does socio-political action to universalize these attributes.

Second, while encouraging redistribution, there is considerable emphasis in Islam on preserving the social structure, in particular that of family. Justice and charity begin from home. Of course, no religion or ethic can claim a monopoly on such matters. Notably, 'charity begins at home', 'duties to parents, elders and ancestors' and 'duties to children and posterity' are among the principles of natural law that C.S. Lewis (1947) identified as held by people in a wide variety of cultures and civilizations. In the particular case of Islam, there are mutual rights and obligations among parents, children and near kin, and there is the obligatory distribution of inheritance among extended family. Also, through the concept of *fard-e-kifaya*, that is, communal obligation, there are rights and obligations of individuals over community and vice versa. Furthermore, there are elaborate mechanisms to institutionalize philanthropy (Hasan, 2007). Together these provisions cultivate and reinforce social capital and create a large space for informal societal and communal modes of governance.

Finally, Islam calls for reforming those market exchanges – constituting the basis of entitlement to earnings – that it considers inherently oppressive; that is, usury, speculation and *gharar*. In this respect, there are parallels not only with other religions in the past (Judaism, Christianity, Hinduism), but also with the present-day 'ethical investment' movement in the West that began with the application of Christian religious principles to investment and now embraces, under a decidedly secular banner, a variety of humanist, environmental and social responsibility concerns. So far, however, it is the case that the Islamic ethical rules are applied to a wider range of financial transactions (banking, insurance and investment funds) than is generally the situation in conventional markets.

SELECTED BELIEFS OF THE HOLY RELIGIONS

This chapter concludes with some prominent fundamental beliefs of Judaism, Christianity and Islam. It starts with the concept of God, and then examines justice and fairness in the Holy religions. It also covers religious teachings towards the concept of wealth and other commercial ethics. Putting this together develops a social framework, including benevolence.

Concept of God

Delineating the concept of God is the founding pillar of the Holy religions which consider God as the ultimate source of existence for human beings. Faith in God takes primacy over all the relationships that people establish and maintain with individuals, groups, community and society at large.

Based on the strictures of Moses, Judaism follows one God (Gen. 1:1). In Deuteronomy and Isaiah six different verses declare the oneness of God as the only supreme authority. YHVH is the only proper 'name of God' in the *Tanakh* (canon of the Hebrew Bible). There are also titles in the Torah that ascribe to God names such as Elohim (god, or authority), El (mighty one), Shaddai (almighty), Adonai (master), Elyon (most high), Avinu (our father), and so on. These names highlight different aspects of God, who had direct relationship with his chosen people and guided them at difficult times. There are many interactions in the Old Testament where God communicates to Adam and Eve, Noah, Abraham and Moses, and so on. The hypostases[5] of the Holy Trinity lies at the core of Christianity: Jesus is the Christ and Son of the Living God (Mt. 16:16–17), together with God the Father and the Holy Spirit, the single substance of the One God. God is the creator of heaven and earth and the ultimate ruling authority on human beings (Col. 1:16–17). The doctrine of the Trinity is important (albeit difficult to understand) because it elucidates the Christian conviction that Jesus can be worshipped along with the Father and the Spirit because each is necessary for the identity of the One God. Each is distinct from the other, yet they are the one in essence (Long, 2010, pp. 7–8).

Tawhid (One God) is the first pillar of Islam. The word *tawhid* literally means 'unification' and is derived from the Arabic verb *wahhada* which means 'to unite, unify or consolidate'. Allah is the term used in Arabic for God. In fact, in Islam, there are 99 names of God which evoke different characteristics. Among these names, the most famous and frequent names are Al-Rahman (the Merciful) and Al-Rahim (the Compassionate). Yousaf Ali's English translation of the Qur'an in English language accounts the word 'God' at 163 places in 151 verses, describing various supreme qualities.

Since God is the only supreme authority, everyone is accountable to him (3:14–15; 4:135). Islamic philosophy is based on a belief that life on earth is temporary and there will be another eternal life thereafter where success is determined upon obeying God's command in this mortal life (2:185; 3:182).

Concept of Justice and Fairness

All of the Holy religions seek to establish socio-economic justice in the society. Worldly resources should be distributed among all stakeholders on the basis of equity and benevolence. In Judaism, the Decalogue (Ten Commandments) provide a starting point for human relationships on the basis of justice. The Torah says not to show any special favour to the rich or poor (Lev. 19:15). Any law which gives advantages in economic matters in fact violates the concept of complete impartiality. Jewish law expects that one must be ethical and even go beyond legal requirements for the establishment of justice (BM 108a), as dictated by the verse 'you shall do that which is fair and good in the sight of the Lord' (Deut. 6:18). No one is above the law (Job 34:17–19) and no one is left outside justice, that is, poor, widows, orphans alike (Isa. 10:1–2).

Christianity in the New Testament extends Judaic law (Mt. 5:17–18) and enjoins the concept of mercy and love with justice to promote peace and social harmony. Jesus preached 'love God and love your neighbour' (Lk. 10:27). God judges each person impartially (1 Peter 1:17) regardless of race, gender, social background and favouritism (Galatians 3:28; James 2:1–9). The Holy Bible blesses those who bear hunger and trust for personal holiness and moral uprightness (Mt. 5:6).

The 'golden rule' is defined in Luke 6:31 – 'and as ye would that men should do to you, do ye also to them likewise'– and is further extended in John 13:34: 'a new commandment I give unto you, that ye love one another; as I have loved you, that ye also love one another'. The definition of love also includes 'love to your enemies' and 'be merciful' (Lk. 6:27–35; 6:36). Lastly, the Bible promises various crowns for faithful Christians at the Day of Judgment, such as a crown of glory for those who serve as faithful shepherds of God's people (1 Pet. 5:4).

The Islamic concept of justice and fairness starts from the position that whatever is created on this earth is for man (2:29). Islam encourages people to work hard and only recognizes legitimate earnings. To ensure justice in society, Muslims are advised to select the best people, capable of the given assignments and abilities to judge with justice (4:58). The Holy Qur'an encourages seeking the opinions of wise and experienced people whenever important decisions are required (42:38), which decisions are to be made in mutual consultation with those involved, based on the principles of *shura* (42:38).

The Holy Qur'an links justice (*adl*) and benevolence (*ihsan*), declaring that they go hand in hand. This leads to a new theory that justice gives birth to benevolence, which ultimately is transformed into a sublime relationship, referred to as treatment of others like a family member (*Ita'i Dhil-Qurba*). In short, justice has a special bond with consciousness of actions and behaviour. Islamic teaching recognizes Muslims as brethren in faith and merciful to each other. The Holy Qur'an ordains 'those who spend (freely), whether in prosperity, or in adversity; who restrain anger, and pardon (all) men; for Allah loves those who do good' (3:134).

At the same time, Islam defines a simple rule of justice that every human being should receive his own share and give to others what are their rights. No one is to be treated with injustice (2:100; 3:128). A Muslim must give witness and stick with the truth even if it goes against his parents and family (4:135). There is a famous saying of the Prophet Muhammad that 'people before you were ruined because they exceeded the limits when punishing the poor and showed excessive compassion when pardoning the rich. I swear by Almighty Allah that if my own daughter, Fatimah, was to steal, I would have her hands cut off' (Ahmad, 2008, p. 227).

Concept of Brotherhood

Judaism gets its name from the land of Judea and is tied to its people. The Old Testament mandates that the descendants of Israel are the chosen people of God (Deut. 14:2) and a Holy Nation (Ex. 19:6). Jews as a community have a special role as a light for other nations (Isa. 42:6). Judaism believes in charity and other acts of benevolence, although almost all are restricted to their own community. As we have seen, the 'Deuteronomic double standard' allows Jews to charge interest from Gentiles but not from fellow Jews (Deut. 23:19–20; Lev. 25:35–37). Also, in the Torah, foreign nations are not treated equally in war (Deuteronomy 20:10–15).

Judaism believes in equal opportunity for all the community members rather than an equal distribution of wealth. The Ten Commandments, along with the created social order, demands looking after the needs of neighbours (Ex. 20:7–12). Jewish law commands charity to the poor, to be fair in business dealings, and not to cheat, deceive, use false weights, and so on.

Christianity is a universal religion and rejects discrimination based upon race, cast or colour, promoting the concept of love and brotherhood for all human beings. The Holy Bible defines brotherhood as 'and all that believed were together' (Acts 2:44). Matthew 19:21 records: 'Jesus said unto him, If thou wilt be perfect, go [and] sell that thou hast, and give to the poor, and thou shalt have treasure in heaven: and come [and] follow me.' The next three verses contain the famous observation that it would be easier for the camel to pass through the eye of the needle than for the rich man to enter the kingdom of God.

A righteous person is defined as whoever pleases the will of God and follows Jesus's advice (Mt. 12:50). Unity under the command of brotherhood is seen as a 'bond of peace' (Eph. 4:3). Thus, the Holy Bible asks all brothers in faith to stand firm and hold to the traditions of their religion, whether it is in the form of spoken words or by letters (2 Thess. 2:15).

Islam introduces the idea of 'Universal Brotherhood', as many verses start from the expression 'O Mankind', such as 'O mankind! We created you from a single (pair) of a male and a female, and made you into nations and tribes, that ye may know each other (not that ye may despise each other) (49:13).

A universal approach is adopted when dealing with other religions, establishing religious rights and freedom and preserving the sanctity of cloisters, churches and synagogues, even during war (22:39–40). Jews and Christians are 'People of the Book', and Islamic law calls them *dhimmas*, which means 'protected' or 'guilty', protected because they have received genuine revelations (via 'the Book') and guilty because they have rejected

Muhammad as a prophet. While they can practise their religions, some-times it is under specified conditions; for example, Christians are unable to distribute Bibles in Saudi Arabia and Iran (*The Economist*, 2007).

The Prophet Muhammad in his famous sermon at the time of his last *hajj* (pilgrimage) declared that all humans are equal regardless of nation, tribe and whatever station of life they may hold, and whether Arab, non-Arab, white or non-white. God has made all brethren one to another. In these respects, Islam bears similarity to Christianity, the New rather than the Old Testament. Both have a broad following across many nations and races.

Concept of Wealth

The Holy religions consider every human being to be a member of God's family and to have an equitable right to share God-gifted economic and material resources. Individual greed and lust for economic gain are replaced with moral traits such as cooperation, brotherhood, affection and mutual respect.

The Old Testament considers wealth as desirable (Eccles 13:24) so long as it is not obtained unlawfully from the needy (Prov. 10:2; 11:16–18; 14; 31), and there are many instances in the Old Testament where God graces its prophets (for example, Solomon and David) with wealth and kingdom. Nevertheless, Deuteronomy (8:11–18) warns that one should not believe that 'my power and the might of my hand had made me all this wealth'. Man is appointed as custodian of God's wealth and is expected to benefit the poor and less fortunate. In particular, all Jews are asked to give 10 per cent of yearly income as tithe. Also, as Wallis (1990, p. 273) points out, the Jubilee year (every fiftieth) in Leviticus results in a regular redistribution of wealth to avoid overaccumulation of wealth in a few hands. He also considers that the Sabbath year (the seventh year) offers a Biblical mandate for the periodic cancellation of debt.

Christianity traditionally has adopted the course of salvation instead of accumulating wealth to seek the blessings of God. Serving God and wealth simultaneously are incompatible goals, and love of money is the root of all evil (1 Timothy 6:10). God knows the basic requirements of human beings. Therefore, people must seek God's kingdom and righteousness, while the worldly comforts will be provided to them automatically (Mt. 6:31–3). Somewhat bizarrely, the idea of divinely endowed financial reward has been picked up in some contemporary Christian theology which borders on a 'corporate mentality', as reflected most particularly in the so-called 'prosperity gospel' and the 'health and wealth gospel' preached in some Pentecostal churches in the United States and Australia, as well as in such churches in the developing world (Abraham, 2011, p. 237). The general message appears to be that faith, the power of positive thinking, and donations to the church will be repaid by God with financial and material rewards (ibid., p. 247). This puts some distance from the early Christian Church when the utopian ideals then being espoused may well have been in actuality lived out (Gonzales, 1990).

The Holy Qur'an declares human beings as greedy, impatient and overpossessive (4:135), and links wealth with the contribution made for the well-being of others. Islam does not consider trade or business to be against religion, so long as it is legitimate with mutual consultation (4:29). In fact, the Prophet Muhammad and his Caliphs were all traders. There are detailed instructions towards the redistribution of wealth via the law of inheritance and compulsory charity (*zakat*). The rate of *zakat* is 2.5 per cent per annum on accumulated wealth, and further ranges from 5 per cent to 10 per cent per annum on agricultural produce, commonly known as *usher* (see Table 5.1 below).

Commercial Ethics

All Holy religions condemn factors such as interest, gambling, hoarding, bribery, fraud, extravagance and miserly behaviour which can disturb the overall circulation of wealth in the society. Alternatively, honesty, hard work, free consent, inheritance, meeting contractual obligations and charity are commended, to ensure the equitable distribution of wealth.

Free Consent

Judaism requires business dealings to be in good faith, and doing what is right in the eyes of God (Ex. 15:26). God has the ultimate authority, and man is born with the ability to make choices but is responsible for his choices as well. In Proverbs, he who sows wickedness reaps trouble (22:8), all hard work brings a profit but mere talk leads only to poverty (14:23), lazy hands make a man poor, but diligent hands bring wealth (10:4). The Torah declares man to be a social animal, and that the family is the foremost basic unit of a society, which converts into communities, communities into states, and states into the world, so that each human is a part of the human family (Gen. 1:26–30).

Christianity is not against commercial trading and creating wealth, although the Catholic Church in medieval times gave that impression, as does the Liberation theology today.[6] It is often overlooked, for example, that when founded in the seventeenth century the Quakers developed extensive financial networks, funding missionary and charitable activities.

They were also involved in banking, including the formation of British banks such as Lloyds and Barclays (Abraham, 2011). One can only wonder what they would think of their progeny today? As the Quaker example demonstrates, Christianity has much to contribute on the issue of charity, the road to salvation and the application of the Golden Rule. The Bible teaches that God is our creator. He has given humans the freedom to obey or disobey him, but there are many things that God does only in answer to prayer (Jas. 4:2).

Islam believes in freedom of selection both in economic and spiritual matters, and human beings are advised to resolve economic issues with free consent and in a spirit of cooperation (4:29). God does not even put any compulsion on people in the selection of religion (2:256). Islamic jurists apply the same philosophy in business and argue that the contracting parties must have all possible knowledge about the marketplace in order to save themselves from fraud, exploitation and other harm (Ibn Taymiyyah, 1976 [1982]).

Right of Private Ownership

In Judaism, trade in property is allowed, but all transactions must be properly evidenced and sealed in the presence of witnesses (Isa. 65:21; Jer. 32:43). In ancient Israel, agricultural land was distributed among various Jewish tribes. Land could be purchased, but the right of ownership expired after 50 years, the Golden Jubilee year. This was not so for urban property. Cities are viewed as works of man; the countryside as a work of God (Wilson, 1997).

The New Testament also mandates that all worldly resources belong to God (Mt. 25:14–30), yet at the same time the sacred text requires individual responsibility and initiative to work hard through labour (Eph. 4:28) and to set aside some money for charity and promotion of their religion (Acts 5:1–4). The Holy Bible further cautions that man should keep himself free from all type of worldly desires, as a man's life is not measured by the number of things he possesses (Lk. 12:13–15).

Islam recognizes a person's right of ownership. However, the Holy Qur'an reminds readers that God Almighty is the real owner of all the resources on earth and man is allowed to enjoy these Godly gifts for a temporary period (7:74; 28:88). Production of wealth is subject to human skill, knowledge and labour applied to the resources which God has provided, to be shared between capital and labour, and also among the communities, especially the poor and needy, and orphans (51:19; 70:24–5). In this way, the Islamic concept of right of ownership is linked with the spirit of brotherhood and cooperation.

Skills and Talent

Judaism considers individuals' talent and skills to be the key behind economic growth, and it encourages people to acquire the latest knowledge and expertise to become professionals in their fields (Ex. 35:35). The Old Testament stresses hard work. Proverbs (13:4) even declares laziness as the major reason to become poor: 'The soul of the sluggard desireth, and hath nothing.'

Personal talent and skills are also appreciated in Christianity, although here the focus shifted from using the talent and earning profit towards the rights of workers and on the timely payment of their wages (1 Tim. 5:18). The rights of poor men should be properly guarded (Jas. 5:4), and in Hebrews (13:5) Christians are asked by St Paul to keep their life free from the love of money.

Islam also recognizes intellectual capacity, and it is argued that if everyone receives the same financial reward regardless of their educational background or training, then intellectual capabilities will start to decline. Indeed, 'And in no wise covet those things in which Allah Hath bestowed His gifts More freely on some of you than on others: To men is allotted what they earn, and to women what they earn: But ask Allah of His bounty. For Allah hath full knowledge of all things' (4:32). Islam links intellectual abilities with the welfare of the poor. The rationale is to share and transfer knowledge and expertise to the needy or poor people who ultimately improve their economic condition caused by unequal distribution of wealth in society (61:10–11). Indeed, this might be construed as an early statement of the 'trickle-down effect'.

Extravagance or Accumulation of Wealth

Conventional economics generally considers acquisition of wealth to be the ultimate measure of success, whereas well-being comes from altruism in the Holy religions. The Old Testament asks people to adopt a moderate living style, being neither a lavish spender (Prov. 21:17) nor a miser (Prov. 28:22). In the New Testament the love of money is also rejected: a man cannot serve money and God at the same time (Mt. 6:24). A good believer must lead a quiet life, mind his own business and work with his own hands (1 Thess. 4:11). Islam asks for moderation in spending habits to seek the blessing of God (5:87). The Holy Qur'an allows Muslims to enjoy wealth, but not to waste it through excess (2:195). Further, a person cannot acquire his own well-being without contributing towards the welfare of others (100:8–11).

Commercial Dealings

The key principles of Jewish ethics in personal and business dealings include the requirements of accurate weights and measures (Lev. 19:35), honesty, fairness in dealing (Ex. 20:15), prohibition on cheating, misrepresentation, lying (Lev. 18:22; 19:11; 19:35–6), conducting business with truthfulness (Ex. 20:15–16) and avoiding activities which lead to depravity and moral decay (Gen. 6:11–13; Ex. 23:7). In similar vein, Christianity regards all types of moral deficiencies in humans as hurdles to reaching God. For instance, 1 Corinthians 6:9–10 says: 'Know ye not that the unrighteous shall not inherit the kingdom of God? Be not deceived.'

Islam requires economic activity to contribute towards a just and equitable society. Bribes, fraud, embezzlement, gambling and speculation are strongly discouraged (11:85; 33:70; 83:1–6), along with activities which involve injustice. Exploitation and gaining at the expense of another party are immoral (2:188). Gambling and speculation are also prohibited (2:219; 5:90). Gambling transfers wealth from one party to another without any real effort and brings harm (11:85). Iqbal and Lewis (2009) noted that the first Muslim state of Medina established an independent department called Al-Hisba. One of the responsibilities of the Al-Hisba was to supervise the behaviour of buyers and sellers in order to ensure smooth functioning of the market.

BENEVOLENT LOANS

A benevolent loan is different from charity. A benevolent loan means the transfer of the use and possession of money to the end user, but not the ownership of money. Charity transfers possession and ownership of money to the recipient. While not disavowing charity, the Holy religions support the idea of benevolent loans to improve the economic health of the poor.

Judaism and Christianity

In the Old Testament, Exodus (22:25) clearly prohibits the charging of interest on loans to the needy. The next two verses even ask to return valuable goods that are pledged as security to seek the blessing of God (Ex. 22:26–7). The charging of interest, especially in the case of commercial loans, may deprive the poor of salary (2 Kgs 4:1–7). One of King David's psalms declared that 'the wicked borrow and do not repay, but the righteous give generously' (Ps. 37:21). The New Testament forbids people from stealing, and encourages them to work and share earnings with the needy (Eph. 4:28). This is the only way to win respect from outsiders and not depend upon others (Thess. 4:11–12).

Talmudic law requires benevolent loans to be extended to all brethren who are in need (BM 64b, BM70b). It considers any gift as a kind of interest if it is received in anticipation of the offering of loans in future, and thus is not permitted. Similarly, accepting a gift even after receiving the loan back is also viewed as another form of interest. The Torah discourages commodity loans in kind for fear that the prices of the commodities may increase or decrease at the time of return. Finally, a mortgagee, even if he is in possession of the mortgaged property, is not allowed to take its produce. He must either return it or sell it off against the capital debt (BM 67a–b).

Gemach is the word used in Hebrew for a benevolent loan with an easy repayment plan. This type of loan is generally for the poorer in society. The Torah treats lending as philanthropic in nature. The idea is to achieve a larger goal: that is, preservation of the family unit and collective survival.

Islam

Islam, similarly to Judaism and Christianity, encourages believers to help their fellows to promote brotherhood among them. Kaleem and Ahmad (2009) argue that the idea of trade is only for productive purposes and for rich people who can afford the risk of losses. Islam's alternative is a benevolent loan (*qard hasan*) for the poor. The Holy Qur'an declares *qard hasan* as a loan to God who himself takes responsibility for the reward (2:245, 64:17). Benevolent loans are provided purely on a goodwill basis to encourage the hard-working and talented people to earn their own living. Here, the debtor is only required to return the principal amount without a prescribed time limit.

Islam defines a clear difference between a benevolent loan and compulsory charity (*zakat*). Benevolent loans are for productive purposes, while charity is mainly to meet the immediate and consumption needs of the poor. The Prophet Muhammad was asked, 'Which are the best forms of income generation?' He replied, 'A man's labor and every legitimate sale' (El-Gamal, 2000, p. 10).

Ariya is another type of benevolent loan where only the usufruct is transferred to the borrower on a temporary and gratuitous basis. The loan article will remain the property of the lender. Lastly, a benevolent loan can also be created if the debtor is in financial trouble. As a first step, the debtor is given some extension in repayment time and later his loan may be converted to charity (2:280). Conversion of the loan into charity is entirely at the discretion of the creditor with only a moral compulsion applying.

Comparisons

Neither the Holy Bible nor the Holy Qur'an seek to abolish loans from society, but instead encourage their followers to extend benevolent loans to the poor in order to seek the blessings of God. This emphasis can be seen to be welfare-enhancing. Charity provides material benefits to the poor, but at the cost of a loss of their dignity. A creditor will likely lend more to the poor if there is a chance of the money being returned. Benevolent loans minimize inefficiency in society relative to money received as charity or a gift.

There are, nonetheless, some differences in the Biblical and Qur'anic approaches towards benevolent loans. Christianity considers benevolent loans as an integral part of grants or charity, but Islam separates benevolent loans from charity. According to the Holy Bible, benevolent loans must be repaid within seven years, after which loans may automatically be remitted. The Holy Qur'an does not impose any time limit in returning money. Lastly, the Holy Qur'an also provides an option to convert a debtor's liabilities into a benevolent loan. The matter is left entirely at the discretion of the creditor, who may also convert his loan into charity. Alternatively, the creditor can claim his loan to be adjusted from the compulsory charity (*zakat*) fund.

CONCLUDING REMARKS

Judaism is the first Abrahamic religion to provide a basic set of beliefs such as One God, the Angels, the Prophets, and the Day of Judgment. It also offers a spiritual, social and moral code of conduct for human beings. Islam is closest to Judaism in terms of basic beliefs. Both trace their ancestries to Abraham: the Jews through Abraham's son Isaac, and the Quraysh of Mecca through Abraham's son Ishmael. However, two differences set these two religions apart. First, Jews believe in the finality of Mosaic law, while Muslims believe in the finality of Qur'anic law. Second, Jews do not believe in the prophethood of anyone after the Prophet Malachi. Muslims believe in the continuity of prophethood after the Prophet Malachi, namely, Jesus Christ and the Prophet Muhammad. Jews also believe in the coming of the Messiah, but they do not accept Jesus in that role.

Christianity grew out of Judaism. Christians seek guidance from both the Old and New Testament. Jesus Christ's teachings about love, forgiveness and charity are reformatory in nature. He had seen many flaws in the interpretation of Mosaic law and tried to correct them. A central tenet is that God is Triune and Jesus is the incarnation of God. Christianity thus believes in the idea of the Trinity: the Son, the Father and the Holy Spirit. These are three separate identities but One God. Judaism and Islam are rigorously monotheistic.

Socio-religious values are essential for any society, such as justice, brotherhood, generation of wealth and commercial ethics. Judaism believes in strict impartiality when delivering justice, regardless of rich or poor. Christianity, on the other hand, promotes love and forgiveness especially towards the vulnerable segment of the society. Islam instructs justice with benevolence, treating people as family members. Considering the concept of brotherhood, Judaism being an ethnically based religion extends the main portion of benefits and privileges towards the Jewish community. Jesus Christ declared the whole world as his family and instructed Christians to 'love their neighbours'. Islam similarly promotes this idea under the slogan of 'universal brotherhood' where rights of Muslims and non-Muslims are alike, but not identical (Muslims vis-à-vis *dhimmas*).

Judaism and Islam both believe in wealth as a gift and reward from God, while Christianity considers wealth as a great responsibility and promotes salvation to seek the blessings of God. Lastly, all three Holy religions hold similar positions towards commercial ethics; for example, free consent in agreement, right of private ownership, acceptance of individual skills and talent, moderation in spending habits, and other social ethics such as prohibition of cheating, fraud, theft, telling a lie, use of false weights. All three strongly advocate the extension of benevolent loans on an interest-free basis. These points of unanimity should not be surprising as all three religions have a firm foundation rooted in ethics and morality. This chapter thus links with the next chapter, which develops and elaborates the common economic policy framework of the Abrahamic religions.

NOTES

1. Some writers are more comfortable using the words 'spirituality' and 'ethics' rather than 'religion'. They argue that instead of emphasizing belief as religion does, the words 'spirituality' and 'ethics' emphasize how values are applied and embodied.
2. The use of Joan Robinson's book as a basis for this discussion suggested itself to us from a reading of Wilson (1997).
3. This section has been greatly influenced by the volume of Long (2010).
4. This section draws on Lewis (2011a).
5. A term used to express that Christ is one person who subsists in two natures; human and divine.

6. Liberation theology of Latin America, endorsed by many South American Catholic priests, eschews North American concepts of economic development, which it considers enriches the rich and makes the poor poorer. Often Marxist in tone, its theological content attempts to reconcile anti-capitalist views with Christian social values. It is thoroughly explored (and criticized) by Michael Novak (1982). See also Wilson (1997) for a discussion.

5. Economic framework of the Abrahamic religions

INTRODUCTION

In the previous chapter we looked at social values promoted by Judaism, Christianity and Islam. Here we consider their views on economic behaviour, a topic which, if not new, is largely ignored in academic research. The Holy religions link material welfare with spiritual development of the community or society. The whole philosophy sees resources as God-given, with man acting as custodian only. In this role, people are guided by various standards, rules and regulations designed to ensure economic well-being and justice in society. But our analysis stays within the nucleus of the religions themselves, and compares the morals and ethical codes, social and economic beliefs, and philosophies of the selected religions. According to Steven Pinker (2018), 59 per cent of people worldwide are religious. Thus a majority have some familiarity with at least one religion, and may appreciate a comparison of it with others.

THE UNDERLYING PRINCIPLES

Our starting point is to consider some general economic principles that underpin Judaism, Christianity and Islam. With the exception of the present volume, the only other study of which we are aware that compares the economic positions of the three Abrahamic religions is that of Rodney Wilson (1997), *Economics, Ethics and Religion: Jewish, Christian and Muslim Economic Thought.* We will review some of the writings that he examined, as well as adding later studies and some of our own additional material.

Judaism

A central tenet of Jewish law is the prohibition of the taking of interest (known as *ribbit*), and much attention is devoted to it. Indeed, Feldman (2010) makes the observation that the practical implications of the prohibition 'fill thousands of pages of the codes of Jewish law' (p. 239). A lender who violates the prohibition is obliged to return the interest to the borrower. The Talmud locates the responsibility in the phrase, 'that our brother may live with you' (Feldman, 2010, p. 245). Domb (2010) argues that Jewish tradition saw wealth as a divine gift, and an illicit transfer of money from one individual to another interferes with the divine plan. Also the Jewish nation was the first to view the purpose of the granting of loans as an act of charity and benevolence.

Some debate emerged amongst rabbinical scholars as to whether such provisions should also apply to loans to Gentiles. However, Maimonides (the influential Rabbi Moshe ben Daimon, 1135–1204) interpreted the interest lending laws actually as an obligation to charge interest to Gentiles, and this became the dominant position. Poliakov (1977, p. 16) saw that this practice ensured that business relations with Christians were kept on a formal level, while at the same time reinforcing the bonds within the Jewish community.

As we saw in Chapter 3, the Torah laid out the prohibition in Exodus 22:24, Leviticus 25:36–7 and Deuteronomy 23:20–21, while the Babylonian Talmud concluded that 'the general principle of *ribbit* is that all payment for waiting is prohibited [amongst Jews]' (Feldman, 2010, p. 40). However, the laws governing economic relations in the Torah embrace much more than the prohibition of *ribbit*. Areas of economic life considered in the Torah are the creation, ownership and distribution of wealth; the laws prohibiting *ribbit* and their implications for banking and finance; markets and good trading practices; and the role of government in regulating economic activity. Making sure that economic actions conform to the religious law constitutes 'right living' under the Torah (Wilson, 1997, p. 24).

Jacob Neusner (1990a), in his *The Economics of the Mishnah*, clarifies the position of the Mishnah – that is, the oral Torah – on the role of markets and allocative matters in general. Essentially the economic order is regarded as permanent, divinely inspired, and should reflect the divine order. Neusner explains that households are the basic economic units for three reasons: (1) they are the cornerstone of economic activity; (2) households own land, which is the means of production; and (3) households undertake consumption. There were also outsider or 'excluded' groups including non-landowning Jews, working as landless labourers, craftsmen and those earning a livelihood from trade and investment, along with Gentiles. They are not governed by the economic laws in the Mishnah, either because they are not landowners, and therefore not guardians of the basic means of production allocated by God to man, or as Gentiles, not subject to the laws designed for Jews (Wilson, 1997, p. 46).

Markets are accepted as the natural order of things in the Torah. Buying and selling are normal everyday activities, with transactions permitted in durable and non-durable commodities, housing and land (the latter, however, subject to the provisions of the Jubilee). Judaism embraces the concept of a just price, referring to not only an honest price, but one that is not exploitative. These conditions only apply to transactions between Jews. Honesty is required in all dealings with Gentiles, but there is no equivalent restraint required if the Jewish partner is in a superior bargaining position to protect the financial position of a non-Jew. As Wilson observes, 'This question of economic discrimination in dealings between Jews and non-Jews is a sensitive issue' (Wilson, 1997, p. 37).

At a broader level, there is the further question of what impact Judaism, and any associated economic discrimination, has had on the rise of capitalism. For elucidating this issue we turn to the debate between Max Weber (1864–1920) and Werner Sombart (1891–1941). Weber (1904–05 [1930]), in his essays on the origins of modern capitalism, *The Protestant Ethic and the Spirit of Capitalism*, expounded the thesis that the Protestant ethic, particularly Calvinism, was the parent of capitalism in the sense that 'the Protestant ethic promoted a work ethic that increased savings, capital accumulation, entrepreneurial activity, and investment' (Iyer, 2016, p. 407). In 1911, Sombart (1911 [1951]) published his response, *The Jews and Modern Capitalism*, in which he sought to show that the Jews had been crucial to the rise of capitalism. (However, it must be recorded that his name is tainted in many circles because he supported the Nazi Party in the latter part of his life.)

In his assessment of the debate, Jerry Muller (2010), in his book *Capitalism and the Jews*, argued that Weber (himself from a family of Calvinist entrepreneurs) saw the distinguishing element of modern capitalism as being 'the rational, industrial organization, attuned to a regular market, and not to political or irrational speculative opportunities for profit' (p. 55). The artisan and business proprietor had long been portrayed as lying at the heart of the nature and culture. Thus the whole realm of finance and investment – which relied on the rational calculation of possibilities for the use of capital, an activity in which Muller considered Jews had excelled – was downplayed in Weber's analysis.

Sombart, by contrast, considered that Jews played a pivotal role in the rise of modern capitalism because they were spiritually and culturally inclined to the rationalistic and calculative mentality so characteristic of capitalism. He also regarded Judaism as predisposing Jews toward capitalism as it was the religion of a rootless, nomadic 'desert people' given to abstraction and a contractual relationship with God, orienting their lives to a distant goal – as required for investment decisions. According to Muller, Sombart portrayed the triumph of capitalism as the replacement of a concrete, particularist Christian community by an abstract, universalistic, Judaized society (Muller, 2010, p. 59).

Some support for this position comes from Hayek in both *Road to Serfdom* (1944) and *The Constitution of Liberty* (1960). Echoing Schumpeter's process of 'creative destruction', Hayek conceived of capitalism as fundamentally dynamic, with dynamism coming from the discovery of new needs and new ways of fulfilling them by entrepreneurs who possessed the characteristic of 'resourcefulness'. The connection with Judaism arose because, in Hayek's eyes, Jews were a striking example of those whose resourcefulness led to the creative destruction that marked, and defined, competitive capitalism. 'Jews are valued precisely for demonstrating the cultural trait of resourcefulness, the intellectual act of discovering new opportunities for the use of resources' (Muller, 2010, p. 70).

But why Jews specifically? Muller (2010) goes on to suggest a number of possible factors:

> As the development of modern capitalism created new economic opportunities in Europe and its colonial offshoots, Jews were disproportionately successful at seizing them. That is because the Jews of Europe were well positioned by their premodern history. Their experience, and the cultural propensities it engendered, predisposed them toward commerce and finance, and toward the free professions. (p. 77)

> Compared to Christianity, Judaism was more favorably disposed toward commerce . . . Talmudic law – which educated Jews continued to study and refine through the ages – was replete with debates about economic matters, including contracts, torts, and prices. (pp. 83–4)

> Another factor that explains Jewish economic success was the propensity to develop social networks . . . The obligation to look after fellow Jews was deeply embedded in Jewish law and culture, and it existed not just in theory but in practice. It took a variety of forms, from simple charity, to mutual aid societies offering low-cost loans to newcomers, to the sharing of information about potential commercial opportunities. (p. 91)

This last characteristic is shared by another ethnic grouping, the Overseas Chinese, notably Hokkien, Chiuchow, Fuzhou Chinese who dominate economic wealth across South East Asia via homeland, family connections and business links (East Asia Analytical Unit, 1995; Lewis, 1999b). In fact, the success of the Chinese in business led to them being described as 'the Jews of the East'.

Christianity

As we saw in Chapter 3, until the advent of Protestant Reformation, the Christian Church had an ambivalent, verging at times on hostile, attitude to business and economic life; notwithstanding the fact that for much of the Middle Ages the Church itself was the largest economic unit and centre of production. Martin Luther was critical of the medieval Church's view that a life devoted to the monastic orders was more holy than participation in political affairs and economic life. Witness to faith could be through honest work, and not by prayer and cutting oneself off from the world through spiritual reflection. Business dealings were to be conducted in accordance with the Ten Commandments, with strict honesty in all transactions, and moderation in consumption. In this respect, the Reformation drew on the teachings of the early Christian fathers, especially St Augustine (354–430), that condemned excess, and saw almsgiving as highly desirable, not so much as to eliminate poverty but to relieve extreme distress. Wealth brings responsibilities, both for wise stewardship, and for good works and charitable deeds (Wilson, 1997, p. 77).

Are we entitled to speak of a Christian approach to business and economic life? Here we turn to the view of some modern Christian writers drawing on the earlier work of Rodney Wilson. Donald Hay (1989), in *Economics Today: A Christian Critique*, highlights three tasks for Christian economists. First, it is necessary to identify from the scriptures those standards which God requires of man. Second, an accurate analysis is needed of the economic and social situation where these principles should be applied. Third, Christians ought to examine themselves and their own motivations, to ensure that they meet the required standards. However, there is no attempt to develop the building blocks of a body of Christian economics. Hay is happy to stay within the fold of conventional, neo-classical, economic analysis. Rather, self-reflection and self-motivation is advocated. For the Christian, the Biblical teachings obviously cannot be ignored, and need to be considered alongside the findings of any economic analysis. Economics is a tool; the scriptures are the guide to how to use the tool and the results obtained (Wilson, 1997, pp. 90–91).

When outlining some of the basic foundations of Christian ethics in Chapter 4, we found it useful to base our discussion around the 'sevens': the seven commandments to Noah, the seven virtues of St Augustine, the seven main beatitudes, the seven gifts of the Holy Spirit and, of course, to be avoided, the seven deadly sins. Two of the books that seek to delineate the Christian approach to economics are based around 'sixes'. J. Philip Wogman (1986), in *Economics and Ethics: A Christian Enquiry*, singled out six features of a Christian theological position on economic matters. Two relate to beliefs, and four to ethics and behaviour. The beliefs concern, first, the physical existence of God's creation; and second, the priority of grace over works. Wogman goes on to explain that the second has important implications for production and distribution:

> If justice, ultimately, is only the proper rewarding of economic behaviour, then we have a clear paradigm for economic organisation. People should simply get what they 'deserve', nothing more and nothing less. But on the other hand if justice is patterned in accordance with the priority of grace, then economic goods should be produced and distributed in such a way as to enhance human well-being and self-acceptance and communal fellow feeling without asking first whether people have deserved what they receive. (Wogman, 1986, p. 35)

Following on from these beliefs, the four issues relating to Christian behaviour are: respect for both physical well-being and social relationships, a sense of vocation, the responsibility of stewardship, and a recognition of original sin with the implication being that economic behaviour can be corrupted by self-interest and self-centredness (Wilson, 1997, p. 98).

The other 'six' dialogue comes from Michael Novak (1982), *The Spirit of Democratic Capitalism*, who applies six theological doctrines to democratic capitalism: the trinity, the incarnation, competition, original sin, the separation of realms, and *caritas*, the compassion and sacrificial love of God as creator. To Wilson, the inclusion of competition seems to sit uneasily with the other five Christian doctrines. However, Novak considers the strength of capitalism to be that it allows space for diversity to flourish. Consider the inspirational hymn 'Onward Christian Soldiers' and even Martin Luther's hymn, 'A mighty fortress is our God, a sure defence and armour'. Both portray the life of a Christian as one of daily battle and combat with sin, in which they must triumph. Competition similarly encourages people to strive to reach new heights of attainment and realize their human potential (Wilson, 1997, p. 111).

Finally, the doctrine of the separation of the realms is to 'give to Caesar what is Caesar's, and to God what is God's' (Matthew 22:21). On the basis of this doctrine a Christian economy or a Christian economics is impossible. The market should be open to all, irrespective of religious belief. Christians should develop their own conception of what constitutes desirable economic outcomes, and ethically acceptable policies to attain these objectives. At the same time, others can apply their own views and ethical standards. The market and Christianity itself is tolerant of diversity.

Islam

It is easier to talk about economics and Islam than it is about the other religions. As we have just documented, there is no Christian economics as such, nor Judaic economics in the form of an integrated analysis. By contrast, beginning in the nineteenth century, Muslim writers sought to lay out the main planks of the discipline of Islamic economics. This subject is very different – indeed the opposite – from the economics of religion. The economics of religion applies the concepts and models of standard economic analysis to study the marketplace for religion (Ekelund et al., 2006; McCleary, 2011). Islamic economics, by contrast, seeks to apply and integrate the religious principles of Islam with economics, with the aim of moulding economic analysis in a way considered appropriate for a Muslim's economic behaviour. The following outline draws on the introduction to the *Handbook on Islam and Economic Life* (Hassan and Lewis, 2014) which in turn was informed by Iqbal and Lewis (2009).

How does the discipline of Islamic economics differ from conventional economic analysis? Utility maximization features in both, but in very different ways. A Muslim accepts revelation as a source of knowledge on metaphysical issues as well as on ethics and justice. By contrast, the whole evolution of standard economic methodology has been in the direction of getting rid of values and ethical theory. In particular, economic theory construes a person as a collection of preferences (attitudes, tastes, actions and laws) that adjust to the changes in the costs and benefits of resources to maximize present utility. In comparison, Islam considers a human being as a servant and vice-regent of God on earth. It is from this perspective that Islam lays great stress on keeping one eye on the material and another on the spiritual.

In Islamic economics the concept of utility is widened in three ways. First, utility or satisfaction is broadened to encompass the spiritual as well as the material. Second, utility is extended temporally from this life to the hereafter. Third, there is explicit recognition of communal obligations, and that well-being cannot be acquired in any true sense without a concern for the welfare of others. The corollary is that the rational being is replaced by the 'faithful' being who pursues personal interests within social bounds and communal interest. The faithful person relies on moral forces such as altruism, cooperation, brotherhood, fraternity, affection and mutual respect to rein in his selfish nature and lust for riches (Ahmad, 1991).

Participation in economic activity in Islamic economics becomes a religious responsibility in which individuals are allowed to pursue their own personal goals while complying fully with the community's norms, values and expectations. In this respect, individual freedom of decision-making is not absolute and has to be moderated and constrained by rules which are designed to ensure that others enjoy similar freedoms. Economic resources and human endeavours are to be employed to seek utility or satisfaction at two levels, the material and the spiritual, so that economic activity is both financially and socially beneficial. This requirement is in recognition that without spiritual enrichment achievement of material fulfilment is ephemeral and ultimately untenable, since a balance of the two is needed for the full development of the individual and society.

In effect, from the Islamic perspective even the most basic decisions about how to organize economic affairs – what commodities to produce, how they will be produced, that is, by whom and with what resources, and for whom the goods are produced – cannot be made without first specifying the purpose of economic life. Put simply, the answer is that the purpose of economic activity is to earn the pleasure of God (Allah). All meaningful human activity, economic or otherwise, is directed towards the Day of Judgment. Any other kind of activity is either meaningless or harmful in distracting one from this purpose. Critics may argue that it may be possible, at least in theory, to reach much the same result by the device of assuming infinitely lived economic agents, but Islam offers a more dynamic and complex view in terms of a battle between conflicting tendencies within the hearts of man. Instead of evaluating people and societies in terms of their ability to produce wealth, wealth is seen as a means of purifying the heart. As a result, Islam seeks to transform society in directions not envisioned in contemporary economic theory, which as Zaman (2014) points out, requires a radically different approach to that which the Islamic paradigm offers.

Nevertheless, the differences between Islamic and conventional analysis can be overstated. In a world of abundant economic resources, relative to demand, there would be no economic problem, as Keynes (1930) noted in his *Economic Possibilities for our Grandchildren*. Accordingly, mainstream economics has its foundations in three building blocks: grappling with the scarcity of resources, pursuit of self-interest in economic activities, and maximization of productive gains from involvement in economic life. These propositions ought not be ignored, but rather viewed from an Islamic perspective. Consider again the three foundations of mainstream economics. First, in terms of scarcity, it is recognized that the provision of resources and their availability to mankind are separate matters. Islamic economics emphasizes that resources are God-given and thus inexhaustible. Yet, their provision to mankind is a function of the application of human knowledge and effort. Second, Islam does not deny self-interest, but requires it to be pursued within the moral and social boundaries of Islam. Acts of selfishness cross those boundaries. Third, and again within the boundaries, there is little quarrel with maximization per se. Maximization is needed for efficiency of resource use in the face of scarcity, and remains a valid method of analysis in Islamic economics (Hasan, 2002).

This broad conception of the discipline needs to be put into practice. The Islamic economic system, like any other, depends on the choices made by individual decision-makers, in this case Muslims, in their everyday activities. A number of writers have set out the central principles that should guide Muslims in their economic activities. Naqvi (1994) in *Islam, Economics and Society* is one such study. Naqvi sees the four foundations of Islamic ethics as unity (*tawhid*), equilibrium (*al adl wal ihsan*), free will (*ikhtiy'ar*), and responsibility (*fardh*). He regards these principles as guiding the rules of economic behaviour in Muslims – in theory if not always in practice – and providing a yardstick for assessing the distribution of income or for observing the nature of consumer behaviour and production in Muslim societies.

Another account is provided by the eminent scholar Umer Chapra (1992) in *Islam and the Economic Challenge*. He sets out an Islamic world view based on three principles: *tawhid* (unity), *khilafah* (vice regency), and *adalah* (justice). *Tawhid* concerns the one unique universe created by God which man must respect. *Khilafah* is the concept of man as God's agent on earth, empowered with considerable discretion to act for good or evil, but with a duty to use the world's resources in an effective and just way. Socio-economic justice or *adalah* implies a duty to live by *Shari'ah* (Islamic law), and avoid all forms of *zulm*, which involves inequality, exploitation and oppression. Wilson (1997, pp. 141–2) describes these as 'lofty ideals' which are, nonetheless, subject to 'divine sanction' which limits the extent of human discretion.

Finally, we come to that old saw, the perennial question of whether and to what extent adherence to Islamic religious rules may have contributed to the Middle East (along with many Muslim majority countries) falling behind the West in terms of economic growth, living standards and technology (although for Muslim countries as a whole, Ariff and Safari, 2014 find evidence of a considerable catch-up over the last 60 years of post-colonial development). It is easy to resort to cultural stereotypes. For example, Max Weber (1904–05 [1930]) in *The Protestant Ethic and the Spirit of Capitalism* suggested that the conservative or mystical nature of Islam stifled curiosity, and the willingness to learn non-Muslim languages or read translations of foreign-language books and other works. In this last respect, little may have changed. The well-known British author Martin Amis records: 'Present-day Spain translates as many books into Spanish, annually, as the Arab world has translated into Arabic in the last eleven hundred years' (Amis, 2008, p. 29). Amis describes Islam as 'autarkic' and exhibiting 'stout self-sufficiency', as it could afford to be for close to a millennium due to a 'chain reaction of conquest and conversion, an amassment not just of territory but of millions of hearts and minds' (Amis, 2008, p. 81).

At a practical level, being a Muslim brings its burdens as well as rewards.

As Amis (2008, pp. 78–9) goes on to point out (perhaps with a degree of exaggeration):

> believers in most religions appear to think that, so long as they observe all the formal pieties, then for the rest of the time they can do more or less as they please. Islam . . . 'isn't like that.' Islam follows you everywhere, into the kitchen, into the bedroom, into the bathroom, and beyond death into eternity.

Certainly, it may impact on economic life, as Rodney Wilson (1997) observes:

> The demands of Islam, not least that to pray five times a day, results, however, in the religion affecting to an enormous degree the lives of believers, who are constantly being made aware of the basis of their faith. These demands, which consume much human energy, inevitably impinge to a great extent on economic activity. It is, in fact, difficult for Muslims to isolate the economic and the spiritual domain in their lives, as both are constantly alternating, with a daily as well as a weekly cycle. (p. 115)

There are, in addition, other interpretations of what Kuran (2011) terms 'the long divergence'. In his essay 'Islamic Institutions and Underdevelopment', Jared Rubin (2014) examines four explanations for why the Middle East fell behind relative to Europe. The first explanation is Avner Greif's (1994) 'cultural institutions' theory, which states that the collectivist social structure of the Middle East was well suited for economic success in pre-modern times, when personal exchange dominated, but was ill suited to support impersonal exchange in a manner akin to the more individualistic Europe. The second is Lisa Blaydes and Eric Chaney's (2013) thesis that the feudal structure of medieval Europe allowed the military to constrain rulers, while the lack of a feudal structure in the Middle East encouraged the use of military slaves, who were not able to constrain Islamic sultans. The third explanation is his own argument which suggests that the significant degree to which Islamic political authorities were legitimized by religious authorities had unintended long-run economic consequences. This theory treats religious authorities as an interest group that placed constraints on the ruler in a manner that favoured themselves and not broader economic success. The final, and most well-cited, explanation is Timur Kuran's (1997, 2001, 2005, 2011) multifaceted hypothesis connecting aspects of Islamic law to the ultimate economic stagnation of the Middle East. Kuran contends that Islamic laws of inheritance, trusts (*waqf*) and partnerships, which were at one point in time optimal responses to the conditions of the Middle Ages, calcified over time and jointly prevented economic modernization.

This last explanation by Kuran is one to which we will return, but a few brief comments are warranted at this juncture. The Islamic inheritance system is egalitarian in spirit by restricting the accumulation of wealth, but the fragmentation of wealth that results – especially of financial wealth – hindered capital accumulation. *Waqf*, a type of pious foundation or an unincorporated Islamic trust, 'used up resources to provide social services that were often unproductive' (Iyer, 2016, p. 426).

A SUMMARY SO FAR

In conclusion, having examined some building blocks for what might constitute a Judaic and Christian perspective on economics, we then explored the nature of Islamic economics and how it differs from conventional economic analysis. In the process, there has been a wide-ranging discussion of some related issues, in particular the relative contributions of Judaism and Christianity in the rise of capitalism, and the multifaceted factors advanced to explain why the once ascendant Islamic Middle East fell behind the West in economic and technological change. It is now time to narrow the focus and consider some specific views of the three Abrahamic religions on economic life. We begin with the major sources of income and expenditure.

RULINGS ON INCOME AND EXPENDITURE

All three religions have, at one time or another, and to a different extent, refused to legitimize interest income as reward for capital investment. Money is considered as an inert factor which cannot grow itself without the aid of entrepreneurial skills. Therefore, human values must be wedded to the money before it produces any results, such as from work and investment.

Work and Investments

Judaism recommends the investment of funds to generate profit that can be used for the benefit of society. The Talmud ruled that traders are not allowed to charge a profit more than one-sixth of the cost price, otherwise the sale is null and void (BM 50b). The Torah also defines rules for labour. Employees are asked to pay their employees on time (Lev. 19:13). Field workers are allowed to eat produce from the field while at work. Likewise, employers are instructed not to send their employees away empty-handed, but with gifts and staple food (Deut. 23:25; 15:13–14). Nor should Jews forget their duties towards God. The Old Testament asks Jews to work six days in a week and take rest and remember God on the seventh day, the Sabbath. Not even animals and servants can be involved in commercial activates on the Sabbath (Ex. 20:8–10; 23:12) although it is always possible to frame questions (for example, 'Wouldn't it be nice if the blinds were closed?') in such a way that the servant voluntarily does so. Perhaps on such bases, the Old Testament railed against the rich class who hid their wealth, did not follow the Sabbath, and refused to pay charity (Isa. 3:14–15; 5:7–8; Mal. 3:5–12).

Likewise, Christianity takes the rights of poor and labourers seriously. Early Christians discouraged profit-making activities, and on one occasion Jesus entered the Jewish temple, overturned the tables of the moneychangers who were busy selling and buying, and declared the temple only as a place of worship (Mt. 20:1–16). Chewning et al. (1990, p.4) pointed out that St Augustine wrote 'Business is in itself evil', and thus created a tension between business and Christianity, which came to the fore in the vigour of the Christian attack on usury (see Chapter 3).

Islam recognizes only profit through legitimate sales (2:275) as reward for capital investment, and defines a true believer as one who spends money both in prosperity and adversity, who suppresses anger and pardons people (3:134), and does not hoard money (9:33–4). Generating income through interest is rejected in favour of a mechanism where both financier and entrepreneur share the outcome of their venture. If there is a loss, both the parties should suffer, and if it turns to a profit, both will participate in those earnings. Such a system demands a high level of caution on the part of the investor (lender), otherwise it may not work. Attempts to implement this pure form have had only mixed success in the context of a modern financial system.

Inheritance

Judaism was the first Holy religion to introduce a law of inheritance. Under Judaic law property or wealth can only be transferred to the eldest male member of a family (2 Chr. 21:3). Moreover, the share of that of eldest son in family property is double that of the remaining children. If a person has two wives and he has sons from both, he must give a double share of whatever he has to the firstborn child (Deut. 21:15–17).

Moses himself defined inheritance law in detail in the Book of Numbers. If a person dies without any male offspring then his daughter is his legal heir. If a person dies without any children then his brothers are considered as his successors. In the absence of brothers, his father's brothers will inherit the property. Even if his father has no brothers, then property shall be transfered to his kinsman (Num. 27:7–11). Mosaic law does not allow transfer of wealth outside of the clan of the father, if a woman is married to an outsider. Women can only inherit property if they marry within the tribe (Num. 36:6–9).

Family leadership is in the hands of the husband. As soon as a Jewish woman gets married she loses control over the property and earnings to her husband. Swidler (1976, p. 142) noted that, after marriage, a husband possesses property which the wife holds, but a wife could not possess anything which belonged to the husband. Epstein (1973, p. 149) observed that in a Jewish family a father first raises his daughter, then arranges a gift or dowry for her husband at the time of marriage. Thus a girl, financially speaking, became a liability not asset for the family. A groom had to present a gift to the bride at the time of their marriage, yet she was owner of that gift only so long as they were married. In the case of the death of a husband, the woman regained premarital property but had absolutely no share in her deceased husband's property.

The law of inheritance further defines that if a person gives some gift to his sons, that gift belongs to them as inheritance. But if the same gift is given to a servant, it will belong to him as long as he is alive. After his death that gift must be returned (Ezek. 46:16–18). Judaism links inheritance with wisdom and righteousness. There is a proverb that a wise man leaves inheritance for his children (Prov. 13:22; 20:21).

Christianity, until the last century, generally followed Jewish tradition. Both canon and civil laws barred daughters from sharing properties with their brothers, and women were deprived of any inheritance rights. To compensate, families offered their daughters a large dowry, and as a result men tried to marry earlier while families often delayed their daughters' marriages (Swidler, 1976, p. 142). Women's rights under English law of 1632 did not allow them to make any independent contract without the permission of their husband. Moreover, they could not sue or be sued in their own names, nor sue their husband. English law believed that a wife legally belonged to her husband and therefore she did not hold property, legal rights or even her family name.

Jesus Christ declared the whole world as his family. That may be the reason why the New Testament does not provide any specific instructions related to inheritance law. We only find two statements in the Gospel of Luke about inheritance:

> And the younger of them said to [his] father, Father, give me the portion of goods that falleth [to me]. And he divided unto them [his] living. (15:12)

> one of the company said unto him, Master, speak to my brother, that he divide the inheritance with me. And he said unto him, Man, who made me a judge or a divider over you? And he said unto them, Take heed, and beware

of covetousness: for a man's life consisteth not in the abundance of the things which he possesseth. (12:13–15)

Christians are advised to turn over whatever they owe to others: taxes, revenue, and respect and honour (Rom. 13:7).

The Islamic law of inheritance is a divinely ordained instrument which, as we have said, discourages the concentration of wealth and economic resources into a few hands, but at the same time may result in uneconomically small holdings and militate against capital accumulation. An individual's power of testamentary disposition is basically limited to one-third of the net estate (that is, the assets remaining after the payment of funeral expenses and debts), and two-thirds of the estate passes to the legal heirs of the deceased under the compulsory rules of inheritance. Here Islamic law (*shari'ah*), providing for every member of the family by allotting fixed shares not only to wives and children, but also to fathers and mothers, aimed at achieving a measure of fairness (for example, a son's share is twice that of a daughter on the grounds that the male is expected to provide for his own family). Islamic inheritance law only disqualifies the legal heir of a deceased person under two situations. First, a Muslim cannot be an heir of a disbeliever, nor can a disbeliever become an heir of a Muslim. Second, one who kills a man cannot inherit from him.

Islam motivates Muslims to work hard rather than rely upon their inherited properties or wealth Furthermore, the concept of inheritance is not confined to legal successors only. Islamic inheritance law encourages Muslims to write a will during their lifetime and also to allocate some portion for the poor, orphans and other financially weak relatives who do not have a direct share in their properties (2:180). Donating or receiving a share in wealth as a gift is another unique characteristics of Islamic inheritance law. A Muslim is allowed to receive or donate a gift (*hiba*) during his lifetime. But the exchange agreement must be unconditional, without involving any commercial interest. A bequest to outsiders in excess of one-third of the net value of an estate is invalid and is not allowed without the permission of other legal heirs.

Marriage is another source of exchanging income or wealth among Muslims. The bridegroom must provide his new wife with a marriage gift or dowry. This gift is the exclusive property of the bride even if she is later divorced. There is no such condition for the bride to present any gift to her husband (4:4). Moreover, Islam allows a married woman to retain her independent legal personality and her family name (but not pass it on to her children, who must bear the father's name).

Income from Land and Agriculture

Judaism defined agriculture laws and announced that all land belongs to God (Deut. 15:8). Distribution of land revolved around the retention of land with the original owners to ensure individual freedom and self-sufficiency in food (Prov. 14:23; 21:25). By tradition, Israelites cultivated land for six consecutive years, leaving the land fallow for the seventh year. Farmers were not supposed to harvest the whole field. They were asked to leave the remains in the fields for the poor, widows and orphans (Lev. 19:9–10) as well as their domestic servants and for wild animals (Ex. 23:11). The Torah did not allow Israelites to sell their agricultural land permanently. They could only sell it on a temporary basis, with the land price linked with its cultivation until the next Jubilee year, after which all land must return back to its original owners and all outstanding debts had to be written off (Lev. 25:14).

The Torah imposed a 10 per cent production tax (the tithe) on the agriculture income after every three years. This income was reserved for the poor, strangers and widows, or those who had no initial share in the distribution of land (Deut. 14:28–9; 26:12–13). The sacred text also defined rules for crop sharing. One-fifth of all crops belonged to the rulers, while the remaining four-fifths went to farmers for their living and to plant next year's crops (Gen. 47:23–4). Mosaic law ruled that God rewarded with improved agriculture output due to high crop yields, lush pastures and rain (Lev. 26:3–5; Deut. 11:15), and punished by what insurers call 'acts of God' such as storms and failed crops (Deut. 11:17; Isa. 3:1; 5:10; Ezek. 4:16; Mic. 6:15).

The philosopher (and agnostic) Bertrand Russell (1923 [1959]) thought that religion would decline with the rise of an industrial society in which people no longer relied on 'the elements' for their living; true perhaps of Western Europe, but not elsewhere. In similar vein, McCleary and Barro (2006, p. 50) note that proponents of the secularization model also predict that religion would decline with 'movements away from the vicissitudes of agriculture and toward greater economic security of advanced urbanized economics'. Indeed, in 'The New Economics of Religion', Sriya Iyer (2016) poses the question (but does not answer it): 'Why is religion still so pervasive and persistent even as countries are becoming richer?' (p. 431).

Mishnah does not permit one to enter into a forward sale agreement unless the seller holds the raw material in his possession, such as grapes for the future delivery of wine and vats of olives for future delivery of oil (BM 72b2). These restrictions help to avoid uncertainty in transactions and to save the sellers from losses due to any upside fluctuation in prices.

BM 65a allows a buyer to demand a discount against future delivery if full payments are made in advance.

Christianity itself does not develop any specific law related to income from agricultural land. Most of its agriculture laws are borrowed either from the Old Testament or from Greek tradition.

Islam encourages Muslims to derive income from agriculture and related activities and also imposes an agriculture tax commonly known as *usher* which means 'one-tenth' in Arabic, levied on the produce of land (6:141). The rate of *usher* tax varies from 5 per cent to 10 per cent per annum, subject to the fertility of the land: 10 per cent if the land is irrigated from natural resources such as rain, springs or streams; 5 per cent of the entire produce if the land is irrigated from artificial means such as wells, buckets, and so on; but no *usher* tax if the crop fails due to natural calamity. It is the responsibility of the cultivator regardless of land ownership to pay the *usher* tax. However, the landlord can be responsible for *usher* tax if the crop is under a sharing arrangement. Note that the *usher* tax is quite similar to the Judaic tithe; the difference is that Islam links *usher* directly with the agriculture outputs, while Judaism allows Israelites to pay the tithe after every third year.

Islamic scholars have identified various techniques to share income generated from land and agriculture. For instance, *mozaraah* is an agreement for joint cultivation. Under this agreement the landlord provides his piece of land to the farmer to cultivate crops. Later, both share the income at a mutually agreed ratio. Alternatively, the landlord can also give his land to the farmer on rent for a fixed period of time. Some jurists object to renting agricultural land, considering a fixed rent to be similar to interest. They suggest that the rent should be set in proportion to income from cultivation (Hussain, 2008).

Welfare of the Family

The Torah declares that God has created male and female in his own image (Gen. 1:27). Jews believe that Abraham was the first patriarch revealed with the knowledge of one God and his will. Abraham was promised a large family network in order to keep the way of God to perform justice and judgment (Gen. 12:5; 18:19).

As noted, Jewish traditional family structures have the husband as the head, responsible for the training and upbringing of his children and to teach them the words and ways of God (Deut. 6:4–9). Parents are responsible for their children up to the age of 20; after that age children must serve the army of Israel (Num. 1:3). Of course, it is also the responsibility of children to obey their parents: the fifth of the Ten Commandments is,

'Honour your father and your mother'. Jewish people are also forbidden to maintain a grudge against their own people; instead, they must take care of neighbours (Lev. 19:18).

Possession of wealth is declared a great responsibility in Christianity. A person can only deserve the adornment of God if he spends money on meeting his family needs and taking care of neighbours and the poor. In fact, Jesus declared the whole world as his family members. He effectively distilled the Ten Commandments into two: one God, and love your neighbour. If a person holds material wealth but does not help his brother in need, how can he find the love of God? (Jn. 3:17). The New Testament defines the qualification to become a bishop: he must be married and have children, and enjoy a good reputation in the society (I Tim. 3:4–7). Thus, a family life is an important criterion to become a community leader in Christianity – a dictate neglected in Catholicism.

Like Judaism and Christianity, Islam put emphasis on the unity of family. Both husband and wife have equal rights on each other (2:228). Nevertheless, Islam makes the husband responsible for arranging the necessities of life, to provide food, shelter and clothing for his family. Both husband and wife are together responsible for the upbringing of their children. The Holy Qur'an also gives instructions to children to take care of their parents, especially when they grow older (16:90).

Compulsory Charity

Inheritance laws and spending on family welfare may divide and subdivide properties so as to prevent the accumulation of wealth in a few hands – not necessarily an unmixed blessing – but they make no provision for the direct relief of poverty and distress. All Holy religions provide an answer through suggesting various types of charities, alms-giving and donations both in cash and in kind. Charity purifies income and wealth of disrepute, by advancing the welfare of the community. Donation and charity do not mean that poor and needy people automatically qualify and are entitled to treat whatever is received as a right. The New Testament says that 'a man shall not eat if he does not work' (2 Thess. 3:10). Similarly, the Qur'an reminds us that God does not like ungrateful people. He (God) is fully aware of what humans do (39:8).

Judaism promotes the concept of charity and donations. In the Talmud, a Hebrew term *tzedakah* is used for both charity and righteousness, meaning that a person cannot become righteous without charity. The Torah suggested a mandatory 10 per cent (tithe) of earnings as a charity tax, regardless of the source of earnings. If a person wants to withdraw some part from the compulsory charity of 10 per cent then he must pay additional charity up to one-fifth of the redeemed amount, imposed as 'plenty' (Lev. 27:30–33; Deut. 14:22–3).

In Christianity a 10 per cent tithe was (and in some cases still is) common amongst devout Christians. Jesus said that it is more blessed to give than receive (Acts 20:35). Christians are advised not to refuse those who beg, and to show hospitality to the poor and strangers, as God likes acts of sacrifice (Mt. 5:42; Heb. 13:2; 16). Kulikovsky (2007) defines the Biblical poor as those who are not economically well off and have no kinsmen to protect them from having their legal and moral rights suppressed. 1 Timothy 6:1–7 provides detailed guidelines about how to spend charity money and who should be assisted, divided into four broader categories: (1) helping widows and orphans; (2) spending during emergency; (3) helping needy people and travellers from other places; and (4) taking care of church workers.

Islam declares *zakat* (compulsory charity) as the fourth of the Five Pillars of Islam, or fundamental observances. Governments impose and collect 2.5 per cent *zakat* per annum on the accumulated wealth (which is in the possession of an assessee for more than one year). The proceeds collected are then used to relieve the poor, needy, salaries of *zakat* collectors, newly converted Muslims, repayment of debt, preachers, and travellers (9:60). Often seen as a tax, this is not strictly correct (Iqbal and Lewis, 2014, pp. 466–7). It is an obligatory charity in return for which no material reward is expected. Therefore, in a broader spiritual context, it cannot be construed as a tax from a giver's perspective, for the very act of giving shows the believer's sense of social responsibility, purifying acquired wealth.

From the viewpoint of the economy, *zakat* has a number of merits, outlined by Ahmad et al. (2006). First, since *zakat* is paid on net worth, regardless of whether the capital is utilized or not, the levy encourages the capital owner to invest in productive activities, both to be able to pay *zakat* from profits, as well as to prevent consumption of capital by *zakat*. Second, the *zakat* levy contributes to economic growth. The exclusion and exemption of the means of production from *zakat* creates an incentive for increased investment in plant and equipment and leads to a high level of capital utilization, which in turn promotes employment. Third, *zakat* contributes to increased consumption through financing the poorest groups in society, providing essential public goods and services to those who would not have sufficient access to them, enhancing the income levels of the target beneficiaries as well as the growth potential of the economy. Most contemporary Islamic economists have laid emphasis on the third point and have directed most attention toward resurrecting *zakat* as an instrument for need fulfilment and poverty alleviation (e.g., Shirazi, 1996; Kahf, 1997).

Table 5.1 The classical zakat system: core items

	2.5 per cent	5.0 per cent	10.0 per cent	20.0 per cent
Mineral production and treasure troves[1]				✓
Agricultural produce[2]		✓	✓	
Livestock	✓			
Trade[3]	✓			
Industry[3, 4]	✓			
Cash, gold, silver and jewellery	✓			
Rents and wages[5]	✓			

Notes:
1. This too is sometimes known as *khums* (one-fifth). Also, some jurists make a distinction between treasures buried by persons and mineral production. It is the former that fetches a *zakat* rate of 20 per cent, while the latter rate is only 2.5 per cent (see, e.g., Maududi, 1994).
2. 2.5 per cent for lands irrigated with artificial systems; 10 per cent for lands irrigated with natural water. The levy is also known as *usher*.
3. Assets and income net of loans, working tools, and permanent fixtures.
4. Given that cash or gold, agricultural produce, livestock, and trade capital virtually exhausted the then existing forms of wealth, the *zakat* rate on manufacturing is considered analogous to trade. On services involving little traditional capital, one may infer, *zakat* is levied on net profits. See Hasanuz Zaman (1991, pp.183–5), for the use, in general, of analogy in *zakat*. For specific juristic details, see Al-Qardawi (1984).
5. Differences of opinion exist on the issue. Hitti (1970), quoting from Sheikh Yaqubi, states that Mu'awiah used to deduct *zakat* at 2.5 per cent, from the fixed annuities of Muslims.

Source: Adapted from Iqbal and Lewis (2014).

Nevertheless, the *zakat* system has a major drawback – its low yield – a point emphasized by Iqbal and Lewis (2014). Table 5.1, drawn from that study, indicates that the scope of *zakat* extends to most major components of gross domestic product (GDP). In addition, there is a levy on wealth. With most income, as well as selected categories of wealth, constituting the base of *zakat*, those authors contend a yield of between 5–10 per cent of GDP ought not to be an overestimate. Actual collections, however, paint a different picture. Zarqa (1995, p.217) estimates that the yield of *zakat* in Syria in 1971 was 3 per cent of GDP, and in Sudan in 1982 was 3.6 per cent of GDP. Based on a study conducted on Pakistan, the low yield can be attributed to three factors. First, there are operational problems, in particular a disinterested and inefficient machinery of government. Second, there is lack of public confidence in the government's use of such funds for the prescribed purpose (Shirazi, 1996, pp.37–40). Many Muslims may prefer to deliver *zakat* on their own rather than through the state, and through preferred institutions (Mustafa et al., 2013). Third, there are differences on the question of the appropriate base of *zakat*. As the composition of national income has changed over the centuries, new forms of income and wealth have become more important. Although there have been attempts (e.g., Al-Qardawi, 1983) to bring these new forms within the ambit of *zakat*, a consensus is still not in sight.

In an earlier study (Iqbal and Lewis, 2009), one solution proposed was that of dispensing with a separate assessment for *zakat* and integrating it with general taxation. The central idea is that, for the directly assessed part of the tax on a taxing unit, the taxpayer be allowed to tender (self-assessed) *zakat* (in lieu of the tax liability) to the government. All monies tendered in the name of *zakat* would be credited to a separate account. In cases where the amounts fall short of a previously stated portion of budgetary allocation for redistribution (say 5–10 per cent of GDP, or 10–20 per cent of total tax take), then funds could be transferred from the general budget to the *zakat* budget. If such targets are exceeded, then funds are transferred from the *zakat* budget to the general budget and the government is allowed to benefit by applying these excess proceeds toward national debt repayments, defence expenditure and public servant salaries.

It needs to be remembered, however, that Islamic teachings are not confined to *zakat* alone. They also promote *sadaqat* or optional charity. A Muslim is encouraged to pay *sadaqat* whenever and wherever it is necessary. If a Muslim makes a contribution openly, that is good; but if he donates secretly, that is even better for him (2:271). Islamic philosophy is to donate the best thing as charity, not items which render one with embarrassment and a sense of shame (2:267). Further, donors should not expect anything in return or reward from the beneficiaries (74:6).

Mining and exploration is a special case of charity in Islam. The religion believes that God has created this world for the benefit of the whole of mankind and all natural resources belong to the nations or communities. No individual can claim exclusive rights on natural resources. Islam has prescribed 20 per cent tax (*khums*) on income generated from mining and that must be used for the welfare of the community. The remaining income goes to finders or discoverers of such minerals. *Khums* is in addition to the *zakat* paid on the accumulated wealth under Islamic law, and it allows the state or government automatically to become part owner in all natural resources under its jurisdiction. The provision can also serve as a corrective measure to manage uncontrolled exploration of natural resources. *Khums* is also levied on what is extracted from the sea, such as pearls, ambergris, and so on. The Qur'an also imposed one-fifth or 20 per cent tax on wealth acquired as war booty. The tax collected could be used for the spread of religion, the welfare of Prophet Muhammad's family, his near relatives, orphans, the needy and travellers (8:41).

Waqf

Islam also encourages establishing *waqf* (endowment funds or trust) purely for certain predefined philanthropic causes. Muslim jurists hold the view that the first ever *waqf* in Islam is the sacred building of the Kaaba in Mecca. *Waqf* is a kind of *sadaq-e-jaria* (endowment fund). Once a property is dedicated as a *waqf*, it remains so until the Day of Judgment. It is perpetual in nature and prohibits the use of reserved properties outside its stated objectives. Kahf (2003) defines five different types of *waqf*: (1) religious *waqf* – spread of religion; (2) philanthropic *waqf* – welfare of the general public; (3) family *waqf* – welfare of the family members; (4) *waqf* of usufruct – only usufruct of the property is used as *waqf*; and (5) financial *waqf* – only the income generated can be used for *waqf* purposes.

Nonetheless, *waqf* are not without their problems. Consider the family *waqf*. Tunku Alina Alias (2014) says that from the available evidence it appears that the family *waqf* may have been used as a vehicle to skirt Qur'anic inheritance rules (Hennigan, 2004, p. 93), although this cannot be taken to be valid for all cases (Doumani, 1998, p. 7; McChesney, 2004, p. 275) She argues that it is necessary to differentiate between a *waqf* established by bequest and becoming operative upon the death of the founder from one established during the life of a *waqif* which is considered as a gift *inter vivos*. The former is subject to Qur'anic inheritance laws, the latter is not (Hennigan, 2004, pp. 93–101).

There is the further charge that Tunku Alina raises, namely that the family *waqf* can be used to avoid arbitrary taxation and appropriation. Taxation goes to the root of the existence of any state. The question to be answered is whether historically the family *waqf* actually eroded the Ottoman tax base by virtue of wholesale conversion of productive lands into *waqf*. As can be seen from the Western approach to charities, the modern argument is that in exchange for any tax benefits, a charitable trust must fulfil its public-services function to justify the support it receives. From this perspective, it is said that family *waqf* do not fulfil this requirement and should not receive public support in terms of tax relief (Kuran, 2001, p. 22).

Benevolent Loans

Benevolent loans are an aspect of religious financing usually missing in conventional finance, extended to needy but competent people without any charges, so that they can start their own businesses. Lenders are instructed not to except any gift or special treatment from the borrowers as reward. Benevolent loans are not linked with any worldly reward; rather, to seek the blessings of God. Judaism, Christianity and Islam have broadly similar views towards benevolent loans. Such loans were considered in Chapter 4.

Noble Causes (Spread of Religion)

Judaism, Christianity and Islam are based upon divine injunctions, which promote spiritual peace among followers. They ask people to spend their wealth for the spread of the religious message of supporting peace and harmony in the society.

Judaism does not accept 'outside' Hebrew people as part of the Jewish community. All financial and other donations in kind are used mainly for the economic and spiritual welfare of their own community. Judaism allows both livestock and crops for offerings to seek forgiveness of sins. Crops, grains, wine and oil are acceptable for offerings as they were the part of ancient rituals (Lev. 23:13–18). Israelites are also instructed to donate their first harvest of crops and the firstborn male cattle, sheep or goats to God (Ex. 22:29–30). Mosaic law also describes in detail the terms and conditions specific to food and eating habits; for example, never to eat any fat and blood (Lev. 3:17).

The New Testament at various places asks Christians to raise funds for noble causes: for travelling ministeries (Rom. 15:24), to supply the needs of God's people (2 Cor. 9:12), for partnership in gospel (Phil. 1:4–5), for assisting ministry needs (Phil. 4:14–18) and for helping those who work for the Church (1 Tim. 5:9–10; 5:17–18). Unlike Judaism and Islam there are no specific food laws, although all Christians are instructed to give thanks to God before and after eating food (Rom. 14:6). Biblical teachings are quite generic and leave this matter for individuals to determine what and how much should they spend on spreading Christianity. Nowadays, at a global level, the spread of Christianity relies heavily on the United States, which supports more missionaries, broadcasting organizations and publishing houses than any other country.

Islam strongly advocates spreading God's message on the earth (2:195), especially through preaching. Two basic rules are given for preaching: (1) 'Invite (all) to the Way of thy Lord with wisdom and beautiful preaching; and argue with them in ways that are best and most gracious' (16:125); and (2) 'Let there be no compulsion in religion: Truth stands out clear from Error' (2:256). And history indicates that Islam was to a considerable degree spread via merchants and religious teachers. However, it must be said that, like the growth of Christendom, expansion was not always peaceful.

Similarities and Differences in the Holy Teachings

In general, the objectives of all three religions are to secure economic and spiritual peace among all communities. Another important aim is to ensure an equitable distribution of wealth to promote harmony and justice in society, related to various permissible sources of generating income and spending money.

Judaism and Islam encourage investments and other business-related activities. Both consider wealth as a gift and blessing from God, and neither have a vow of poverty. Christianity initially took a different position, declaring that a man cannot serve two masters at the same time. Either he can serve God or he can accumulate wealth, and the New Testament put emphasis on serving and helping the poor, earning the blessing of God.

Distribution of inheritance property is a second major source of income. Islam sets out specific inheritance laws for distribution among all family members, whereas Judaic inheritance law relates predominantly to the male members of its community. Christianity followed Mosaic law for the distribution of wealth and did not itself develop any separate inheritance laws until the nineteenth century. Later it adopted common law and accepted the rights of women in deceased property.

Judaism provides detailed rules in the case of income from land and agriculture, covering taxation, harvesting and land sales. So too does Islam, although the tax varies with land fertility. It also includes taxation on mining.

Charity is encouraged in all three religions. Judaism promotes a tithe or 10 per cent for charity. Christianity leaves it to the individual, but in practice a tithe of 10 per cent is common amongst devout adherents and fundraising is strong amongst Evangelicals who constitute 80 million of Christians in the United States.[1] Islam asks Muslims to pay 2.5 per cent of their net wealth in compulsory charity (*zakat*), and also urges optional charity. We have noted some issues surrounding *zakat* collection.

Benevolent loans are another major source to help the poor. Judaic law allowed benevolent loans for a maximum period of seven years after which all loans are automatically remitted. Christianity encourages benevolent loans but does not define any specific time limit for return. The same is the case for Islam. Lastly, Christianity and Islam, being more universal religions, encourage followers to spend money for the promotion and spread of religious teachings.

CONCLUDING REMARKS

We began this chapter with the observation that, with the exception of this analysis, the only other study that we know of that compares the approaches to economic issues of Judaism, Christianity and Islam is that of Rodney Wilson (1997). Our review of his literature has been supplemented with later material (including our own) on a wide-ranging discussion of the contribution of Judaism to the expansion of capitalism, the definition and nature of the discipline of Islamic economics, recent work on *zakat* and family *waqf*, along with revisiting whether the Islamic religion itself held back economic development in the Middle East. Nevertheless, the central conclusions remain. First, beliefs shape economic behaviour. Religious belief in particular encourages people to behave in certain desirable ways, offering a standard to judge right from wrong. Second, religion provides rules to govern economic life, reinforcing and being reinforced by the conscience of the individual follower. Third, despite some differences in doctrine and practice between the Abrahamic religions, the moral compasses they offer in the economic sphere are not so different: honesty, justice in economic transactions and a concern for the situation of the poor mark all three. Fourth, there is a moral concern about the working of modern financial systems, and the perceived failure of personal responsibility on the part of those allocating capital resources. This is apparent when recent financial crises and behaviour are considered in the next chapter.

NOTE

1. Evangelical churches also have a strong presence outside of the United States. Notably, Mr Scott Morrison, the Prime Minister of Australia (as of late 2018), is a leading member of an Evangelical church in Sydney, New South Wales.

6. What the Abrahamic religions say about contemporary financial practices

THE ATTITUDE OF THE RELIGIONS

Not surprisingly, given their common heritage, the ethical positions of Judaism, Christianity and Islam on finance differ little. All have strong views about financial advice and misleading contracts. In Judaism, the giving of ill-suited advice (*lifnei ivver*) and creating a false impression (*geneivat da'at*) are violations of Jewish business ethics (Pava, 1998; Tamari, 1987; Levine, 2010b, 2010c). Many aspects of Jewish law carry over to Christianity through Mosaic Law and the Old Testament. In addition, in the encyclical *Caritas in Veritate*, Benedict XVI (2009) mandates the need for 'truth telling'. In Islamic law, *gharar* signifies ambiguity, uncertainty or lack of specificity in the conditions of a financial contract and is strictly forbidden in Islam, which insists that information must be easily and equally accessible to all transactors, which was clearly not the case during the global financial crisis of 2008 (Lewis, 2010, 2014b).

There is now an extensive literature on what took place in the run-up years to the financial crisis of 2008. However, it is important to recognize that this event was not the end of it, for financial malpractices have continued, as evidenced by the attempt of banks to manipulate the London Interbank Offered Rate (LIBOR) and the Australian bank bill swap rate. At the time of writing (September 2018) ongoing misdeeds are being revealed before the Australian Banking Royal Commission, which ought to be much to the banks' embarrassment, but the culture of entitlement and arrogance is such that it is not. Through subsidiaries, banks have sold 'dud' insurance, against which they are reluctant to pay claims. Sky-high up-front and trailing commissions have been paid to mortgage brokers, and to used car dealers, for business to be directed to the banks. Banks have made large loans to pensioners and low-income earners, often against application forms filled in by the broker or forged, that borrowers have no reasonable means to repay. What is perhaps worse is that not many observers are surprised by any of this, reflecting the low esteem in which bankers and financiers are held.

It has been a sorry tale, and while few would condone the unconscionable financial practices that have come to light, there are some who might shrug their shoulders and say *caveat emptor*: let the purchaser beware (that is, he buys at his own risk). In the same way, judges sitting on cases of borrower restitution have held that existing laws must not be used to provide compensation to investors because of their own negligence or bad decisions. At the same time, however, it has been recognized that banks due to their position of power have a duty of care to protect vulnerable borrowers and investors, such as retirees and the less financially savvy, and not simply to pursue the biggest commission or bonus. Yet, even this last position does not go far enough for the Holy religions, which insist on a strict moral code governing behaviour, drawing no distinction between financial and other activities.

By standing back and considering the financial crisis (and later events) it is apparent that the religious strictures were violated in the following ways:

- Financial planners and mortgage brokers played up the potential gains and misled their clients about the downside risks to contractual arrangements to which they were signing up. Such behaviour constitutes ill-suited advice and fails to meet the requirements of truth-telling and access to full information.
- *Caveat emptor* does not apply in religious codes. Responsibility for discovering the risks cannot be shifted onto the borrowers. In the case of Jewish law (and by inference Christianity), such a transfer would violate the prohibition against oppressing someone and causing needless mental anguish (Lev. 25:17).
- Lenders made loans based on borrowers' stated income (often inflated by the borrower, the broker or the loan salesman) without requiring verification in the form of tax returns, payslips or audited records. Such a contact is illegal under Jewish law because of the 'good faith' imperative. It also violates the requirements of Jewish and Islamic law insisting on the need for witnesses.
- Brokers and lending institutions lending against property or using property as collateral overstated property values, and also pressured valuers and appraisers to boost the value of mortgage collateral. This practice, hardly truth-telling, would seem to be inimical to the interests of borrower and lender alike, but these checks and balances were blunted by the quest for commission and fees, and because risks could be passed down the securitization chain.
- In turn, however, the securitizers failed in the duty to disclose to investors the potential 'hidden flaws' in the mortgage-backed securities (MBSs) and collateralized debt obligations (CDOs). Synthetic

CDOs took this process one step further by having the investor rely on the credit default swap (CDS) to generate income flows.

- A needed step in the securitization chain comes from the role of the credit rating agencies, who in giving an AAA rating to 80 per cent of the tranches of the securities did not reveal the hidden assumptions and flaws in MBS and CDOs, and might be considered to have breached the Biblical injunction, 'And Thou shall take no gift; for the gift blindeth the wise and perverteth the words of the righteous' (Ex. 23:8).

It follows that if the theologically based strictures – that is, those requiring truth-telling, eliminating *gharar* and requiring full and clear information, preventing ill-suited advice and exercising good faith imperatives – had been followed, the subprime and 'low-doc' and 'no-doc' loan markets might never have developed and grown to a size such that their collapse would imperil the global economy.

Yet, it was not only breaches of the religious rules regarding misleading contracts at fault. There were other ways in which adherence to the religious laws could have averted the crisis, namely with respect to speculation, governance, debt and leverage, financialization and, of course, greed.

SPECULATION

Speculation may violate Jewish law's *hin tsedek* 'good faith' imperative since speculative intentions and activity are masquerading as a conventional commercial transaction. Pope Benedict XVI (2009) addressed the issue of speculation in unequivocal terms in *Caritas in Veritate*. He spoke of 'the damaging effects on the real economy of badly managed and largely speculative financial dealing' (para. 21), 'the speculative use of financial resources' (para. 40), and the need for regulation of the financial sector to 'discourage scandalous speculation' (para. 65). Here the Islamic position is equally forthright. Speculative transactions and all forms of gambling are prohibited in Islam because they destroy the moral, economic and social fabric of socio-economic life. Gains are made by one person at the expense of another, encouraging a concentration of wealth in the hands of a few and socio-economic inequalities.

Amongst conventional banks, the reality was very different from that envisaged in the Islamic prohibition (and some Islamic bankers themselves got caught up in unwise real estate development loans in Dubai and other locations). The 'old' model was that commercial banks took little or no risk other than credit risk, and it has to be said that even credit risk got them into more than enough trouble, as the Third World debt crisis of the 1980s and the commercial property crash of the early 1990s revealed (Lewis and Davis, 1987; Lewis, 1994). Over time, however, commercial banks evolved to be significant risk-takers and moved into market risk and investment risk, expanding their trading activities in derivatives and other financial products. Underpinning the reliance on risky trading was a compensation system whereby executives and traders helped themselves to profits when the market was booming, and shareholders bore the bulk of the losses during the bust. One of those executives, Citigroup Chief Executive Officer (CEO) Vikram Pandit, has declared that he now accepts (in principle) the so-called Volker rule, which aimed to get United States banks to return to the basics of lending to the real economy, rather than indulging in the kind of proprietary trading that contributed to the crisis and left a legacy of many current woes. He said: 'bank capital should be reserved for use for our clients and it shouldn't be there for us to put to use ourselves' (Gluyas, 2012).

Investment banking also changed. The traditional model was one in which risks were limited to short-term underwriting risks at the time of the securities float, and the main income came from fees for organizing the flotation, handling the share trades and engaging in mergers and acquisitions. In the new model, investment banks too became risk-takers on a grand scale. From 2000 to 2006, trading income rose from 41 per cent to 54 per cent of revenues for the Big Five, with proprietary trading in stocks and bonds, currencies, oil futures, junk bonds and other speculative vehicles accounting for most of the increase in revenue (Tully, 2008). Underpinning the reliance on risky trading again was a bonus system, which meant that employees of the Big Five took home 60 per cent of the firms' revenue in 2007. Later losses sheeted home to shareholders outweighed these profits, dubbed 'the banking bonus racket' (*The Economist*, 2009, p. 3).

GOVERNANCE

Governance issues arise at every turn in contemporary banking systems, and the religions have a lot to say on this topic, but with different emphases. According to Van Biema (2008), medieval Jewish jurists such as Maimonides identified a specific kind of bad advice: the hidden flaw. 'If you sell an animal, you had to disclose to the buyer what the hidden flaw is.' Not only that: 'the disclosure has to be made so that a reasonable, or average man can decide whether to buy'. This led to a demand for full fiscal disclosure, a good starting point for governance issues. *Caritas in Veritate* emphasizes that the economy needs a moral character (para. 34), and requires ethics for it to function correctly (Benedict XVI, 2009, para. 23). The encyclical also calls for 'a moral foundation for free markets', 'greater corporate moral codes of conduct' and 'financiers whose consciences are attuned to the requirements of the common good' (para. 71). Islam also looks for a moral regeneration and greater inner fortitude on the part of market participants to enhance governance. In addition, Islamic financial institutions have external governance mechanisms imposed in the form of the discipline provided by Islamic religious auditing, backed by higher authority in accountability to God and the community (Iqbal and Lewis, 2009).

During the financial crisis the failure of governance systems is evidenced most clearly by the way in which 'the banking system was metamorphosing into an off-balance sheet and derivatives world – the shadow banking system' (Gorton, 2009, p. 41). In this system:

> 'Regulatory arbitrage' evolved into a business model. Required risk capital was reduced by creating the 'shadow' banking system – a complex network of off balance sheet vehicle and hedge funds. Risk was transferred into the 'unregulated' shadow banking system. The strategies exploited bank capital rules. Some or all of the real risk remained indirectly with the originating bank. (Das, 2008)

Certainly this was the experience of banks such as Citigroup, UBS and Goldman Sachs, which ran into difficulties with the specific-purpose geared investment vehicles (conduits, structured investment vehicles – SIVs) established off balance sheet. As runs on them began, the SIVs were absorbed back onto the balance sheets of the sponsors. Not only did this off-balance-sheet activity seemingly escape the regulators' attention, but banks' boards also went missing and failed in their governance duty to look after shareholders' interests, as revealed when the losses came out of the shadows and appeared on the banks' balance sheets. Good governance in this context would mean:

> No more 'structured investment vehicles' that hold zero capital and fund their long-term lending by borrowing short-term funds. No more banks pretending they are not backstopping these entities and thus do not have to maintain a capital cushion against that lending – and then taking the failed loans on to their books anyway. (Wessel, 2008)

The scale of the problem that hung over the banks is indicated by the observation of Mervyn King (2010), Governor of the Bank of England, that the shadow banking system in the United States (US) 'grew in gross terms to be larger than the traditional banking sector' (p. 4). This system helped to spawn the exotic and risky securitized products that triggered the financial meltdown in the United States and Europe (Kodres and Narain, 2012). Although the shadow system has gone, the profit-driven greed has not.

GREED

All three religions strongly disapprove of greed. In Judaism, Meir Tamari (1987), described by Wilson (1997, p. 25) as 'the most lucid Jewish writer on the implications of Judaism for economic activity', argues that the Hebrew concept of modesty, *tzniyut*, goes beyond not wearing revealing clothing and refers also to moderation in the consumption of food and the acquisition of personal belongings. Ostentatious and luxurious living are regarded as undesirable ends, not just because of the social jealousy that may result, but because such lifestyles are considered to be inappropriate for devout Jews. While avarice, ambition and greed are recognized as forces for advancing society, they are phenomena that need to be harnessed for the good of the individual and society (Ohrenstein, 1970). Wealth and possessions can encourage people to neglect worship and forget their debt to God. For example, the Mishanic laws of agriculture rule that a farmer's time might be better used spent in worship or studying the Torah rather than reaping the last grain of the harvest. In particular, overharvesting is to be avoided, especially if this is a consequence of material greed (Wilson, 1997, p. 31).

In Christianity, Pope Benedict XVI has spoken of greed and selfish behaviour in the context of the global financial crisis on a number of occasions. In a general audience before 35 000 people in St Peter's Square in April 2009, the Pope said: 'greed, which views possession and appearance as the most important things in the world, is the real root of the current global economic crisis', and again pointed to a 'vice' of the human heart as the profound cause of the economic situation. He also cited with approval the views of Ambrose Autpertus, an eighth-century monk and later abbot, who spoke of greed as the sole root of all vices, echoing the message in St Paul's first letter to Timothy: 'the love of money is the root of all evil' (1 Timothy 6:10).[1] The Pope expressed such views repeatedly, for example in Luanda, during his trip to Africa in March 2009, when he spoke of 'the greed that corrupts the heart of man', or at the beginning of April 2009 when in a message to the G-20 summit he wrote that in the origin of the crisis there is also a 'failure of correct ethical behaviour' (Asia News, 2009).

Earlier, on 26 February 2009, in a preview of his encyclical *Caritas in Veritate*, the Pope highlighted 'the shortcomings of a system founded on selfishness and the idolatry of money' (Moynihan, 2009). In the encyclical itself, published in July 2009, the Pope noted that 'every economic decision has a moral consequence' (Benedict XVI, 2009, para. 37) and that 'honesty and responsibility cannot be ignored or attenuated' (para. 36). Continuing:

> Economy and finance, as instruments, can be used badly when those at the helm are motivated by purely selfish ends. Instruments that are good in themselves can thereby be transformed into harmful ones. But it is man's darkened reason that produces these consequences, not the instrument *per se*. Therefore, it is not the instrument that must be called to account, but individuals, their moral conscience and their personal and social responsibility. (para. 36)

In Islam, the quest for material possessions may produce earthly rewards, but these are not what really matter:

> If any do wish for the transitory things (of this life), We readily grant them – such things as We will, to such person as We will: in the end have We provided Hell for them: they will burn therein, disgraced and rejected. Those who do wish for the (things of) the Hereafter, and strive therefore with all due striving, and have Faith, – they are the ones whose striving is acceptable (to God). (*Al Isra*, S17:18–19)

Acts undertaken by a person to take unfair advantage of another are strictly banned. Instead, economic activities must be based on moral and legitimate foundations. Individuals are expected to feel socially responsible for others in the community, allowing the protection of the essential dignity that God conferred on all humanity.

GREED IN ACTION

Some blame China for the financial crisis of 2008 by flooding US financial markets with liquidity and driving down long-term interest rates. Others blame the Greenspan Federal Reserve Bank (the Fed) for creating the dollars that China pushed back to the United States.[2] What is not in question is that the crisis played out initially in the US mortgage market in terms of what the Harvard historian Niall Ferguson (2009) called the 'subprime surprise'.

Salient features of the events that led to this 'surprise' are well known and need not be repeated here in great detail. It will suffice to say that there were many banks willing to oblige homeowners' desire to borrow for consumption purposes against the rising value of their houses ('mortgage equity withdrawal'), and they assisted others to become first-time home-buyers by making loans that in nearly half of the cases were up to and exceeding 100 per cent of valuation, and lent to those with little chance of repayment once the initial 'teaser' rates adjusted to the much higher contracted levels, so giving birth to the 'NINJA' borrower (no income, no job and assets). By 2006, nearly 50 per cent of new US home loans were ones that did not qualify for insurance by the mortgage insurers, Fannie Mae or Freddie Mac ('subprime' loans) or loans that were higher quality than subprime but did not qualify for insurance because of little ('low-doc') or no ('no-doc') documentation (the Alt-A mortgages). Collateralized debt obligations (CDOs) then packaged these individual loans into securities so complex that they misled credit rating agencies, investors and the banks themselves.

Greed can be seen up and down this mortgage chain, beginning with the Wall Street (and other international) bankers buying mortgage loans aggressively, often with little scrutiny, in search of fees from underwriting, bundling and distributing MBSs, many repackaged to create triple-A-rated securities. In the decade to mid-2007, 37 000 structured finance issues in the United States were awarded this grade by the credit rating agencies. In 2006, Moody's reported that 44 per cent of its revenues came from rating structured finance products (Coval et al., 2009). Often the CDOs did not contain actual mortgage securities, but derivatives such as CDSs linked to mortgages. Investment banks liked these synthetic CDOs comprising CDSs because they avoided having to purchase the underlying securities, while enabling the banks to create a large number of CDOs related to the same mortgage-backed bonds.

Greed led to a market for the CDOs among hedge funds and other professional investors, while on the other side of the ledger banks originated loans to less creditworthy customers. Greed extended down the chain to mortgage brokers who signed up perhaps 80 per cent of the mortgages and, as incentive, often received higher commissions for originating mortgages that promised the higher returns (that is, subprime and Alt-A mortgages).

Finally, greed went all the way back to the homebuyers. They were attracted by the low-doc or no-doc loans (so-called 'liar loans') by the low teaser rates on offer and, in some cases, by the 'put option' that no-recourse loan provisions provided in many US states. In this case, borrowers could bet on the continued increase in home prices, safe in the knowledge that they could return the keys to the bank at no cost to themselves if housing prices fell.

MISLEADING CONTRACTS

In all three religions, commercial contracts are regarded as both legal promises and moral commitments. Honesty and fair dealing are virtues in business as in all walks of life, and the Jewish, Christian or Muslim business person should therefore be a person of high moral values who would not set out to deceive or exploit others. Failure to live up to the standards is a violation of ethical principles and a matter for severe approbation.

Consequently, Judaism, Christianity and Islam have strong edicts on the subject of misleading information conveyed in contracts and in business dealings generally. In Judaism, giving ill-suited advice (*lifnei ivver*) and misleading someone by creating a false impression (*geneivat da'at*) are violations of Jewish business ethics. According to Van Biema (2008), this ethical stance flows out of Leviticus 19:14, which reads: 'Thou shalt not curse the deaf, nor put a stumbling-block before the blind.' From an early date, rabbis expanded this into a general prohibition on bad advice. In time, it became part of the language specifically regarding loans, mostly regarding the need for witnesses, but now applies to the whole loan process. Regrettably, there are a lot of financially 'blind' people in the markets, and 'a lot of people badly advised them' (Van Biema, 2008, p. 1). In his encyclical *Caritas in Veritate*, Benedict XVI (2009) saw the need for 'truth-telling', and argued that without mutual trust the market cannot completely fulfil its proper economic function. He went on to add that 'today it is this trust which has ceased to exist, and the loss of trust is a grave loss' (para. 35). For Muslims, *gharar* is strictly forbidden. By failing or neglecting to define any of the essential pillars of a contract relating to the consideration or measure of the object, the parties undertake a risk that is not indispensable to them, and is deemed unacceptable.

Before considering how these strictures and ethical principles were violated in practice, it is worth noting some relevant features of the US mortgage market during the mid-2000s. Option adjustable rate mortgages (ARMs) became a staple of the subprime lending saga and were described in *Business Week* as perhaps 'the riskiest and most complicated home loan product ever created' (Der Hovanesian, 2006, p. 71). Created in 1981 for well-off homebuyers who wanted flexibility in repayment, the product was transformed from a financial planning tool for the wealthy into an affordability tool for aspiring homeowners. 'With its temptingly low minimum payments, the option ARM brought a whole new group of buyers into the housing market, extending the boom longer than it could have otherwise lasted' (ibid.).

An option ARM generally comes with a number of payment choices, ranging from full amortization to interest-only and other low payment options. There is usually a minimum payment which does not cover the interest charges. In the meantime, the interest rate adjusts every month (say from an initial rate of 7.38 per cent p. a. rising to 7.95 per cent p. a. during the first year). When borrowers make the minimum payment, the shortfall is added on to the balance, a situation known as negative amortization. Once the balance increases by 10 or 15 per cent, the loan resets and the new balance is then amortized over the remaining life of the (generally 30-year) loan. At that point, making a minimum payment is no longer an option. The problem was that 80 per cent of option ARM borrowers made only the minimum payment, and once housing prices started to fall, borrowers could no longer rely on rising home equity to act as a buffer. Anecdotal evidence suggests that many (but not all) did not understand that the low payments were only temporary and that the less a borrower pays initially, the more is added to the balance of the mortgage (Der Hovanesian, 2006).

In these circumstances, most option ARM borrowers were not in fact paying down their loans; they were underpaying them. Interestingly, however, under generally accepted accounting principles (GAAP), the lending banks that kept option ARMs on their books (rather than securitizing them) could by virtue of accrual accounting count as revenue the highest amount of an option ARM payment, that is, the fully amortized amount, even when borrowers made the minimum payment. Through such deferred interest, banks can bring forward future revenue and create what has become known as 'phantom profits', since the interest may never be paid. While defending the accrual accounting standard, the Financial Accounting Standards Board ventured the opinion that it is 'concerned that the disclosures associated with these types of loans [are] not providing enough transparency relative to their associated risks'. More telling still, from a religious standpoint, is the observation in *Grant's Interest Rate Observer* that negative-amortization accounting is 'frankly a fraudulent gambit. But what it lacks in morality, it compensates for in ingenuity' (Der Hovanesian, 2006, p. 74).

Viewed from the perspective of Judaism, Christianity and Islam there were breaches of ethical principles and lapses in morality in every step of the mortgage chain. There were borrowers who overlooked the importance of truth-telling and provided misleading information about their credit position, and who broke the 'good faith' imperative by taking on mortgage debt that they well knew they could not repay. Mortgage brokers, for their part, went along with the deception and, at the same time, misled borrowers about the contractual obligations to which they had signed up. They were guilty, under Judaism, for example, of offering ill-suited advice and creating a false impression. Worse, they did not care (McDonald and Robinson, 2009).[3] Banks did not verify the information about borrowers' income and assets with which they were supplied. Brokers and lending banks also pressured real estate appraisers to inflate the value of the property so that larger loans could be made while reporting healthy loan-to-valuation ratios. Banks hid behind GAAP and did not report the true earnings and income flows from mortgage lending. Investment banks failed to disclose the hidden assumptions and flaws in CDOs, while credit ratings agencies did not explain how they could give an AAA rating to 80 per cent of the tranches of mortgage-backed securities. Finally, investors did not heed the advice of Pope Benedict XVI and act in a responsible way (Benedict XVI, 2009, para. 65).

DEBT AND LEVERAGE

The Abrahamic religions have well-known views on usury and prohibit the generation of profit from the process of lending, although profit from deferred payment or advance payment sales is allowed. Profits on these debt-based instruments are legitimized because all the relevant parties share the risks related to real goods (Wilson, 1997; Lewis, 2007). The religions are thus opposed to interest-based debt and the leverage that comes from its use.

In prohibiting usury, the religions seek to establish a society based upon fairness and justice. A loan provides the lender with a fixed return irrespective of the outcome of the borrower's venture. It is much fairer to have a sharing of the profits and losses, free of the potential for exploitation and injustice, where the reward is governed by the return on the individual project which is being funded. Historically, the primary test for usury has been whether the lender can collect interest regardless of the debtor's fortune (Jones, 1989).

Although the religions saw usury as an unnatural activity, harmful to debtor and creditor alike, and to society at large, their concern for the overall structure of the economy gains credence from a literature owing to Sir Ralph Hawtrey (1932, 1950), Irving Fisher (1933) and Bernanke and Gertler (1986) that emphasizes the potential for debt and leverage to magnify small economic shocks into larger investment and output fluctuations. Irving Fisher's debt-deflation hypothesis seems particularly apt. He argued that the severity of the Great Depression of the 1930s resulted from poorly performing financial markets. What made the economy initially so vulnerable, in Fisher's view, was the high leverage of borrowers in the wake of the prosperity preceding 1929. In his words, 'they [debts] were great enough to not only "rock the boat" but to start it capsizing'. The downward economic shock was magnified by a 'debt deflation' transmission mechanism involving, *inter alia*, debt reduction, falling asset prices and reduced net worth, higher interest rate premiums, falling confidence, lower profitability and output, contracting money and credit, and reduced velocity of money (in effect, increased money demand). The fact that the massive deterioration in borrower balance sheets occurred simultaneously with that of output and prices lent credibility in his eyes to the debt deflation view.

This analysis resonates in terms of the 2008 crisis. High leverage among borrowers and banks alike was a striking feature of the housing market and investment banks in the United States. Among US households, low household saving and high investment in housing meant that the 'net acquisition of liabilities' by households rose to 13.4 per cent of disposable income in 2005, double the post-war average (Iley and Lewis, 2013). The old Big Five investment banks' leverage, measured by assets as a multiple of equity, jumped from 30:1 in 2002 to 41:1 in 2007, with the banks relying on a constant stream of short-term debt funding to finance their portfolios. A study by Brennan et al. (2010) examined the financial leverage of 15 large US, United Kingdom (UK) and European banks in 2007. As shown in Table 6.1, with one exception (JP Morgan Chase), the leverage ratios exceeded 20, and in two cases (UBS, Deutsche) they actually exceeded 50. These are remarkable numbers. The problem of high leverage is that the

Table 6.1   Financial leverage and write-downs of selected LCFIs*

	Leverage		Write-downs	
	2007	Change 2007/04 %	End-Q1 2010 (US$ bn)	As % of common equity
Citi	24.5	22.9	58.0	51.1
Bank of America	20.6	19.1	20.6	14.5
JPM	17.6	4.4	13.6	11.0
Barclays	37.8	36.4	22.9	56.6
RBS	31.2	22.1	26.5	32.6
HSBC	21.3	11.8	9.4	7.3
UBS	58.1	16.6	50.8	163.9
Deutsche Bank	52.1	15.7	15.6	28.7
SocGen	43.2	49.9	7.8	20.3
BNP Paribas	39.7	18.2	4.6	5.9
Credit Suisse	39.2	−11.6	13.8	35.6
Merrill Lynch	35.3	–	58.6	212.6
Morgan Stanley	27.8	–	20.7	68.6
Lehman Brothers	27.6	–	16.3	76.2
Goldman Sachs	25.0	–	10.3	25.8

Note: * LCFIs are large complex financial institutions.

Source: Brennan et al. (2010).

banks are considerably exposed, with even small movements in asset values sufficient to wipe out their equity and leave them insolvent. For example, if a bank's portfolio is leveraged at 33:1, it takes only a drop of 3 per cent in the value of the portfolio to wipe out the bank's entire capital; hence the scale of the bank bailouts needed in the US, UK and Europe. These highly leveraged positions created fragility in 2008 and bedevilled recovery as banks needed to rebuild their balance sheets. Hence the 'balance sheet recession' that has been the result (Claessens, 2012).

FINANCIALIZATION

Growth of finance in the West has been described as 'financialization', in which the structure of advanced economies has shifted towards the provision of financial services and where the value of financial assets greatly exceeds that of tangible assets (in some European countries, many multiples of gross domestic product). As a result, there is a decoupling of financial activity from productive tangible asset investment, and as part of this change, managerial culture and behaviour, corporate governance, executive remuneration and the distribution of income and wealth are all substantially modified by the demands of financial capital (Martin, 2002; Stockhammer, 2004; Froud et al., 2006; Foster, 2007). These developments have not only been a source of considerable instability, but one study (Cecchetti and Kharroubi, 2012) also found that it has lowered productivity growth, as resources are diverted from more productive uses.

Judaism and Christianity have relaxed their long-standing antagonism to usury either by redefining usury as exorbitant interest (Christianity) or by the legal fiction of partnership agreements to circumvent the prohibition on interest for inter-Jewish loan transactions (Judaism). Islam still maintains its stand against usury. However, debt has proven to be as indispensible to Islamic banking as it has to conventional finance.

On a strict interpretation there is no scope for interest or discount-based financing instruments in Islam. Interest – that is, any stipulated excess (increase) on the principal amount in money lending – is prohibited. The ideal replacement for interest-based loans is interest-free loans (*qard hasan*) for a charitable cause, and profit and loss sharing (PLS) arrangements for commercial purposes. Given the teething difficulties of operating PLS contracts in developing economies, however, jurists adapted some contracts for finance that in the classical interpretation were meant for engagement in the real business of buying and selling of goods. Broadly speaking, the prevailing instruments of interest-free finance along these lines relevant for financing can be divided into three categories: the different buying and selling mark-up type arrangements adapted for credit financing through the process of *ijtihad* in the last three decades such as *murabaha*, *bai'muajjal*, *istisnaa*; leasing (rental) operations (*ijara*); and, most recently, Islamic bonds (*sukuk*) and the controversial *tawarruq*. Details of these will be given in later chapters.

For the present we note that these financing instruments, which often bear rates of return explicitly referenced to LIBOR and other market interest rates in the conventional system, seem to many observers to be like interest lending in another guise. But there are two important differences from conventional finance (Chapra, 2007). First, because the seller of goods (the financier) must legally own and possess the goods being sold, Chapra argues that speculative short selling is ruled out, helping to curb the type of excessive speculation that takes place and has been so evident recently in conventional financial markets. Second, the sales-based financing methods do not involve direct lending and borrowing but comprise purchase or lease transactions based on real goods and services. Financing in the Islamic system thus tends to expand *pari passu* with the growth of the real economy, constraining excessive debt and credit creation and limiting one of the causes of instability in the international markets. Stated alternatively, unlike many financial systems in the West, Islamic financial markets are not as yet marked by a decoupling of financial activity from tangible asset investment.

The importance of giving attention to the real economy has been stressed by Pope Benedict XVI. In his annual peace message in 2008 he emphasized that 'the most important function of finance is to sustain long-term investment and development' (MailOnline, 2008). In *Caritas in Veritate*, the Pope recalled the example of John Paul II, who taught that investment always has moral, as well as economic significance:

> What should be avoided is a speculative *use of financial resources* that yields to the temptation of seeking only short-term profit, without regard for the long-term sustainability of the enterprise, its benefit to the real economy and attention to the advancement, in suitable and appropriate ways, of further economic initiatives in countries in need of development. (Benedict XVI, 2009, para. 40)

POST-CRISIS POLICY

The precepts of the Holy religions on financing are in the way of preventative medicine. The body politic has been made to suffer because of greed (on the part of homeowners, mortgage brokers, originating banks, investment banks and securitizers, hedge funds and other investors), unwarranted hazard and misleading information in financial contracts, excessive speculative trading, poor governance of banks and other institutions, too much leverage and debt, and an explosion of financial activity relative to real tangible investment. On the other hand, if greed can be tempered internally by self-restraint, if mortgage borrowers had fully been made aware of their contractual obligations, if speculation and risky trading is forbidden, if ethical and religious principles are written into bank supervision and governance, and accountability is to God and the community, if usury is banned and financing based on concrete assets, and if the financial sector does not grow much faster than real activity, then the conditions that arose might have been avoided and the crisis might not have happened.

Being preventative, rather than prescriptive, medicine carries the corollary that the religions may be able to offer few prescriptive insights as to how to get out of the morass and put economies on to a path of sustainable growth. As we noted in Chapter 1, former US Treasury Secretary Larry Summers (2016) has spoken of the present as 'The Age of Secular Stagnation', while Christine Lagarde (2016) warned of the risk of economies trapped in a 'new mediocre of growth'. So far, central banks have adopted more of the same, lowering policy interest rates to zero or near zero in two dozen countries in order to encourage increased bank lending by lowering borrowing costs. These policy settings have been supplemented by quantitative easing (QE), expanding central bank (base) money via large-scale asset purchases, in order to drive down longer-term rates even more (Lewis, 2011b, 2014b). It does seem paradoxical to rely on past excesses of borrowing (and lending) being cured by engaging in yet another round of borrowing that can be maintained only at unsustainably low interest rates.

In fact, it is far from clear that increased borrowing will occur in current circumstances, for a number of reasons. First, an ultra-low interest rate policy relies on there being borrowers who want to take up the loans. Many households are saddled with excess debt and are in the slow process of shedding debt (deleveraging), rebuilding their net worth and restructuring their loans (Claessens, 2012). Second, many prospective homebuyers cannot obtain mortgages due to tight lending standards, impaired creditworthiness or because their current mortgages are in negative equity. Third, even at very low loan rates, borrowers must have confidence in the future. Personal borrowers and small businesses need to be confident about house prices and overall demand. Firms are unlikely to borrow for investment or restocking if they are not sure of future cash flows. If the future is so rosy, why are interest rates so low?

If, due to a combination of such factors, there is no (or little) response of bank credit, the base money pumped in presumably ends up in a build-up of cash reserves at the central banks (either desired or excess) earning interest for the banks, or in banks purchasing more government bonds, so giving the federal government cheap financing. There are questions that could be asked of a policy that so obviously helps banks and the government.

In particular, there are aspects of the policy with which the Holy religions would be concerned. A clear consequence of the ultra-low interest rates is that it has been 'hell on savers' using bank deposits for investment in or toward retirement, who must cut down on consumption and 'save now rather than starve later'. Of course, to the extent that the low rates pump up the stock market, shareholders gain at the expense of the less wealthy saving via bank accounts, but at the cost of having a more risky investment profile.

In evaluating the effectiveness of ultra-low interest rates and QE there are many considerations that need to be taken into account, given the divergent interests of savers, borrowers and superannuants; the variety of pension schemes in operation (annuities, defined contribution, defined benefit); and the redistribution of income from those with perhaps a high marginal propensity to consume to those with a lower propensity when wealth is transferred to the wealthiest by the young and the poor.

From the viewpoint of the Holy religions, however, the issues are in much clearer focus. All three religions place great emphasis on justice and fairness in economic affairs, and encourage partnership arrangements in which there is profit and loss sharing, with the interests of users and suppliers of funds balanced. A policy in which the balance is tilted so far in favour of borrowers to the potential detriment of savers, and actual and would-be pensioners, cannot be endorsed.

CONCLUDING REMARKS

This chapter links social values and business ethics defined in previous chapters with the global financial crisis of 2008, post-crisis policy responses and (regrettably) continuing financial misbehaviour by the banks and other financial institutions. Ethics consist of general principles which help to determine rules of conduct. Rules can be based on natural law, they can stem from the law of the land, or they can also derive from religious laws, such as those which shape the business ethics for Jews, Christians and Muslims. Religious rules have been the focus here, and answers have been sought to the following questions. What would Judaism, Christianity and Islam say about the financial behaviour exhibited in the lead up to the financial crisis, and subsequently in policy responses? Might the crisis have been avoided if religious precepts had been followed?

Considered in this light, while the crisis was not entirely about ethics, it most certainly had a large ethical component, and should be seen to have had its true origins in greed, misleading contracts, speculation, a lack of leadership and governance, usurious behaviour and a financial sector divorced from real activity. These moral failings have been exacerbated by monetary policy responses in the wake of the crisis that arguably do not meet the fairness test that the religions demand.

The religious traditions require one to ask: 'how can I make money and simultaneously be a responsible member of the society in which I live, protecting the interests of both buyer and seller [or borrower and lender]' (Van Biema, 2008). All three religions – Judaism, Christianity and Islam – deem that in order to prevent a repetition of the global crisis and rid the banking system of financial misconduct, a new 'moral compass' is needed to guide business and financial behaviour.

On the face of it, there would seem to be some encouraging developments in this direction. In the UK *Today* programme lecture in 2011, the CEO of a major British bank spoke of the importance of trust and integrity and said: 'corporate culture is difficult to define and even more so to mandate, but for me the evidence [of it] is how people behave when no one is watching'. This is certainly true. Unfortunately, however, the CEO concerned was none other than the now disgraced Bob Diamond of Barclays Bank, whom the Governor of the Bank of England in July 2012 demanded be dismissed for having manipulated the interbank interest rate, LIBOR, to Barclays' advantage, when no one seemingly was watching. There is certainly a moral here.

Finally, two observations are made in conclusion. First, the precepts of Judaism, Christianity and Islam set out in this chapter are striking both in terms of their similarity and in how much they conflict with actual behaviour. However, they are in the way of preventive medicine designed to alter behaviour in a way that might prevent a crisis and financial malpractice from happening. Second, being preventive, rather than prescriptive, medicine carries the implication that the religions offer few prescriptive insights as to how to get out of the mess. Yet, there is one matter on which they might agree. The religions look for the interests of users and suppliers of funds being balanced, whereas in the aftermath of the crisis, policy interest rates were lowered to near zero in major developed countries. A leading critic of this policy is Thomas Hoenig, President of the Federal Reserve Bank of Kansas City (cited in Barrett and Lanman, 2010, p. 78):

Wall Street banks and large corporations are currently able to borrow for almost nothing and either hoard cash, make acquisitions, or invest in long-term Treasuries for a guaranteed profit. Retirees and other bank depositors effectively subsidize this borrowing and earn almost nothing on their savings. It's a distortion, and it favours the large institutions over smaller ones and Wall Street over the saver. I just don't like it. It's not fair.

Chapters 7 and 8 focus on different types of equity-based and sales-based debt financial instruments and examine their relevance with the teachings of Judaism, Christianity and Islam. This is especially important in the case of religious and ethically minded people who sometimes stay away from interest-based banking due to their personal beliefs. Coming chapters are an effort to initiate a unified holistic approach or develop general principles to provide financial solutions (including possible usage of benevolent loans as alternative financial instruments) that are acceptable and understandable for the followers of all Holy religions and those who advocate a society based upon a fairer and equitable distribution of wealth and more support to the poor and needy. Chapter 9 focuses on and considers the future of Islamic finance, since Islam maintains that it is the only religion upholding the age-old prohibition on interest. A brief conclusion then follows in Chapter 10.

NOTES

1. This verse is often misquoted as 'Money is the root of all evil', thanks no doubt to the pop song of that title popularized by the Andrews Sisters in the 1940s.
2. For analyses of these two alternative views (which, however, can be combined), see Lewis (2009) and Iley and Lewis (2011a, 2011b).
3. McDonald and Robinson (2009) talked in 2006 to some 'bodybuilders' (salesmen) working for New Century Financial in California, all earning between $300 000 and $600 000 on commissions selling mortgages.

> Possibility of defaults? *Not our concern, pal. Our job is to sell the mortgage policy. Period. Right after that it's someone else's problem.*
> Proof of income or assets? *Hell, no. They just need to state their income. No docs. That's why we work here.*
> No-doc borrowers taking the money and not making payments? *I just told you, it's not our problem. We're salesmen. New Century makes it easy for us.*
> Attraction of New Century stock? *Look man, right here we got a great company and we're killing them out there in the market. Let's just fly with it. Three of our top guys have made $74 million over four years, with cash and stock. That's a goal for all of us. And New Century's gonna make that possible. Universal home ownership, right? That's our target. New Century for the new century. You gotta love it.* (p. 185)

As noted in Chapter 1 (note 1), New Century Financial filed for bankruptcy on 2 April, 2007.

7.   Partnership-based equity instruments

INTRODUCTION

Having examined the objections of the Abrahamic religions to interest-based traditional banking and having demonstrated how far many contemporary financial practices in modern-day banking differ from the social and economic norms that the religions embody, it is now time to turn our attention to modes for commercial financing that appear, at least on the surface, to be in accord with the religions' ethical financing standards. These are partnership equity-sharing arrangements and debt instruments that are sales or commodity-based.

Considering in this chapter the first of these, the concept of partnership is different from pure lending, where the lender gets a guaranteed return regardless of economic outcomes of the venture financed. A partnership allows the transferring of funds from financier to an entrepreneur while ensuring participation of both the parties, if not necessarily in the management, then in the process of risk-sharing. In addition, it develops a spirit of cooperation, group decision-making and the idea of brotherhood (Paris, 1998, p. 97).

Broyde and Resnicoff (1997, p. 2) identify five features needed for the establishment of a partnership. First, all parties must intend to create a partnership and be in agreement with the terms of the contract. Second, the parties must engage in profit-seeking commercial activities. Third, each party must have proprietary interest in the partnership itself. Fourth, partners must participate in the profits of the business. Fifth, partners must be at risk if the business sustains losses.

Partnership-based contracts existed in the Middle East well before the emergence of even Judaism. The main contributions of religious teachings are to provide guidance based upon equal opportunity, justice and societal development. Partnerships require a high level of business ethics, trust and commercial expertise among all partners. Simple spiritual and religious association among partners cannot alone make the commercial ventures successful. A successful partnership relies upon regular monitoring and follow-up, especially if the business is spread over multiple geographical locations. Another aspect might be the hiring of the right type of professionals and employees, those who are dedicated, competent and hard-working. These conditions constitute a considerable challenge.

PARTNERSHIPS IN JUDAISM

Judaism was the first to define social and economic boundaries for its believers regarding partnership contracts. Partnerships are a well-explored area under rabbinical law. Two or more persons can create a valid partnership by actually mixing their products or jointly hiring a property. Each partner is bound to evaluate the market value of the investment or assets before bringing them into partnership, and then appraise their profit and loss accordingly. A mere promise to bring in money does not create a valid partnership. Similarly, if two proprietors decide to share their income only, again a valid partnership is not created. The rule applies that a person cannot transfer ownership of an article which is not in existence. A valid partnership can only be created, for example, if both jointly create a fund, then purchase raw material from that fund, prepare an article and sell in the market. Now they are partners, and whatever they earn as income from their work is divided equally between them. *Halacha* law allows partners mutually to decide the profit and loss sharing ratio. In the absence of any predefined agreement, partners must share their profit in equal proportion even if they invested their money in different proportions.

According to Dani Rapp (2010, p.438), Judaic law permits creating a partnership for a stipulated period of time. Each partner can prevent his colleague from dissolving the partnership before the agreed time period. Likewise, no partner is allowed to withdraw their investment or even profit before the termination date. In the absence of any agreement related to a stipulated time, any partner can dissolve the partnership. Assets under the partnership, if they are of a nature which cannot be divided or are fixed such as involving property or machinery, then such items should be sold in the market and the income distributed.

Our primary concern, however, is with non-interest financing arrangements. Another type of partnership occurs when one or more persons make an investment and another person controls the business. This type of partnership is called *iska* (an investment agreement or joint venture), comprising an active partner who manages the project and a silent partner who supplies financing for the project.

It is this combination of the active and inactive that constitutes the defining feature of an *iska*. The reason for this condition being the case is the presence of *avak ribbit*, that is, 'the dust of interest' (Levine, 2010a, p.663). In an ordinary partnership in which both partners are active, each is considered to be supplying equity to the venture and consequently the question of interest (*ribbit*) does not arise. By contrast, the situation where one partner supplies finance and the other supplies only human capital is a different matter and was regarded as problematical for the Talmud when viewed from the perspective of *avak ribbit* (Callen, 2010).

To overcome this problem, rabbinical scholars forged a solution, namely that the *iska* contract be considered half loan and half equity. The *Babylonian Talmud* (1935, p. 104b) characterizes the *iska* as a 'semi-loan and a semi-trust' (BM104b). In effect, one-half of the capital supplied by the silent partner is deemed to be a loan to the active partner, which the active partner then invests in the joint venture, and one-half is deemed to be the silent partner's equity in the joint venture. In the event of a profit (loss), each partner would end up with half of his capital investment plus (minus) half of the profits (losses), which apparently, according to the rabbis, gives each potential partner sufficient incentive to initiate an *iska* joint venture to the benefit of both the debtor and the creditor. Callen (2010, p. 96) gives an example:

> If the silent partner finances one hundred in the joint venture and there is a gain of forty, the silent partner gets back his fifty on loan and seventy on equity while the active partner ends up with twenty in total. In the event of a loss of forty, the silent partner again gets back his loan of fifty and thirty of his equity investment, so that each partner loses twenty. In the event of a loss of the entire capital of one hundred, the active partner pays back the loan of fifty to the silent partner, so that each loses fifty.

Nevertheless, as Callen goes on to note, the Talmud still saw a potential interest problem with the 50:50 allocation, since the active partner would be working for the silent partner's equity portion in addition to the work undertaken for his own capital input (that is, the loan). Since the only apparent reason that the active partner would be willing to work for the benefit of the silent partner is in recompense for the loan, this would fall under the prohibition of *avak ribbit*. Thus, the rabbis suggest as one potential solution that, in addition to the 50:50 profit or loss allocation, the active partner should be compensated for his time for each day that he works in the joint venture.

Essentially, the rights of the working partner (seen as the weaker partner) are further protected through regular wages apart from the share in profit (BM 5:4; BM 65a). That is, the Talmud's suggestion is for the active partner to be awarded with a contract involving a fixed salary plus an equal portion of any profits or losses.

Additionally to this contract, the Tosefta, a collection of teachings of Mishnaic-era authorities, proposes another solution to the potential interest impropriety of the *iska* arrangement. These are discussed in more detail by the Talmud in a case in which a deceased man was an active partner in an *iska* and the contract did not explicitly provide a fixed salary compensation beyond the 50:50 allocation. To quote the Talmud:

> The sons of R. 'Ilish were faced with a written *Iska* contract in which the allocation was 50 per cent of the gains and 50 per cent of the losses. Rava said: R'Ilish was a great man and he who would not have caused others to sin. Therefore, on the one hand, where the contract explicitly states that he receives half of the gain, it is understood (implicitly to mean) that he suffers only one third of the losses. On the other hand, if the contract explicitly states that he suffers half of the losses, it is understood (implicitly to mean) that he benefits two thirds of the gains. (*B. Rava Meta'a*, 686-69a, cited in Callen, 2010, p. 97)

Callen further observes that, interestingly, the Talmudic notion that the active partner should be compensated an additional third in the case of a loss in order to avoid *avak ribbit* finds expression in non-Jewish medieval *commenda* contracts. Pryor (1977) points out that the allocation in which profits were divided 50:50, but the silent partner bears two-thirds loss and the active partner one-third loss, is typical for bilateral sea *commenda* contracts at the ports of Genoa, Venice, Amalfi, Marseilles and Barcelona. Apparently, no rationale for the one-third is provided by either Jewish or non-Jewish sources, except for the Talmud story above.

To summarize, in order to obviate any element of indirect usury or unfair advantage, the rabbis declared that the agent must always have a larger share in the profits than in the liability (Udovitch, 1962). The Talmud mentions two possible combinations of liability and profit: (1) an equal division of profits between both parties, with the investor bearing the liability for two-thirds, and the agent for one-third of the principal; (2) an equal division of liability, with two-thirds of the profit for the agent, and one-third for the investor. In the post-Talmudic literature, Maimonides in his codification of Jewish law in the Mishnah Torah declares that almost any division of profits and liabilities is permissible, providing only that the agent's share of the profit is greater than his share of the liability. Yet the agent's liability still remains to an extent.

In earlier chapters we saw that a well-known biblical prohibition forbids Jews from lending to each other on interest. As stipulated in Exodus 22:24, 'If you lend to any of my people with you who is poor, you shall not be to him as a creditor, and you shall not exact interest from him.' The biblical words are simple and direct: it is unfair to take advantage of a poor person by charging him interest. Loans were an act of kindness on the part of the lender. Any gain by the lender was forbidden. But the Torah did not take into account loans of a commercial nature, and this particular biblical law against lending on interest refers to personal loans. The intention of the prohibition was to prevent the wealthy from exploiting the unfortunate. In the Talmud, however, this prohibition was applied to business transactions. In the course of time, it was seen to have consequences that militated against the economic welfare of Jewish society as a whole. As a result, Jewish law (*halacha*) has over the centuries relaxed the biblical injunction, allowing interest charges despite the biblical prohibition. This evolution in Jewish law due to economic forces is examined in detail by Gamoran (2008).

Describing the current state of affairs, Bleich (2010, p. 202), in his chapter in the *Oxford Handbook of Judaism and Economics*, concludes:

> The primary device recognized by Jewish law as an acceptable means of avoiding the prohibition against extending or receiving an interest-bearing loan is known as a *hetter iska*, or 'permissible venture'. Its function is to substitute some form of profit-sharing representing a return on invested funds for what would otherwise have been structured as an interest-bearing loan.

Callen, in his chapter in the same *Handbook*, writes: 'In modern times, the *hetter iska* has essentially neutralized the prohibition against *ribbit* even though that was not the original intent' (Callen, 2010, p. 95, n. 14). In fact, the earliest version of *hetter iska* was 'composed' by a sixteenth-century Polish scholar, R. Mendel Avigdors of Cracow. The *hetter iska* is a document that specifies the terms and conditions under which money is advanced by one individual to another. Its legal purpose is to create a partnership agreement as distinct from a debtor-creditor relationship (Bleich, 2010, p. 198).

As we noted earlier in Chapter 3, there appears to be a widespread practice within some Jewish business circles simply to use a standard promissory note and write the words '*al pi hetter iska*' (in accordance with *hetter iska*) with the intent to nullify explicit references in the instrument to a loan and interest by declaring the actual purpose to be a joint venture and shared profit (Bleich, 2010, p. 209). Present-day banks in Israel use *hetter iska* (partnership clause) to make interest-based loans among Jews perfectly legal and blameless and to avoid the biblical prohibition of *ribbit*. Jewish community members can create a credit agreement through a signed *hetter iska*. A sample of such a contract is set out in Box 7.1. *Hetter iska* is generally created for commercial loans, although according to Broyde and Resnicoff (1997) many Jewish authorities allow this arrangement for consumer financing as well.

BOX 7.1   SAMPLE *HETTER ISKA* CONTRACT

Preamble

Jewish Religious Law prohibits the paying or receiving of interest on loans made between Jews. However, when monies are advanced as part of a business venture arrangement, an agreement may be entered into, whereby the provider (investor, financier) and recipient of these funds are considered to be equal partners. This partnership is based upon the stipulation that, upon request, every loss must be attested to by two trustworthy witnesses, and all profits verified by oath. All consequent profits and losses are then equally shared on a 50 + 50 basis. However, in order to avoid these stringent requirements, the provider of the funds, under this *Hetter Iska* contract, agrees to waive his share of the profits in lieu of receiving a fixed percentage of the money advanced. This percentage is then considered profit, rather than interest on a loan. Such an agreement becomes effective when the recipient of the funds executes a form as set out below.

The Agreement

Under this Agreement made this _____ day of _____, I (we) the undersigned do hereby state that I (we) have received from _____ the sum of $_____ to be returned _____ which shall be used in the form of a joint business investment venture. I (we) obligate to utilize this sum in a manner which it is believed will generate profits. All of the profits that I (we) earn as a result of the said $_____ which is to be used in the business venture, shall be divided equally, i.e. 50 per cent shall go to the benefit of myself (ourselves) with the other 50 per cent going to the financier. The same shall apply to any losses incurred in the above business venture.

In the event that there is a loss, the only way that the matter may be proven will be through the sole basis of having testimony of two reliable and trustworthy witnesses under conditions acceptable to an Orthodox Jewish court of law. Any claim regarding the amount of profit generated by this business venture shall be verified under solemn oath, before an Orthodox Jewish court of law.

It is agreed, however, between all the parties that in lieu of _____'s share of profits, _____ herein shall accept my (our) payment of _____ per cent annually. Based on the acceptance of the said amount the financier shall have no claim against me (us) even if the actual profit is higher than the amount stated above. This agreement is in effect until the whole principal amount is returned.

In consideration for my (our) efforts, I (we) have received a token payment of $1.00, receipt of which is hereby acknowledged.

It is agreed that any dispute which may arise in connection with this agreement shall be submitted before _____. Judgment rendered by the aforesaid authority may be entered in any court having jurisdiction thereof. This agreement shall follow the guidelines of *hetter iska* as explicated in *Sefer Bris Yehudah* and has been made in a manner which effects a legal transfer and obligation, known as *kinyan sudar.**

It is further agreed that all conditions and terms contained in this contract shall supersede any and all contracts entered into between the same parties.

Signed this _____ day of _____ _____

_____Recipient(s)

Witness _____

I (we) agree to all the above-mentioned terms and conditions

_____Investor(s)

Witness _____

Note: * *Kinyan sudar* is a legal form of acquisition of objects or confirmation of agreements, executed by the handing of a scarf (or any other article) by one of the contracting parties (or one of the witnesses to the agreement) to the other contracting party as a symbol that the object has been transferred or the obligation assumed.

CHRISTIAN ATTITUDES

Finance in Western Europe, and later the Americas and elsewhere, was marked by the birth, first, of banking, then bond markets (especially for government finance) and stock markets, and most recently, derivatives. Christianity, as we have seen, at least nowadays, has strong opinions about some of the goings-on in these markets and institutions, but such objections did not stop the development over time of those financing avenues. Even at present, the Church can see that they have value in creating a more prosperous society able to afford to help those who are less well-off, but it wishes to realign the 'moral compass' of participants in them, while worrying about the inequalities of wealth that can result.

Of these developments, the growth of the stock markets, particularly when allied with the formation of the joint stock company, can be seen as watershed events, for they allowed the pooling of funds from many sources to fund large-scale, long-term, major investments. Moreover, the marketability and the liquidity thereby given to stocks enabled what William Baumol (1969 [1995]) called 'an act of magic'. In his words:

the market performs an act of magic, for it permits long-term investments to be financed by funds provided by individuals, many of whom wish to make them available for only a very limited period, or who wish to be able to withdraw them at will. Thus it imparts a measure of liquidity to long-term investments that permits their instruments to be sold at a price that yields a lower rate of return than would otherwise be required. (p. 3)

Despite the significance of the joint stock company in the development of the West, the creation of the partnership can be seen as a precursor, or 'ancestor' in the description of Charles Kindleberger (1984) in *A Financial History of Western Europe*. To quote:

> The earliest form of business organization above the sole proprietorship was the partnership. It could be a true partnership in which the partners each provided both capital and services, or one or more partners, but not all, could be silent. In the *commenda* (in Italian, in French the *commandite*, in German the *Kommanditgesellschaft*, in English the silent partnership), one partner, assuming only two, dominated the other. The partnership could be, in effect, a disguised loan in which labor hired the capital, or a disguised principal/agent relationship with capital hiring the labor. (p. 195)

As we saw in the Judaism section of this chapter above, the rabbinical scholars laboured on this very point, and rules in the *iska* came to a balancing between the position of the active and silent partners. However, to continue with the quotation from Kindleberger:

> On occasion, partnerships became complex, as in Scottish banks with over 300 'partners', who were actually shareholders using the old nomenclature, or in the Hanseatic practice, shared elsewhere, of merchants forming a large number of short-range and shifting partnerships to diversify interests in various ships and voyages as a form of real insurance in the absence of effective financial institutions.
>
> As the scale of transactions became larger and their nature more complex there developed in Britain the regulated company, a loose federation of merchants associated for limited purposes . . .
>
> Various other ancestors of the joint-stock company, and ultimately of the corporation, consisted in: the maone, a large partnership to finance petty conquests of one city-state by another during the Middle Ages; of associations that grew up to provide loans to city-states in return for special privileges, as in the Casa di San Giorgio in Genoa in 1408, the first bank in Europe; various municipal affairs that required charters from monarchs or local lords, paid for them and obtained bundles of rights which gave a city or borough a quasi-corporate character; the guild, with a wide variety of purposes of a socio-religious nature beyond trade and crafts, essentially a monopoly that excluded non-members. (Kindleberger, 1984, pp. 195–6)

In what follows we focus initially on the *commenda* and the attitude to it of the Catholic Church. Clearly, however, developments such as those listed by Kindleberger were pushing the partnership concept to the limits of the instrument, paving the way to further financial innovations.

Trading and business-related activities initially were not greatly encouraged in Christianity. During the medieval period, the Catholic Church played a central role in generating and enforcing legal norms throughout

Europe. According to Callahan (2004, p. 221), the Catholic Church until the medieval period 'stood at the apex of society as a centralized, hierarchical institution'. The Church considered that commercialization, urbanization and the growth of the marketplace would endanger its followers' souls. An old saying of medieval times, referred to in Chapter 3, was that 'the merchant can scarcely or never be pleasing to God'. As an alternative, the Church promoted a path of salvation which slowed down the growth of commerce and trade. This was the time when Europe was emerging from manorial society. Profits from agriculture and textile production were seen as positive, while profits from banking and finance were regarded with suspicion.

Meanwhile, the Catholic Church was gradually transforming itself. Noonan (1957) considered that the Church had good reason to change its attitude towards business. Merchants frequently donated money for the construction of churches, and helped churchmen ready to adopt poverty as the purifying path to salvation. A second reason was that medieval Europe was divided among small states and powerful rulers. The Church was the only truly transnational organization. This feature gave the Church jurisdiction over pilgrims and travellers involved in key economic issues (monasteries with their almost identical layout were the equivalent of international hotels today). Another reason for change in the Church attitude was the rise of modern universities to rival traditional monastery schools. Writings of the Church fathers, decrees of the Church and other sacred books dominated parts of the universities' syllabi and administration (Berman, 1983, p. 163). As is the case now, universities rely on endowments from wealthy benefactors.

Bekar (2000) studied the various sources of raising finance amongst farmers in medieval Europe, concluding that a pooling of resources was the most efficient way of generating funds. The Catholic Church encouraged pooling arrangements rather than borrowing and lending on interest. Farmers mostly lacked assets to participate in the emerging capital markets. Participation in income-sharing arrangements required only social capital. Pooling of income was a powerful arrangement to smooth consumption among farmers and over time.

Ecclesiastical courts in the twelfth century monitored all commercial transactions under their jurisdiction, especially over usury. Although merchants devised various techniques under credit and forward sales and resale agreements to evade anti-usury laws, the Church policed these devices vigorously. Trade, and especially banking activities, were largely condemned and the only flexibility available was on partnership financing which was allowed under the Church's moral norms.

The turning point came after the work of St Thomas Aquinas, whose writings justified profit from business as a partner, provided that the same person participated as well in the losses (Henning, 2007, p. 41). His imprimatur in turn led to the formation of partnership law, with merchants using *commenda* agreements to raise funds from their first appearance in tenth or eleventh-century Italy. *Commenda* continued for several centuries to be one of the basic legal instruments, especially for overseas commercial ventures, for the pooling of capital and for bringing together investor (*commendator*) and manager (*commendatarius*).

Udovitch (1962) describes the arrangement in the following terms, drawing on Lopez and Raymond (1955, p. 175):

> The simplest form, the universal *commenda*, is an arrangement whereby an investor or group of investors entrusts capital or merchandise to an agent-manager, who is to trade with it, and then return to the investor(s) the principal and a previously agreed upon share of the profits. The remaining share of the profits goes to the agent as a reward for his labor. Further, the agent is in no way liable for any loss resulting from the exigencies of sea-travel or from an unsuccessful business venture. This is borne exclusively by the investor(s), the agent losing only his expended time and effort. (Udovitch, 1962, p. 198)

An interesting aspect of the *commenda*, as Udovitch highlights, is that it melds the advantages of a loan with those of a partnership, while containing elements of both. Like in a partnership, profits and risks are shared by both parties, the investor risking capital, the agent his time and effort. But in the *commenda* there is no social capital formed, and the investor does not become jointly liable with the agent in transactions with third parties. As in a loan, the *commenda* entailed no liability for the investor beyond the sum of money or quantity of merchandise handed over to the agent, and in the event of its successful completion, the agent returned the capital plus a share of the profits. Nevertheless, the agent's complete freedom from any liability for the capital, in the event of partial or total loss, except for 'acts of God and public enemies', is a novel and distinctive feature of the *commenda*.

Commenda-based trade agreements resolved many concerns of the Church and helped to develop a state of trust between the Church and merchant community. On one side, this fulfilled the Church requirements of 'sterility of money and the associated fixed standards of values' (Callahan, 2004, p. 230), yet on the other side it helped merchants to raise the required capital. According to Cizakca (1996, p. 14), it was clearly established in the thirteenth century that financiers received three-quarters of the profits while the ship owners (entrepreneurs) took the remaining share. With the passage of time, ship owners themselves established trading skills and accumulated wealth, and the profit-sharing ratio with financiers reduced to one-half. There were clearly principal–agent issues at stake in terms of the relative freedom of action given to the agent. However, *commenda* allowed financiers to travel with their goods to avoid any agency problems.

With this arrangement, trade and commerce in Europe flourished. Meanwhile, the nature of trading agreements was also changed with time. Some of the business risks were transferred from the financiers towards the ship owners who themselves started contributing to the capital. Europeans used the term *societas* for this new arrangement. Callahan (2004) noted that the merchants of that time defined the fiduciary duties of each partner under *societas* agreements. First, *societas* were operated on an equality basis where all investing parties were liable for gains or losses. Second, partners in common were liable for any harm done to their businesses. Liabilities of all the partners were unlimited even if losses were made due to the act of any single partner. Third, the share of each partner was clearly stipulated subject to his business contribution in terms of both capital and entrepreneurial skills. Similarly, if one partner withdrew his share before transferring into common funds, he was held liable for any delay and thus paid damages to other partners. In a nutshell, *societas* agreements contributed towards later developments in partnership laws covering a variety of relevant issues such as rights, duties, responsibilities, profit-sharing ratios, and so on.

European merchants also introduced the concept of limited liability in *societas* or partnership agreements. Merchants created separate pools of funds to finance business ventures. All losses were compensated or settled from these pools of funds. For instance, Bonsignore Company of Siena suspended the concept of joint liability and made each partner liable only up to their original investment in the company. In other words, partners were not liable for losses made by other partners beyond certain limits (Sapori, 1948, p. 66). This amendment effectively converted a general partnership into a limited partnership, so laying the groundwork to some considerable extent for the concept of limited liability in a company.

The Christian Church also approved the *census*, an annuity on fruitful goods. Although the charging of interest on a loan (*mutuum*) was prohibited, the usury laws did not apply to the medieval contract of *census*, which allowed one party to buy a stream of annual payments from another (Ferguson, 2009, p. 74). Such contracts provided regular income to buyers throughout their lives. *Census* contracts were designed to sell present goods against future goods. According to Noonan (1957, p. 157), the Church authorities themselves were involved in sales of *census* contracts as money raised from the *census* contracts were even more lucrative than from *societas* agreements. There were many types of *census* contracts in Europe during the eleventh to thirteenth centuries. Life *census* linked future income with the life of buyers. Perpetual *census* was issued for an indefinite period.

Similarly, temporary or fixed *census* had predetermined maturity periods, much like mortgage loans. *Census* contracts had an option to redeem at the request of both buyers and sellers. With the passage of time, *census* contracts eventually converted into modern-day annuities and became a source of regular income for European governments.

Another interesting development in partnership agreements of the thirteenth century was the inclusion of 'God share' in business. In his 1948 article, Robert Lopez pointed out that medieval merchants extended commercial credit unchecked by ecclesiastical authorities. Instead, they generously donated to churches and charities. The classical example was of the Bardi who included God, 'Messer Domeneddio', among other partners and assigned dividends pertaining to his share. Because the Catholic Church maintained a strict attitude towards usurers and often seized their properties as punishment, moneylenders typically wrote '*Cocchi-Compagni*' in their wills, donating certain amount of their incomes to the Church as gifts. The Church in turn showed them some leniency.

Such financial agreements provided some protection to the moneylenders themselves, but not enough safety to their capital. The solution devised was in the form of insurance contracts which secured their principal investments against losses. The Church allowed both partnership and insurance contracts separately, but declared them illegal when offered together as one contract. The new decree was not in accordance with concurrent commercial practices, and many Italian merchants objected to the decision. Their argument was that one partner can insure his other business partners against any expected risk of losses to their capital. The argument was eventually accepted in the fifteenth century and became part of civil and common law (Henning, 2007, p. 43).

Once this point of view had been established, the next step was obvious: if a partner could insure his principal amount, he would also earn a guaranteed minimum profit. The transaction eventually known as *contractus trinus* (triple contract) in which the investor first entered into a silent partnership, next insured his principal amount through purchasing an insurance contract and then assured a fixed return by selling uncertain future profit for a certain fixed profit which was also legal (Salin, 1948, p. 196). Three different financial contracts when combined together yielded a fixed return. Thus the triple contract was nothing but a modern form of interest-bearing loan. Henning (2007, p. 43) explained the same concepts with the help of following example:

> the first contract would call for A to contribute R100 to a partnership between himself and B for one year. In the second contract A would then sell back to B the right to any profit over and above R30 for a fee of R15 to be paid by B.

Finally, in the third contract, A would insure himself against any loss of wealth at a cost to A of R5, paid to B. The net result of these three simultaneously agreed contracts was an interest payment of R10 (R15 minus R5) on a loan of R100 made by A to B.

While the arrangement put the Church in a quandary, prompting a denunciation by Martin Luther in 1585, the idea gained popularity among the merchant community.

Overall, partnership-based contracts had been well established in Europeans ports and commercial cities by the fifteenth century. Business families such as the Medici and Peruzzi, who were active in international trade, established trading houses and their own banking companies in prominent port cities (Usher, 1943, p. 19). According to Kohn (1999, p. 5) the entities enjoyed strong ties with the Catholic Church. The remittances of papal taxes were among the major sources of funds for them. Apart from capital contribution from the regular partners, other sources to raise capital were: (1) additional funds provided by the partners (*sopracorpo*); (2) reinvested earnings; and (3) deposits from their customers. Trading companies treated *sopracorpo* as debt and extra funds. Partners were allowed to earn money on extra capital, but to avoid interest, the extra payments were voluntary rather than contractual. In addition, the companies routinely retained profits to be distributed later when the partnership was terminated.

Traders nevertheless faced limitations in terms of the frequent transferring of shares to liquidate positions or to convert investments into cash or even to take loans against their investments. The problem was resolved with the development of *carati*. The new instrument was a more complex form of partnership agreement and can be traced back to thirteenth-century Italy. Under this arrangement, financial values of outbound ships were divided into multiple shares and investors were asked to invest. *Carati* shares were free to float, changed hands or even used as collateral against loans. Interestingly, *carati* shares guaranteed investors through limiting their liability up to the amount of their investments.

In this way, *carati* shares developed into a new organizational form: joint stock companies, a partnership with transferable shares. Among the early joint stock companies were the English and Dutch East India Companies, founded in 1600 and 1602, respectively. These companies were developed through their own capital and had horizons longer than one voyage. The chartering of these companies also provided regular finance and supported the maritime trade of the respective countries. Shareholders supplied funds for longer periods and committed investments over an extended number of years. Joint stock companies also raised additional funds through loans and retained earnings (Kuran, 2003, pp. 426–7).

Kuran (2003) further noted that early joint stock companies were managed mainly by the partners themselves. The situation raised many legal disputes as the activities of all partners proved impossible to monitor. This problem was resolved with the development of the corporation or *corpus* where liabilities of the shareholders were limited but at the same time management was also independent from shareholders on a day-to-day basis. Newly developed corporations could now sue or be sued by others in their own corporate names (Munro, 2006, p. 55). Corporations also provided better protection to minority shareholders who previously had no voice in the companies' affairs.

ISLAM AND PARTNERSHIPS

Trading and its related activities were practised in Peninsular Arabia well before the advent of Islam. This tradition was further validated from the Qur'anic injunctions encouraging income from trade rather than earning interest income from loans. Throughout the history of Islam, jurists adopted trading as a source of income and living. For instance, Prophet Muhammad, his first wife, Khadija, and the first four rightly guided Caliphs were all traders. Imran Abu Hanifa, the famous Islamic jurist who also led the Hanifi school of thought, was also a well-known trader. There were numerous events in Islamic history when local governments themselves entered into commercial partnership agreements. For instance, Caliph Umer, on behalf of the government, used to invest the orphanages' money in different businesses on a partnership basis (Cizakca, 1996, p. 6). Islamic legal doctrine which oversees matters related to commercial transactions remains the same from its beginnings until today. Cizaka (2010) explored the reasons behind the survival of the Islamic partnership in its original form during the Ottoman Empire. He extensively translated archives related to commercial partnerships and concluded that small-scale private firms and the flexible nature of partnership contracts were motivating forces behind its existence and durability.

The Islamic partnership is broadly divided into property or proprietary partnership (*sharikah al milk*) or contractual or commercial partnership (*sharikah al aqd*). The former is inclusively linked with the joint ownership of property and the latter created purely for sharing profit and loss through investments.[1] Islamic jurists further classify property or proprietary partnerships (*sharikah al milk*) into optional and compulsory partnerships. An optional partnership is created when the owners jointly and freely purchase property. Compulsory partnerships are automatically created upon receiving joint property in inheritance or as a gift (Yasseri,

1999, p. 232). Apart from joint ownership of property or wealth, property or proprietary partnerships are not necessarily created only for commercial venture purposes, whereas the contractual partnerships are exclusively created with a profit motive.

A partnership in Islam can be established for both general purposes and specific purposes, or for a specific period. Once the specific purpose is achieved such partnerships cease to exist. A partnership is also automatically terminated at the death of any partner regardless of whether it was created for a specific purpose or a defined period. Partnerships can also be terminated after giving due notice. All undividable assets may be sold out in the market and sale proceeds can be distributed among the partners. Nevertheless, if the remaining partners are interested in continuing their joint business, they can simply calculate and pay out the share of the outgoing partner. Islamic jurists agree that partners can refuse to terminate partnership if their investments are of a long-term nature and a profit is yet to materialize. They justify such condition on the principle laid down by the Prophet Muhammad in his famous saying, 'all conditions agreed upon by the Muslims are upheld, except a condition which allows what is prohibited or prohibits what is lawful' (Usmani, 2002, p. 91). Some of the main types of Islamic partnerships are given below, drawing also on Lewis and Algaoud (2001).

Mudaraba

A *mudaraba* can be defined as a contract between at least two parties whereby one party, the financier (*sahib al-mal* or *rabb al-mal*), entrusts funds to another party, the entrepreneur (*mudarib*), to undertake an activity or venture. This type of contract is in contrast with *musharaka* in which there is also profit-sharing, but all parties have the right to participate in managerial decisions. In *mudaraba*, the financier is not allowed a role in management of the enterprise. Consequently *mudaraba* represents a profit and loss sharing (PLS) contract where the return to lenders is a specified share in the profit or loss outcome of the project in which they have a stake.

The *mudarib* becomes a trustee (*amin*) for the capital entrusted to him by way of *mudaraba*. The *mudarib* is to utilize the funds in an agreed manner and then return to the *rabb al-mal* the principal and the pre-agreed share of the profit. The *mudarib* keeps for himself what remains of such profits. The following are the significant characteristics:

1. The division of profits between the two parties must necessarily be on a proportional basis and cannot provide for a lump sum or guaranteed return to the *rabb al-mal* (beneficial owner).

2. The *rabb al-mal* is not liable for losses beyond the capital he has contributed.
3. The *mudarib* (labour partner) does not share in the losses except for the loss of his time and efforts.

These contractual arrangements may be either simple or complex, and restricted or unrestricted. A simple *mudaraba* may have two parties to the contract, an investor and an entrepreneur or 'worker', or it may have more than one party on either side, that is, a number of investors and a number of workers, and the arrangements may vary. Complex *mudaraba* may take several forms; for example, the investor may be a partnership and the worker may be a partnership. The unrestricted or absolute type is one in which the capital is handed over and neither of the type of work that is to be done, nor the location, nor the time, nor the quality of work, nor those with whom he is to trade is determined. The restricted type is one in which some or all of these things are determined.

Considering its origins and historical validity, the word *mudaraba* has been derived from *darb fi al-ard*, which means those 'who journey through the earth (*yadribuna fi al-ard*) seeking the bounty of Allah' (S73:20). Because of his work and travel, the *mudarib* becomes entitled to part of the profits of the venture. In terms of the *sunna* (that is, information concerning the practices of the Prophet and his Companions), jurists rely on the precedent of the contract of *mudaraba*, concluded by the Prophet with Khadija prior to his marriage, as a result of which he travelled to Syria. Thus the legal evidences employed in support of the arrangement rest on both the Holy Qur'an and the *sunna*.

When defining a *mudaraba*, jurists focused on it as a 'participation in profits' (Nyazee, 1999, p. 244). Those who wanted to distinguish *mudaraba* from the other types of partnerships, within this broad definition, added the words: 'with wealth from one side and work from the other'. Al-Quduri said: '*Mudarabah* is a contract for participation in profits with wealth from one partner and work by the other' (Al-Quduri al-Baghdadi, n.d.). According to the terminology used by the jurists of Medina, *mudaraba* is also called *muqarada* or *qirad*.

A feature of a *mudaraba* comes from the dual roles of the *mudarib* as agent and partner. The *mudarib* is the agent of the *rabb al-mal* in whatever transactions he undertakes in the wealth of the *mudaraba*. The *mudarib* then becomes a partner of the *rabb al-mal* when profit emerges, because *mudaraba* is a partnership in profit, and an agent is not entitled to profit on the basis of his work after the emergence of profit, but he becomes a partner in this situation due to the contract of partnership. The wealth of the *mudaraba* becomes a joint ownership between *mudarib* and the *rabb al-mal*, and the share of the *mudarib* is now on the basis of his undivided share in co-ownership. All division of profit must be expressed as a ratio or as a part of the total profit. The profit cannot be expressed as a percentage of the capital invested. This principle is the *sine qua non* of a valid contract. Any deviation from it or condition that leads to uncertainty in this requirement will render the contract unenforceable.

Although profit-sharing and interest lending may seem alike, the differences are clearly more than semantic ones. The yield is not guaranteed in profit-sharing, while, in interest lending, the loan is not contingent on the profit or loss outcome, and is usually secured, so that the debtor has to repay the borrowed capital plus the fixed (or pre-determined) interest amount regardless of the resulting yield of the capital. Thus, with interest lending, the financial losses fall most directly upon the borrower. Under *mudaraba*, financial losses are borne completely by the lender. The entrepreneur as such loses the time and effort invested in the enterprise, and the reward for his labour. This distribution effectively treats human capital equally with financial capital.

Musharaka

Under a *musharaka*, the entrepreneur adds some of his own capital to that supplied by the financial investors, so exposing himself to the risk of capital loss. In this respect, the entrepreneur's own financial contribution defines the difference between the two profit and loss sharing modes of financing. Because the agent also contributes to the capital, he can therefore claim a greater percentage of the profit. In most other respects, the *musharaka* bears the same characteristics as the *mudaraba*.

Formally, *musharaka* (from the Arabic *shirkah* or *sharikah*) implies partnership in a venture, and can be defined as a form of partnership where two or more persons combine either their capital or their labour, to share the profits, enjoying similar rights and liabilities. It can take the form of a *mufawada*, meaning an unlimited, unrestricted and equal partnership in which the partners enjoy complete equality in the areas of capital, management and right of disposition. Each partner is both the agent and the guarantor of the other. A more limited investment partnership is known as an *'inan* (*shirkah al-'inan*). This type of partnership occurs when two or more parties contribute to a capital fund with money, contributions in kind or labour. Each partner is only the agent and not the guarantor of his partner. An *'inan musharaka* is limited in scope to the specific undertaking.[2] For both the partners share profits in an agreed manner and bear losses in proportion to their capital contributions.

Such contractual partnerships can be considered proper because the parties concerned have willingly entered into a contractual agreement for joint investment and the sharing of profits and risks. The agreement need not necessarily be formal and written, it could be informal and oral. As in *mudaraba*, the profits can be shared in any equitably agreed proportion. The basis for entitlement to the profits of a *musharaka* are capital, active participation in the *musharaka* business and responsibility. Profits are to be distributed among the partners in business on the basis of proportions settled by them in advance. The share of every party in profit must be determined as a proportion or percentage. Losses must, however, be shared in proportion to the capital contribution. On this point all jurists are unanimous.

Musharaka has well-defined rules in Islam. The contract allows any person (without any restriction of religion or caste, as is the case of Judaism) to join in partnership including differences in gender and marital status provided that the contract takes place with the free consent of all parties and without any fraud or misrepresentation. *Musharaka* allows each person to take active participation in the business. Each partner is bound and responsible for the acts of other partners. For instance, if any partner takes a loan in his official capacity the remaining partners are also liable and responsible for the timely return of that loan. Furthermore, all partners must participate in the profit and loss. Any condition which forbids any partner to participate in the profit renders the whole partnership contract invalid.

Islamic partnership rules allow partners to become a sleeping partner or inactive partner in the business. Under this scenario a sleeping partner should not claim profit more than his investment in the overall capital (Usmani, 2002, p. 87).[3] Similarly, liabilities of sleeping partners can also be limited up to their investment (ibid., p. 216). For instance, if a sleeping partner invests 50 per cent of the total capital, he can only claim profit up to 50 per cent. There is no restriction on a maximum share in profit on active partners. But all terms must be settled before the commencement of the partnership. Finally, *musharaka* prohibits any predefined and guaranteed return on investment.

Islamic laws allow Muslims to enter into partnerships with non-Muslims to encourage interfaith harmony. Some jurists, however, believe that non-Muslims can only become a sleeping partner with Muslims or vice versa, but all active partners must be from the same faith (Kuran, 2003, pp. 420–422). The rationale behind this decision is to avoid investment in activities which are strictly prohibited in Islam, such as, among other things, the sale of wine and pork. Kuran (2003) concluded that during eleventh century, although majority partnerships were formed between the same ethno-religious group such as Turks with Turks, Arabs with

Arabs, Jews with Jews, and so on, there were also examples where Muslims entered in partnerships with Jews. Even judges of Islamic courts at certain places entered into agreements with non-Muslims. Further evidence in this context comes from Yasseri (1999, p. 232), who pointed out that *mudaraba* and *musharaka* were extensively used by the Jewish community who lived side by side with Muslims in Arabia. Merchants, regardless of religious affiliation or ethnic background, recognized that the supreme goal of commercial transactions was to attain profit.

Islamic jurists also identify *sharikah al aamal* (partnership in service) under *musharaka* financing. This partnership is created when partners jointly provide some specific services to their customers against service charges. The fees, commission or service charges earned have to be distributed among all partners in a predefined sharing ratio. For example, two partners mutually decide to start a tailoring shop and whatever they jointly earn will go to a common pool of earnings. Later they can distribute income or profit irrespective of the work done by each partner.

Credit Partnership

Sharikah al-wujah (credit partnership) is the third type of Islamic partnership. It is a unique concept in Islamic finance where two or more entrepreneurs establish a partnership without having any investment capital. Here all partners make a joint agreement that whatever capital they borrow from third parties would be their joint liability. Such a credit partnership restricts partners to share profit strictly in proportion to their liabilities (Udovitch, 1970, p. 299). This stipulated condition is different from the other mentioned partnership agreements where active partners are at liberty to agree upon any profit-sharing ratio.

Credit partnership was well established in the late eighth century. It was named *sharikah al-wujah* which means 'partnership in good reputations'. Here people only extended credit to those parties who enjoyed good repute among them. The partnership was also known as *sharikah al mafalis* ('partnership of the penniless'). In modern times, Udovitch (1970) translated an Arabic papyri deed from the eleventh century, recovered from Cairo. He narrated the following example to explain credit partnership:

Musa bin Bishr and Hiba formed a partnership for the production and sale of bread. The initial capital making this enterprise possible consisted of a loan of four dinars from Bi Ar-Rida . . . All work, profit and losses were to be shared between the partners equally, as was the responsibility for repayment of the investment loan . . . the partners did not succeed in generating enough profit to provide both a livelihood for themselves as well as surplus from which the original investment could be repaid. When the creditor, Abu Ar-Rida claimed his debt, Hiba, one of the partners who had apparently dissociated himself, or otherwise lost interest in the joint enterprise, refused to accept responsibility for his share of the four dinar debt ... Musa bin Bishr sought redress against his former partner Hiba before the Rabbinical Court, presumably to force the latter to pay his share of two dinars. Instead of his full claim being satisfied, a compromise settlement was agreed upon by which, instead of an equal liability of outstanding debt, Musa bin Bishr paid three-quarters and Hiba one-quarter. (Udovitch, 1970, pp. 293–4)

Bayt al-Mal

Unlike in Europe, there is no prominent example of the development of large-scale private corporations or the establishment of private banking firms in the Islamic world before Western colonialism, an issue discussed further at the end of Chapter 8. The only close parallel was the *Bayt al-Mal*, the main objectives of which were to finance trade, to make profitable investments and to maintain public finances of the state. In the early years of Islam there was no permanent *Bayt al-Mal* in Medina. Whatever amount collected was immediately distributed among the needy people. The state of Medina had not employed any permanent staff and maintained no regular expenses, and the need for a separate treasury department arose during the time of the Second Caliph (Umer) when large amounts were transferred to Medina after new conquests. After consulting his cabinet, Caliph Umer decided to construct a separate building by the name *Bayt al-Mal*. He also set up a separate department to maintain a record of all official spending.

Other underlying objectives of the *Bayt al-Mal* were to provide welfare services and act as guardian to the poor, orphans, widows and other deserving citizens. The Islamic state provided regular stipends from its income. Similarly, affluent members of society also contributed financially to support welfare projects. The *Bayt al-Mal* further provided benevolent loans to the poor so that they could start their own businesses, and also invested government funds in profitable ventures.

Partnerships Employed in Banking

While *musharaka* is the term used to describe partnerships that are formed for various commercial activities, the basic concept of a *musharaka* has also been used as a technique for Islamic financial institutions to provide finance to commercial enterprises. For example, the features of *musharaka* can be used to structure a working capital facility for a company, or it can be used for joint investment in activities such as real estate development and rural finance. In Western countries, diminishing *musharaka* has been used by Islamic banks for residential property financing.

Islamic bankers have adapted and refined the *mudaraba* concept to form the two-tier or triple *mudaraba* (sometimes called re-*mudaraba*, *mudarib yudarib*). In this arrangement, the *mudaraba* contract has been extended to include three parties: the depositors as financiers, the bank as an intermediary, and the entrepreneur who requires funds. The bank acts as an entrepreneur (*mudarib*) when it receives funds from depositors, and as a financier (*rabb al-mal*) when it provides the funds to entrepreneurs. The main conditions associated with a *mudaraba* contact are as follows.

The bank receives funds from the public on the basis of unrestricted *mudaraba*. There are no constraints imposed on the bank concerning the kind of activity, duration and location of the enterprise. However, a *mudaraba* contract cannot be applied to finance *haram* activities which are forbidden by Islam. Such a contract is considered null and void.

The bank has the right to aggregate and pool the profit from different investments, and share the net profit (after deducting administrative costs, capital depreciation and Islamic tax) with depositors according to a specified formula.[4] In the event of losses, the depositors lose a proportional share or the entire amount of their funds. The return to the financier has to be strictly maintained as a share of profits.

The bank applies the restricted form of *mudaraba* when funds are provided to entrepreneurs. The bank has the right to determine the kind of activities, the duration and the location of the projects, and to monitor the investments. However, these restrictions may not be formulated in a way so as to harm the performance of the entrepreneur. When a project is undertaken, the bank cannot interfere with the management of the investment and take part in the daily operation of the business. Thus loan covenants and other such constraints usual in conventional commercial bank lending are not allowed in Islamic banking.

Under a *mudaraba*, the *rabb al-mal* cannot demand any guarantee from the *mudarib* to return the capital or the capital with a profit, since the relationship between the investor and the *mudarib* is a fiduciary one and the *mudarib* is a trustworthy person. Accordingly, the bank cannot require any guarantee such as security and collateral from the entrepreneur in order to insure its capital against the possibility of an eventual loss. Such a condition makes the *mudaraba* contract null and void. But it is allowable for there to be a guarantee from an independent third party.

The *mudaraba* contract should assign a profit rate for each party. The rate should be a ratio, and not a fixed amount. Assigning a fixed amount to either party invalidates the *mudaraba* due to the possibility that the profit realized may not equal the sum so stipulated. Before arriving at a profit figure, the *mudaraba* venture should be converted to money, and the capital should be set aside. The *mudarib* is entitled to deduct all business-related expenses from the *mudaraba* capital.

The liability of the financier is limited exclusively to the capital provided. On the other hand, the liability of the entrepreneur is also restricted, but in this case solely to his labour and effort. Nevertheless, if negligence or mismanagement can be proven, the entrepreneur may be liable for the financial loss and be obliged to remunerate the financier accordingly.

The entrepreneur shares the profit with the bank according to a previously agreed division. Until the investment yields a profit, the bank is able to pay a salary to the entrepreneur. This salary is determined on the basis of the ruling market salary.

Mudaraba and *musharaka* constitute, at least in principle if not always in practice, the twin pillars of Islamic banking (Ariff, 1982). The two methods conform fully with Islamic principles, in that under both arrangements lenders share in the profits and losses of the enterprises for which funds are provided. The *musharaka* principle is invoked in the equity structure of Islamic banks and is similar to the modern concepts of partnership and joint stock ownership. Insofar as the depositors are concerned, an Islamic bank acts as a *mudarib* which manages the funds of the depositors to generate profits subject to the rules of *mudaraba*. The bank may in turn use the depositors' funds on a *mudaraba* basis in addition to other lawful (but less preferable) modes of financing, including mark-up or deferred sales, leasing and beneficence loans considered in the next chapter.

However, there are some incentive issues to consider. A *mudaraba* loan contract is a device for directly linking the remuneration to capital to the outcome of the project. A *riba* contract, by contrast, creates an explicit relationship between the input and remuneration of capital. This is the formal position. But the differences between the two might go beyond this formal distinction and may extend to economic incentives and managerial performance. Under a standard incentive compatible *riba* contract, the manager is left free to choose the individually optimal level of effort contingent on the specified level of investment. *Mudaraba*, on the other hand, allows there to be a relationship between capital investment and the outcome of the project. Lowering the specified return from the project in the bad state under state preference theory (and therefore the associated level of effort) below that which may be desirable given the level of investment, provides an inducement for the manager in the good state truthfully to report the investment prospects. With this second instrument for achieving incentive compatibility, *mudaraba* might act to reduce inefficiently large fluctuations in capital investment (Presley and Sessions, 1994). However, it would seem that, in reality, these inducements may not be as significant as the theoretical argument they presented suggests could be the case. We take up this issue again in Chapter 9.

CONCLUDING REMARKS

Trade and its related activities were recognized and appreciated in Talmudic and Qur'anic teachings but did not receive much support in Christian literature, which for some considerable time considered money as being opposed to salvation. Despite these differences, history tells us that trading activities flourished under the umbrella of Judaism, Christianity and Islam, using different names and under diverse terms and conditions. Partnerships and equity-type arrangements were the preferred instruments.

The Talmudic concept of *iska* is quite similar to the Christian concept of *commenda* where the entrepreneur has to bear some of the associated risks in the case of loss. However, *commenda*, unlike *iska*, did not emphasize regular wages for entrepreneurs. Likewise, the Islamic system of *mudaraba* adopted a similar view towards regular wages as *commenda*.

The concept of *societas* was parallel to Islamic *musharaka* where all parties had to share in the profits and losses at pre-agreed ratios. Whereas liabilities of partners were unlimited in *musharaka*, *societas* contracts linked financiers' liabilities with their original investments. Lastly, the word *carati* is quite near to an Arabic term of *qirat* which is an alternative word for *musharaka* (Cizakca, 1996, p. 27). *Carati* was an ideal agreement used for risk diversification, and can be regarded as a foundation stone for the formation of joint stock companies in Europe.

European-based partnership arrangements provided initial support towards the evolution of banking and joint stock companies in Europe. Early-period banking was partnership-based, where each partner contributed his share in capital – the *corpo*. Partners sometimes also contributed additional capital called *sopracorpo*, a sort of subordinated debt to earn interest. In addition, all partners received regular wages, while their shares in profit were retained until the termination of the partnership (de Roover, 1942). It was customary among merchants to terminate partnership contracts after a certain number of years and simultaneously to sign new partnership contracts, often with the same partners. Medici and Peruzzi in Italy were leading examples of medieval period partnerships. Both companies successfully ran their businesses, but later failed due to heavy loans granted to the rulers who eventually defaulted on timely repayments (Kohn, 1999).

In the Islamic world, we do not find a single prominent example where partnership contracts evolved into large-scale businesses or corporations or Muslim trading houses which lasted for centuries. Muslims preferred to conduct trade within their social circles or by establishing limited-scale partnership contracts. Why Europeans successfully converted trade into large-scale corporations, and why the Muslim Middle East failed to maintain its momentum in terms of financial innovation, is an interesting question to which various answers were suggested in Chapter 5, including the contribution of Islam itself. However, we prefer to focus on current day issues in what follows, rather than to dwell too much on the past.

NOTES

1. Excellent accounts of profit and loss sharing partnership techniques are contained in Al-Harran (1993) and Nyazee (1994, 1995, 1999). We follow Nyazee in dividing the traditional law of business organization into two categories, both being types of contract partnership. In the first category (for example, *musharaka*), management and participation is stipulated for all partners, whether or not all partners actually participate in the management. In the second category (for example, *mudaraba*), management is stipulated for one of the partners and the other partners are simply investors who share the profits in return for the capital they have provided.

2. Contractual partnership (*shirkah al-ugood*) has been divided in the *fiqh* books into four kinds: *al-mufawadah* (full authority and obligation); *al'-inan* (restricted authority and obligation); *al-abdan* (labour, skill and management); and *al-wujuh* (goodwill, credit-worthiness and contracts). *Shirkah al-abdan* is where the partners contribute their skills and efforts to the management of the business without contributing to the capital In *shirkah- al-wujuh* the partners use their goodwill, their credit-worthiness and their contracts for promoting their business without contributing to the capital. Both these forms for partnership where the partners do not contribute any capital, would remain confined essentially to small-scale business only.

3. The Hanbali school allows the sleeping partner to claim profit more than investment percentage in the total capital. It is worth noting that there are different opinions among the scholars as to whether the ratio of profit must conform to the proportion of capital invested by each partner. The principle of proportionality between the capital contributed and share of the profits is visible in all categories of partnership according to the Malikis, except the *mudaraba*. This is stated in the *Mudawwanah*: 'Partnership (sharing of profits) is not permitted, except in proportion to the *amwali* (capital contributed)' (Sahnun, 1905, Vol. 5, p. 41). However, this view has not won general acceptance. The Shafis do not allow the profit-sharing ratio to diverge from the capital contribution ratio (and thus there is no need for it to be specified in advance), but there is considerable flexibility in the basis for determining the ratio amongst the Hanafi and Hanbali schools. However, one of the most fundamental principles of *fiqh* is that losses from an investment must be divided in proportion to the initial capital contribution.

4. Two types of accounting policies are typically applied by Islamic banks. The first approaches separate the equity and invested amount completely. The second covers those deposits for a set period, which may be 3, 6, 9 months, one year or two years. The revenue and expenses of that type of investment are allocated according to the proportional share of investment. For example, if the bank bought or constructed a building as an investment 'common portfolio' the income will be allocated between the investors and shareholders according to the proportional share. If a particular investor enters into a deal with the bank as a 'specific investment', the total income of this deal is allocated for the investor and the bank charges its fees.

8.   Sale-based debt instruments

DEBT INSTRUMENTS

This chapter considers the teachings of Judaism, Christianity and Muslims about debt financing. To this end, it explores various types of debt-based financial instruments approved by each religion. Another aim of this chapter is to examine how Christian and Muslim governments, having in the past used interest-free debt techniques to finance budget deficits, were led towards interest-based instruments.

Debt-based financing falls into three broad categories. The first type of debt is that created mainly through lending or borrowing activities. All three religions have traditionally opposed the interest income generated through this process, demanding that lenders ask only for the return of principal. In particular, they encourage unconditional interest-free debt to help poor and needy people. A second type of debt is established through trading activities, such as credit sale and advance payment sale. Jurists from all three religions unanimously allow income generated as result of deferred payment or advance payment contracts, albeit subject to certain specified conditions and restrictions. For example, lenders are not allowed to charge additional amounts in the case of late payments as an extra source of income. Islam allows merchants to charge a higher market price than the spot price in the case of a credit sale; Judaism prohibits such transactions if the spot price of the similar commodity has already been established in the market. In general, any profit raised from sale is legitimized so long as relevant parties appropriately share risks related to the transacted goods.

Leasing is the third type of debt financing, where the lessee can only use the object (the usufruct) for a specific period against predetermined rent. Ownership of the asset remains with the lessor (owner) during that period. The Old Testament allows a temporary sale until the next Jubilee year (Lev. 25:14–17). There is no direct reference in the New Testament or Holy Qur'an about lease financing. Nonetheless, all three religions have approved of, and used, this financial instrument. In Islamic banking, the term *ijara* is used for leasing which is quite similar to an operating lease. Islamic jurists allow an operating lease but disapprove of a financial lease, considered as a mere exchange of money.

JUDAISM

By way of introduction we note that Judaic law evaluates a loan from the perspective of both the borrower and the lender. One reason for a borrower taking a loan is the need for ready cash, perhaps for consumption. Or the loan may be taken out in order to invest in a business. Obviously, the purpose for the loan will govern the size of the loan and the conditions attached to it, such as the types of guarantees that the creditor will seek. There are a number of ways to guarantee a loan and the Talmud discusses them in detail, starting with a personal guarantee: guarantor, mortgaging assets, general responsibility and taking out a mortgage. The latter was popular and the Talmud offers a number of possibilities; some are permissible, others are prohibited, and some are open to discussion. Rivlin (2010) considers them at some length.

Naturally, the lender is hardly disinterested in these caveats, but is also interested in profits and obtaining a return on his funds. At this point the prohibition of *ribbit* poses a major stumbling block in the case of a person wanting some advantage on his money, as Jewish law prevented the taking of interest. There were various types of prohibitions of interest and various possible solutions. One key issue is whether the transaction in question can be regarded as a sale rather than a loan.

Here, for an explanation, we defer to Rivlin (2010, p. 595):

> if A sells his field to B, B, the new owner, can benefit from the produce from the field, even if A still intends to buy it back. There are only two types of transactions in which the owner of the field can benefit from its produce. If the first transaction between A and B was not the purchase of the field, but rather a loan to A and the transfer of the field to B as security for the debt, then B is not entitled to the produce, since this is considered interest. In both cases the same money changes hands at the same time, but the first transaction is a sale and permissible, whereas the second is a loan and prohibited.

Continuing:

> The possibility of calling a transaction a sale was preferred by many debtors who wished to disguise the loan as a commercial transaction. This was an appropriate solution for a creditor who wanted to benefit from the produce of the field until the loan was repaid. The debtor feared this solution, since, unlike a mortgage, it transferred ownership of the asset to the creditor. The debtor obviously had no interest in giving up his field forever and tried to ensure the return of the field after payment of the debt, using a reversible sale. The structure of such a transaction is: 'I sell you my land but I buy back tomorrow.'
>
> However, this approach negates the illusion of a sale and reveals the loan beneath. The Sages therefore permitted this transaction only if the return of the asset is not built in.

Overall, Jewish teachings classify loans into two main categories, that is, interest-free loans (Elkin, 2010) and loans created as result of sale (Berger, 1935; de Roover, 1942). Interest-free loans are further divided into: (1) a loan secured with collateral; and (2) a loan without mortgage or pledge. Similarly, sale-based loans are divided into advance payment sale and deferred payment sale. Judaism encourages making loans rather than giving charity. In general, lending to the poor is seen to be a more meritorious deed than giving charity, as loans protect their self-respect and avoid any embarrassment involved in accepting charity.

The Old Testament recommended two types of interest-free loans. In the first kind, the loan was valid for a maximum period of seven years or until the Sabbath period, after which an outstanding amount was automatically remitted if it remained unpaid. No collateral was required in this type of loan and it was offered mainly to the poorest of the poor to meet their basic needs, or to those who could not offer any security as collateral. The second kind of loan was for a longer duration and offered to people who had some agricultural land to sell. The Old Testament allowed temporary sale of agricultural land subject, as we saw, to a buy-back arrangement. Here the price of land was subject to harvest, and before the Jubilee year (Lev. 25:14–17). This loan allowed the debtor the right to repurchase his land if he recovered financially. Alternatively, the debtor could seek help from his relatives to repurchase the land. In their absence, the land could remain in the ownership of the buyer for a maximum period of 49 years. The fiftieth year was declared as the Jubilee year, a time of freedom and celebration when all properties had to be returned to their original owners and slaves were to be set free to go home (Lev. 25:10–13). Meanwhile, the buyer could use the agricultural land for his own cultivation during the purchase period, which resulted in an implicit form of return on the loan. According to Wright (1990, p. 124), the aim of Jubilee was 'to restore the tenure of land to the smaller household units within the "kinship group" . . . an attempt to preserve, or periodically to restore, the economic viability and independence of the smaller family-plus-land units'.

Judaism also allowed debts to be created as result of business transactions such as credit sale or advance payment sale. These two sale transactions were well established among Jewish merchants, who sometimes mixed deferred payment sales with buy-back agreements to avoid usury, which the Catholic Church strictly policed and punished. For instance, pawnshops of Lombards in Bruges specialized in consumer credit against pledges of personal properties. They normally charged mark-ups at the weekly rate of 2d per pound or 43⅓ per cent per annum (de Roover, 1942). Judaism permits profit on debt created in the process of credit sale, provided that the transaction must be unconditional. Likewise, a sale price

Religion and finance

once mutually agreed upon cannot be changed unilaterally by any party. According to Lister (2006), additional charges in the case of late payment are forbidden as a reward for waiting. Even charging a higher price in the case of late payment is forbidden provided that the same commodity is currently available in the market at a lower price and is known in the market (BM 65a).

Gemara encourages full disclosure of cost and the profit margin at the time of sale agreement (BM 5:2). For example, the Baba Metzia (V:2) from the Jewish Talmud includes the passage: 'a credit sale where the buyer, in return for the privilege of delaying payment, pays the seller a premium over the cash price is not permissible because it is usurious, but a discount for pre-payment is permissible' (Houkes, 2004, p. 88). However, assets sold will remain in the ownership of a seller until the settlement of final accounts.

As an alternative to a credit sale, debt can also be established through advance payments where goods are to be delivered in future. Judaism allows a buyer to seek a discount in the case of advance payments. The only condition is that the transaction must be unconditional and real. For instance, a tenant may ask to pay rent below the market rate if he pays one year of rent in advance (BM 65). Similarly, advance payments to farmers against future delivery of crops or fruit do not fall under interest if future prices are unknown at the time of contract. A possible rationale behind this permission is that lenders expect higher prices of commodities in future, while farmers who sell crops in advance are expecting lower future prices. In short, actual commodity prices may be either high or low, and subject to market conditions which keep on changing and are unknown. Talmudic law considers advance payments as a loan until farmers actually deliver the crops or fruit as per the agreed contract.

Gamoran (1976) tried to distinguish between usury and business loans under Talmudic teachings. If a person leases property at a predetermined rent, that is allowed. If the same property is purchased through a borrowed amount where the installment is equal to the rent, then that is not allowed. Why is rent allowed but interest not permitted? He reasoned that interest is prohibited as loans are mostly related to the poor, but rent is normally paid in business transactions and has nothing to do with assisting poor people. Extending a loan can be an act of charity, but rent is purely a business deal. Additionally, termination of a rental agreement allows the lessor to take back possession of the original assets. A loan does not require the returning of the originally borrowed coins. Offering the equivalent currency or amount is good enough to settle outstanding debts. A lease agreement requires the lessor to bear all of the depreciation cost, while a lessee is responsible for any theft and lost items but is not held accountable for unavoidable events such as natural catastrophes. In the case of a loan, the borrower has to return the loan in full, regardless of theft or unavoidable events. Gamoran (1976) further pointed out that Talmudic teaching allows family members to borrow from each other. Any additional payment will be considered as a gift and does not fall under the definition of interest.

There are certain loans which were highly discouraged among ancient Jews. For instance, they were not allowed to accept 'iron flock' from fellow Jews, but such agreements could be made with outsiders. 'Iron flock' was a partnership cum debt agreement where investors lent money to entrepreneurs with an understanding to participate in profits only as per an agreed ratio, and enjoyed complete immunity from participation in losses. Since investors did not share in losses, such contracts were declared illegal and thus prohibited (BM 69b and 70b).

As an alternative to iron flock, a new contract named *hetter iska*, discussed in previous chapters, was developed to validate specific partnership contracts and to transgress the usury prohibition. The new contract exposed investors to risk of losses but at a minimal level. *The Oxford Handbook of Judaism and Economics* defines *hetter iska* as:

> An elaborate form of the *iska* business partnership wherein conditions are attached with the design of protecting the financier from absorbing a loss on his principal and increasing the probability that he will realize a profit as well. These clauses are structured in such a manner that *ribbit* law is not violated. (Levine, 2010a, p. 666)

If investors only receive a share in profit without sharing risk, then there was no *hetter iska*. For example, in modern banking, loans are normally secured through lien or charges on borrowers' properties or other assets. In such cases, banks are not exposed to significant risks and whatever returns earned are merely reward for their waiting period.

Being an *iska* in form, *hetter iska* is half investment and half deposit. Unlike iron flock where the investor did not participate in losses, now the investor contributes half in losses, if any, but shares equally in profit with the entrepreneur. Since both parties participate in expected losses, this makes the *hetter iska* legal. The contract further allows the entrepreneur to charge regular salaries against his labour before sharing profit with investors. Indeed, *hetter iska* is considered as an alternative to a loan and provides creditors with a lawful way to charge profit on loans. *Hetter iska* satisfies the concerns of rabbis towards charging interest from fellow Jews, and have grown in popularity to meet credit demands.

CHRISTIANITY

Christianity, following the Old Testament, holds similar views to Judaism towards the prohibition of interest. Christian theology in older times even imposed a ban on excess profits generated through either credit sales or advance payment sales. This injunction was further implemented with the institution of 'just price theory' which declared all oppressive bargains to come under the description of being usurious. According to Callahan (2004), the idea of a 'just price' was established to regulate markets and to establish effective Church control over economic affairs.

Berger (1935) recorded that Pope Alexander III in 1176 condemned the sale of dearer goods under the device of excessive credit price. He further quoted a statement of Gregory IX (Pope from 1227 to 1241) who declared: 'a man is to be counted a usurer, not only if he charges interest, but if he allows for the element of time in a bargain, by asking a higher price when he sells on credit' (quoted in Berger, 1935, p. 155). A clear definition about usury was first given by King Henry VII (1494) in an English statute which particularly forbade two specific types of financial transactions, that is: (1) lending of money; or (2) sale of property with an immediate buy-back arrangement at a lower price to create a loan. The law imposed harsh fines and penalties on usurers but failed to eradicate usury at large from the society. Henry VIII (1545) redefined usury and allowed a sale with repurchase agreement with the same party. He also allowed lending of money provided that the stipulated interest rate was below 10 per cent. Subsequent rulers further relaxed rules and ultimately anti-usury laws lost importance with the rapid commercialization and industrialization in Europe. Note that this development preceded the rise of Calvinism and Lutheranism. However, with the establishment of those religions the game was really up, as we noted in Chapter 3. Nevertheless, it is worth noting some other contracts that were used.

Advance payment agreements were another option specifically designed by the merchant community to avoid medieval anti-usury laws. Not only were they approved by the Catholic Church but they were also frequently employed by local rulers and even the Church itself to raise additional finance. For instance, Edward I of England when introducing a tariff on wool in 1275 sold exclusive rights to Ricciardi[1] in exchange for an advance payment. Thirteenth-century Italian traders took over the wool trade from English and Flemish merchants due to their ability to pay in advance, commonly a year (Kohn, 1999). Ekelund et al. (1989, p. 326) recorded that even the Church 'routinely borrowed advances against the collection of revenues, then raised taxes to cover the cost of loans'.

Another prominent example of advance payment was the *census* contract, mentioned in the previous chapter: an advance sale arrangement where delivery of goods was made in the future. According to Burke (2011, p. 12):

> A census contract is an exchange of money for the fruits of productive property, originally attached to a piece of land. The seller of a census owns the property and by extension the fruits of it, and the buyer purchases these fruits. While the census is a sale, it is similar to a loan, in which the seller, who receives money, is the borrower, and the buyer, who receives an annual return, is the lender.

European merchants in the twelfth century also traded in bills of exchange to remit money from one place to another. It is important to note that bills of exchange were an important source of creating debt due to time lags in receipts and payments. European merchants combined foreign exchange with credit to conceal interest rates in terms of a high exchange rate (Ekelund et al., 1989). This practice was examined in Chapter 3.

A sea loan was another type of debt financing source used to support maritime commerce. Repayment of this loan was subject to the safe arrival of the ship. No loan was repaid if the ship was lost, destroyed or plundered during the voyage. This loan did not specifically mention any interest amount. In practice, lenders used to transfer lesser amounts than amounts received at the time of repayment. This discounted amount varied according to cargo destinations, time and risks involved during voyages. Typical interest rates started from 15 per cent and increased sometimes up to 50 per cent per annum (Hoover, 1926).

The decline of the sea loan started in 1236 when Pope Gregory IX declared it usurious. Until then, it had been regarded as free from usury due to the risk of loss involved. Another immediate effect of the papal decree was an increase in the popularity of bills of exchange, which involved risk of fluctuation in the exchange rate when the bill was drawn in one currency while payments at the destination were made in another currency. Another reason behind the decline of the sea loan was the easy availability of other financial instruments, that is, *commenda*. Lara (2002) examined the reasons why European merchants shifted from sea loans towards equity-based *commenda* contracts (considered in the previous chapter). Both financial instruments were used to raise additional capital to finance overseas trade. Again, both instruments protected borrowers if losses were incurred due to unavoidable incidents at sea or from the hostile action of people such as sea pirates or corrupt local officials. Lara argued that the increased presence of European trading houses or overseas colonies (*fondaco*) made it difficult for Europeans merchants to hide their actual profitability. Legal authorities with better and accurate information could confiscate profits if merchants tried to cheat or did not fulfil their contractual obligations. This development pushed shipowners to shift towards *commenda* contracts, which were better instruments to access risks and joint liabilities.

ISLAM

Islamic jurists agree that debt can be created either in the form of interest-free loans (*qard hasan*) or in a process of sale and purchase such as deferred (credit) payment transactions and advance payment transactions. Islamic jurists legitimize different trading agreements where extra profit is earned as direct result of credit sale and advance payment transactions. Unlike Judaism, Islam allows sellers to demand a premium price in the case of credit sale agreements. Similarly, buyers can ask for discounted prices in the case of advance payments (Udovitch, 1975). This section now considers various debt instruments which were either adopted from earlier religions or later developed in the Islamic world. But first we start with the elemental principles and the basic building blocks of Islamic financing, again drawing on Lewis and Algaoud (2001).

The basic principles of commercial law are laid down in the four root transactions of: (1) sales (*bai, bay*), transfer of the ownership or corpus of property for a consideration; (2) hire (*ijara*), transfer of the usufruct (right to use) of property for a consideration; (3) gift (*hiba*), gratuitous transfer of the corpus of property; and (4) loan (*ariyah*), gratuitous transfer of the usufruct of property. These basic principles are then applied to the various specific transactions of, for example, pledge, deposit, guarantee, agency, assignment, land tenancy, *waqf* foundations (religious or charitable bodies) and partnerships.

Partnerships play an important role in Islamic financing and were considered in detail in the previous chapter. Briefly:

- *Shirkah al-'inan* (limited partnership). In this kind of partnership, partners contribute capital, property and/or labour. Profits and losses are shared in an agreed manner. Each partner is only the agent and so a partner is not liable for a debt contracted by his co-partners and is only able to sue someone with whom he has contracted.[2]
- *Musharaka.* When two or more people combine their resources to invest in an enterprise, a *musharaka* partnership is formed according to Islamic law. In this category of partnership, management and participation is stipulated for all partners, whether or not all partners actually participate in the management.
- *Mudaraba* or *qirad* (dormant partnership). In this category of partnership, management is stipulated for one of the partners and the

other partner(s) are investors who share the profits in return for the capital they have provided. Thus a *qirad* is a contract whereby one person (the dormant partner) gives funds or property to another on the basis that the financier will share in the active partner's profits in a proportion agreed upon in advance. The dormant partner remains the owner of the capital, but takes no active part in the enterprise. The trader is responsible only for negligence or breach of contract.

Musharaka and *mudaraba* and their traditional counterparts *muzarah* and *musaqah* are all Islamic investments based on the principle of profit and loss sharing (PLS). *Muzarah* is the traditional counterpart of *mudaraba* in farming in which the farmer takes agricultural land on a share-cropping basis. Banks hand over to farmers land which they own or which is otherwise in their possession. The plot of land has to be completely specified in the contract and must be given for a specified period. The output from the land is shared by the bank and farmers in an agreed proportion. *Musaqah* is the counterpart of *musharaka* in orchard keeping, and an arrangement is made for planting and tending fruit trees. The harvest of the orchard or garden is divided among the contracted parties (bank and farmer) in a specified ratio, normally according to their respective contributions.

But not all uses of funds are amenable to PLS, and certain alternative financing modes are available; and in practice, Islamic banks have often shown a strong preference for these other less risky modes. These alternative methods, which are meant to be applied by Islamic banks when the PLS principles cannot be utilized, include mark-up (*murabaha*), instalments (*bai bi-thamin ajil*), deferred payment (*bai'muajjal*), pre-paid purchase (*bai'salam*), manufacturing (*istisnaa*), leasing (*ijara*) and lease-purchase (*ijara wa iqtina*), and beneficence (*qard hasan*). In some cases these overlap; in others (such as for housing finance) they are combined with PLS techniques. Almost all are based on the charging of a fixed cost rather than an allocation of profit and loss.

Murabaha (Cost Plus Mark-Up)

The most commonly used mode of financing is the 'mark-up' device which is termed *murabaha*. In a *murabaha* transaction, the bank finances the purchase of a good or asset by buying the item on behalf of its client and adding a mark-up before reselling the item to the client on a 'cost-plus' basis profit contract. This contract form is used especially for foreign trade and working capital financing for circumstances in which banks will purchase raw materials, goods or equipment and sell them to a client at cost, plus a negotiated profit margin, to be paid normally within a fixed period of time or in instalments. When a *murabaha* sale is made on a deferred payment basis, it is called *murabaha-bi-muajjal* (Ahmed, 1997). With *murabaha*, Islamic banks do not share in profit and losses, but instead assume more of the role of a classic financial intermediary. In the traditional *murabaha* in *fiqh* (jurisprudence) books, the mark-up differs from interest in that it is not to be explicitly related to the duration of the loan but instead computed on a transaction basis for services rendered and not for deferring payment. Consider, for example, trade financing through *murabaha*. This might be arranged under a letter of credit requesting the bank to purchase or import the goods specified. The bank will issue the letter of credit, and pays the proceeds to the negotiating bank. The bank sells the goods to the customer on their arrival.

It may appear at first glance that the mark-up is just another term for interest as charged by conventional banks, interest thus being admitted through the back door. Yet the legality of the traditional type of *murabaha* is not questioned by any of the schools of Islamic law (although there are disputes about some forms of *murabaha* which have come into use where the factor of time commitment is added). What makes the traditional *murabaha* transaction Islamically legitimate in *fiqh* books is that the bank first acquires the asset for resale at profit, so that a commodity is sold for money and the operation is not a mere exchange of money for money (Wilson, 1983, pp. 84–5). In the process the bank assumes certain risks between purchase and resale; for example, a sudden fall in price could see the client refusing to accept the goods. That is, the bank takes responsibility for the good before it is safely delivered to the client. The services rendered by the Islamic bank are therefore regarded as quite different from those of a conventional bank which simply lends money to the client to buy the good.

While the *murabaha* is employed in the context of trade financing, the technique has been adapted for a variety of other uses. It is utilized as a vehicle for syndication, on the classic lead manager and co-managers format, enabling a number of banks to participate in the financing. One such application involved the acquisition, and financing on a deferred basis, of equipment for a power generation project. Another has been to finance home purchase whereby a designated residence is purchased at a specified price by a financial institution which, in turn, resells the property to the consumer, with the purchase price (including a profit component) to be paid in instalments over a period of five years.

Murabaha can also used by Islamic banks for the investment of idle funds on a sale and repurchase basis, much as a conventional bank might do with a 'repo' but using commodities rather than *riba* instruments (Rahman, 1999). The bank's agent contacts a commodity broker and obtains a quotation for the purchases of permissible commodities (often metals) at a set price for delivery against payment. At the same time, the agent enters into a transaction for the simultaneous resale of the same commodities to another broker, delivery to be made on a current basis but payment to be deferred for a specified time period (generally one, two or three months). The difference between the higher deferred purchase price and the original price represents, after the agent's fee, the rate of profit to the Islamic institution. This rate of return is an Islamically acceptable alternative to placing (that is, lending) money in an interest-bearing time deposit or using a bond repurchase.

Bai bi-thamin ajil (BBA)

This is similar to *murabaha* except that BBA is a deferred payment by instalments while *murabaha* is also a deferred payment but in a lump sum. With *murabaha* the purchaser should be aware of the cost price, which is in contrast to BBA. Some Islamic economic authors make no reference to BBA as it is incorporated into *murabaha*, for example in Pakistan (Yasin, 1997). However, in Malaysia, BBA is used separately and distinctly from *murabaha* for the specific purpose of the acquisition of assets such as buildings and machines for a longer period of time (for example, 10 to 30 years), while *murabaha* is for financing working capital (that is, within 30 to 120 days).

Bai'muajjal (Deferred Payment)

Islamic banks have been resorting to purchase and resale of assets, products and properties on a deferred payment basis, which is termed *bai'muajjal*. Both BBA and *murabaha* fall under this category of sale, because this transaction allows the sale of an item on the basis of deferred payment in instalments or in a lump-sum payment. The price of the product is agreed to between the buyer and the seller at the time of the sale and cannot include any charges for deferring payments. It is considered lawful in *fiqh* (jurisprudence) to charge a higher price for a good if payments are to be made at a later date. The general *shari'ah* rules on sales apply, namely that the object must be in existence, be owned and possessed by the bank, the sale is instant and absolute, and the price is certain, with no conditions attached. According to *fiqh*, this does not amount to charging interest, since it is not a lending transaction but a trading one. This system is widely used in Pakistan and Bangladesh.

Bai'salam (Prepaid Purchase)

Reference must also be made to 'advance payment sale' or prepaid purchase of goods, which is termed *bai'salam*, as a means used by Islamic banks to finance production. Here the price is paid at the time of the contract but the delivery takes place at a future date. This is a method which is really the opposite of the *murabaha*. There the bank gives the commodity first, and receives the money later. Here the bank pays the money first and receives the commodity later. It is a method which is normally used to finance agricultural products. The bank pays the value of the crops in advance, at a predetermined price, and receives the product later at the harvest time. The method is, of course, applicable to other trade activities that the bank may be interested to finance, and where there is a 'necessary sale' denoting the need of the contracting parties to enter into this type of 'advance sale'. This mode enables an entrepreneur to sell his output to the bank at a price determined in advance. Islamic banks, in keeping with modern times, have extended this facility to manufactures as well.

Istisnaa (Manufacturing)

This is a contract to acquire goods on behalf of a third party where the price is paid to the manufacturer in advance and the goods are produced and delivered at a later date. It is a contract for production of specified items where a person or a company may ask the bank for production of such items, with inputs provided by the maker, at an agreed price. Such contracts are used for the financing of aircraft manufacture, equipment installation of factories, construction, and so on, where the subject matter needs manufacturing (while in *bai'salam* this is not necessarily the case).

Ju'alah (Commission)

Derived from the Arabic word *ju'l*, originally 'reward' and now meaning 'fees', *ju'alah* means a transaction on a commission basis. The concept of *ju'alah* is similar to *istisnaa*. In *istisnaa* the seller provides a physical commodity, but in *ju'alah* the seller provides a service. In a *ju'alah* contract, a seller will offer a definite service to be provided as agreed upon, whereas the buyer will pay a definite price for this service under the principle of *al-ujr*. This mode usually applies to transactions such as consultations and professional services, fund placements and trust services.

Ijara and *ijara wa iqtina* (Leasing)

Leasing or *ijara* is also frequently practised by Islamic banks. *Ijara* literally means 'to give something on rent', and technically it relates to transferring the usufruct of a particular property to another person on the basis of a rent claimed from him. The difference between sale (*bai*) and *ijara* is transfer of ownership vis-à-vis transfer of the usufruct (*manfa'a*). That is, the leased property remains in the ownership of the lessor and only its usufruct is transferred to the lessee.

Consequently, an *ijara*, or operating lease, is based on a contract between the lessor and lessee for use of a specific asset. The lessor retains the ownership of the asset and the lessee has possession and use of the asset on payment of specified rentals over a specified period. An *ijara wa iqtina*, on the other hand, is more like a financing lease. The rentals during the term of the lease are sufficient to amortise the leasing company's investment and provide an element of profit.

Under this mode of financing, the banks would buy the equipment or machinery and lease it out to their clients who may opt to buy the items eventually, in which case the monthly payments will consist of two components, that is, rental for the use of the equipment and instalments towards the purchase price. The original amount of the rent for the leased assets should be fixed in advance, but some incentive related to business success can be added. The client can also negotiate for the purchase of the asset at the end of the period. In such a case, the lease rentals paid in advance will be part of the price less the bank remuneration.

The profit element in an *ijara wa iqtina* is permissible, despite its similarity to an interest charge. According to Islamic jurists, the *shari'ah* allows a fixed charge relating to tangible assets (as opposed to financial assets) because by converting financial capital into tangible assets the financier has assumed risks for which compensation is permissible. An *ijara wa iqtina* can either have a purchase option or a purchase obligation at the end of its term.

Since the distinguishing feature of *ijara* is that the assets remain the property of the Islamic bank, it has to put them up for rent every time the lease period expires so as not to have them remain unutilized for long periods of time. Under this mode of finance, the bank bears the risk of recession or diminishing demand for these assets. Leasing also has been justified on the grounds that by retaining ownership the bank runs the risk of premature obsolescence. The rental equipment is often used in a transient manner, whether the situation is one of 'rental' or 'rent', the lessor is charged with the responsibility for maintenance. In the case of 'rental' especially the lessor is also charged with the responsibility for coping with the product's obsolescence, so that it may be regarded as a service-oriented business.

Islamic leasing is a major activity for Islamic banks. Although used primarily to finance high-valued equipment, such as aircraft, it is also being used increasingly to finance smaller items of equipment, such as medical equipment required by medicos in their private practice, or for purchasing property.

Ijara thumma al-iqtina/al-bai' (Hire Purchase Finance)

This, as we have noted, is one application of *ijara* in modern Islamic banking, when the bank rents the asset to the customer, who promises to purchase the asset within a specified period. The rental payment could be a fixed amount or a percentage directly tied to the cash flow of the project (important for project finance), and consists of the bank's share in the net profit plus the rental charges. When the total rental charge equals the cost of the asset, ownership of the asset transfers to the customer.

Qard hasan (Beneficence Loans)

Recalling our earlier discussion in Chapter 4 on benevolence finance, *qard hasan* is the zero-return type of loans that the Holy Qur'an urges Muslims to make available to those who need them. The borrower is obliged to repay only the principal amount of the loan but is permitted to add a margin at his own discretion. The *qard hasan* borrowers also benefit from various services and financial and moral support rendered by the bank. This loan is often provided to charity institutions for the financing of their activities. Repayments are made over a period agreed by both parties. A levy of a modest service charge on such a loan is permissible provided it is based on the actual cost of administering the loan and is not related to the amount or maturity of the loan.

Qard hasan funding may also be a way of cementing and facilitating existing business relationships. Al-Harran (1993, p. 99) gives examples of circumstances where it might be advisable for Islamic financial institutions to make use of *qard hasan* finance:

1. In the case of *musharaka* between the institution and the client, it often happens that not all of the institution's shares in the project can be earmarked for the right to participate in profits. The institution's participation may be split into two parts: one constitutes a share in the partnership capital, and the other a share in the working capital provided through *qard hasan*. However, under Islamic law, a question

mark would exist about this *qard* because there is benefit derived out of it.

2. A *qard hasan* can also be provided to a client with cash flow problems.
3. A third use of *qard hasan* may occur when a customer who has a blocked savings account, which generates no interest, encounters an urgent need for short-term finance.

Sukuk

All of the instruments so far examined (with the exception of *qard hasan*) feature in the financially engineered technique of *sukuk* (Lewis et al., 2014, pp. 63–4). Commonly referred to as an 'Islamic bond', *sukuk* means participation certificate. Techniques similar to conventional structured finance securities are employed, with *sukuk* akin to pass-through certificates. A *sakk* simply represents a proportional or undivided ownership interest in an asset or pool of assets (McMillen, 2007). Although it is not an essential feature (for they can be held to maturity), Islamic bonds, like conventional bonds, are more useful if they can be traded on the secondary market to gain liquidity. A difficulty, however, is that in Islam, debt obligations can be traded only at face value. Instead, to be traded the bonds must constitute property of an approved asset. Such a bond is obtained through the securitization of the asset, the property of which is divided into equally valued units and incorporated in the *sukuk* certificates (Radzi and Lewis, 2015). The value of the *sukuk* thus remains connected to the value of the underlying asset, the productivity and return of which is linked to the profit of the underlying asset and not to an interest rate (although an interest rate such as the London Interbank Offered Rate, LIBOR, can be used as a benchmark or indicative rate).

Consider, for example, the case of the *sukuk al-ijara*. The originator holds assets (land, buildings, aircraft, ships, and so on) that are to constitute the basis of the returns to the *sukuk* investor. These assets are sold by the originator to a special purpose vehicle (SPV) and then are leased back at a specified rental. The SPV securitizes the assets by issuing *sukuk* certificates that can be purchased by investors. Each *sukuk* certificate represents a share in the ownership of the assets, entitling the investor to periodic distributions from the SPV funded by the originator's rental payments on the leased assets. The returns can be either fixed rate or floating rate (often referenced to LIBOR as a benchmark) depending on the originator.

In fact, the basic structure of a *sukuk* is very flexible and can be varied in a number of ways. The underlying assets that are pooled and securitized can be *ijara*, *murabaha*, *istisnaa* or *musharaka* receivables, or combinations of them, and the rates of return can be fixed, floating or zero coupon. The

Accounting and Auditing Organization for Islamic Financial Institutions (AAOIFI) has issued standards for 14 types of *sukuk* (AAOIFI, 2003). These can be broadly grouped into *sukuk* that bear predetermined returns and *sukuk* that allow for profit and loss sharing. To date, most issued *sukuk* have borne predetermined returns, such as *sukuk al-ijara*.

It is the potential for tradeability that makes for the popularity of *sukuk al-ijara*. *Ijara*, though less commonly employed than *murabaha* as an asset in Islamic banks' balance sheets, offers much greater flexibility for the Islamic bond market due to their legitimate tradeability. Each security called *sukuk al-ijara* represents a pro rata ownership of physical assets embedded in the SPV structure, as compared with a pro rata share in financial claims or debt in the case of *sukuk al-murabaha*. While debt can only be transferred at par, ownership in physical assets can always be transferred at a mutually negotiated price (Obaidullah, 2007). Hence *sukuk al-ijara* allow for creation of a secondary market since they represent a share in the ownership of a physical asset. As such they, along with the other *sukuk* types, constitute a new investment avenue for Islamic banks as well as for investors.

GOVERNMENT FINANCE IN THE WEST

The West has simply got used to governments financing budget deficits by the issue of government bills and bonds to the public. A vast expansion of central banks' balance sheets in the wake of the global financial crisis of 2008, and its aftermath in the form of the pursuit of quantitative easing policies to stimulate sluggish economic growth, has opened up another financing source as central banks have, in effect, printed money and bought government debt.

Only occasionally is concern expressed about this trend, in which it would seem that the 'old world' is rapidly heading into the territory where, as Reinhart and Rogoff (2009, 2011) have documented, unusually high levels of government debt begin to have a long-run impact on economic growth. They identify 90 per cent as an important threshold for the government debt to gross domestic profit (GDP) ratio. When debt is above this level the authors find that median growth rates fall by 1 per cent, and average growth falls by even more. The validity of this finding has been questioned, but Reinhart and Rogoff have two telling rebuttals. First, they do not pretend:

> that growth will be normal at 89 per cent and sub par at 91 per cent of GDP any more than a car crash is unlikely at 54 mph and near certain at 56 mph.

However, mapping the theoretical notion of 'vulnerability regions' to bad outcomes by necessity involves defining thresholds, just as US [United States] traffic signs specify 55 mph. (Reinhart and Rogoff, 2011, pp. 33–4)

Second, they note that, in their large sample of 2317 annual observations for advanced economies (dating back to 1790 in some instances), about 92 per cent of observations fall below the 90 per cent threshold. Only about 2 per cent of their observations are at debt-to-GDP levels at or above 120 per cent. As they observe:

> if debt levels above 90 per cent are indeed as benign as some suggest, one would have expected to see a higher incidence of these over the long course of history . . . if debt to GDP levels over 90 per cent are so benign, then generations of politicians must have been overlooking proverbial money on the street. (Reinhart and Rogoff, 2011)

Far from leaving 'money on the street', the developed world seems to have been catapulted by the 'great recession' into what can only be labelled a 'debt-trap' (Iley and Lewis, 2013, p. 125). As of 2018, debt to GDP ratios for most of the G6 countries are either above or approaching the 90 per cent threshold; in Japan the ratio is over 200 per cent and in Italy it is about 130 per cent. Governments effectively face Hobson's choice. Where austerity has been tried, debt ratios have continued to climb. Where austerity has been skirted, debt ratios have also continued to climb.

In the distant past, a variety of approaches were pursued to reduce debt. Governments often used debasement of coins to finance their budget deficits, which provided temporary relief but caused inflation in the long run. Leasing of state lands against fixed rent was another major and permanent source of revenue. Governments sold lease contracts to landlords or nobles against a certain portion paid upfront in cash. These landlords sometimes were also given responsibility or authority to collect farm taxes from local farmers on behalf of governments. It was customary among landlords to deduct a certain percentage from the collected income as their commission, before remitting the remaining amount to the royal treasuries. Religious forces also permitted and supported rental incomes as an alternative to state loans. Thus, the earlier ban on usury put significant obstacles on the path of fashioning government debt-based financial instruments and systems.

Munro (2003) pointed out that Italy in 1164 was the first European country which established a permanent debt fund in the form of *prestanze* or forced loans. It imposed fixed levies on its general public depending upon their ability to pay. The amount collected was then used to finance wars. Although Italian and other European governments had easy access to *prestanze* contracts and other interest-based loans due to the significant presence of Jewish communities in major urban settlements, such deals apparently did not satisfy the Church and the consciences of religiously motivated traders. Therefore, the authorities had to find alternative but more secure and acceptable anti-usury financial instruments. These efforts resulted in the *rentes* (annuity) contract in the early fifteenth century. The concept was derived from the Old Testament, which allowed demanding a premium price or discount price in the case of lease agreements and linked fair price with the number of years of purchase (Lev. 25:14–17).

Rentes contracts quickly spread across Europe (Munro, 2006). They were designed to resolve the issue of a fixed return against a predefined time period which fell within the definition of usury. According to Christian theology, interest was calculated according to the length of the loan, and it can therefore be considered as a 'theft of time' which belongs to God alone; a serious sin, as we noted in Chapter 3. *Rentes* was not a loan but a legitimate sale contract and a form of public debt as it allowed governments to borrow for indefinite periods. Here the state (by legislation) used excise taxes or consumption taxes to make annual payments. Munro went on to note that, although many theologians criticized *rentes*, Pope Innocent IV as early as 1250 ruled that these contracts cannot be declared usurious, subject to fulfilment of two basic conditions. First, investors did not reclaim their original investments while linking annual rental payments directly with real properties. Second, the Church allowed the state to redeem *rentes* whenever possible but again only at par value. Further, annual rental income must not exceed 10 per cent of the original investment.

Rentes contracts provided guaranteed low risk but a regular stream of income to the general public. From the 1690s *rentes* laid down the foundations of modern public finance, in the form of annuities. Instruments such as *rentes* were like perpetual annuities (or consols) and were redeemable at any time during their lifetime. These contracts were different from loans which have specified expiry dates and are commonly redeemed upon expiry. Further, *rentes* were initially issued by the local governments or on behalf of kings who took personal responsibility for repayments.

Munro (2003) claimed that modern-day interest-bearing public debt is among the few phenomena which are without roots in the ancient world. In the United Kingdom, the first public debt was issued in 1694 when the government borrowed money from the Bank of England[3] to finance the ongoing war with France. The original licence was issued with the permission of Parliament. New debt constituted neither municipal nor private obligations, but national liabilities which were freely negotiable and transferable all over the world. Hamilton (1947) maintained that it was only the British Empire which devised a long-term solution for the ever-increasing expenses of modern warfare. The Empire created a large and diversified customer base for the holding of government debt issues, easily transferable and tradeable through establishing an efficient Stock Exchange in London.

That was the beginning of the golden period of public debt financing in the United Kingdom, and other European countries that also followed the same route. Yet, budgets for a long time were kept under control. For more than a century and a half, beginning roughly with the publication of the *Wealth of Nations* by Adam Smith in 1776 (Smith, 1776 [1937]), both in Britain and in the fledging United States budget deficits and public debt were viewed with disapprobation and resorted to only in emergencies such as wars. Invariably, the resulting debt was retired through budget surpluses in normal times. In Victorian Britain, budget protocol aimed at balancing the annual accounts of the central government at the lowest possible figure (Taylor, 1972, pp. 60–62). Christianity undoubtedly played a significant role in all of this, for this was an era when Protestantism was pervasive in cathedrals, churches and chapels across the country, underpinning 'Victorian values'. In addition, it must be admitted, the gold standard was in full force and kept a leash on government budgets. It was not until 1971 that the link of currencies to gold was finally severed by President Nixon (Lewis and Mizen, 2000, p. 43).

Under well-defined circumstances, government budget deficits can be employed to support economic activity and employment. Yet, the risk remains that, within the modern political decision-making framework, such definitions will be stretched liberally, creating an expanding public sector needing to be financed. In effect, in the words of Buchanan (1992), 'the idealized Keynesian policy set – deficits in depression, surpluses in booms – proved to be unworkable in democratic politics. The regime of apparently permanent debt-financed deficit spending was born' (p. 231). This 'birth' can be said to have led ultimately to the present fiscal dilemma and debt trap.

How can the public finances be brought under control? Here countries come face-to-face with the 'iron law' of economics, for there are only five ways that the government debt:GDP ratio can be brought down (Taylor, 2012):

1. austerity, that is, reduce the numerator by tax increases or spending cuts (including lower entitlement benefits), or both;
2. boost economic growth, that is, increase the denominator;
3. default or debt restructuring;
4. using inflation to lower the real value of the debt (itself a form of taxation on monetary assets);

5. 'financial repression' (creating a captive market for debt amongst households or financial institutions).

The fourth and fifth methods were used extensively in the early post-Second World War years (when many insurance policies were rendered nearly worthless, and savers betrayed), but work best in a closed economy with an unsophisticated financial system. While the first and the second are clearly the preferred options, it is becoming apparent that there are inherent tensions between the two. Austerity has been pursued in the United Kingdom, and in those eurozone economies for which financial assistance has been made conditional upon the implementation of budgetary reforms; but as Iley and Lewis (2013) observed, these economies have discovered that, in the short term at least, contractionary fiscal policy is just that: contractionary.

By elimination, option three – default and debt restructuring – necessarily comes into focus. Greece has already given the eurozone its first sovereign default. History suggests that Greece may not be as 'unique' as eurozone policy-makers would want us to believe. As Reinhart and Rogoff ominously point out: 'the high debts of the First World War and the subsequent debt associated with the Depression of the 1930s were resolved primarily through default and restructuring' (Reinhart and Rogoff, 2011, pp. 37–8).

This last option is unlikely to hold much appeal for the major developed countries, which are then faced with choices. Do they treat unemployment as today's problem, and debt as tomorrow's? Or, by not acting today, do they run the risk of making things much worse tomorrow? Some, we suspect, may be tempted to use 'cheap money' to lower the financing costs of government debt through financial repression, and pass the problem on to future generations. In this case, the assessment in 2011 of Johan Norberg, the Swedish historian, is sobering:

> All governments are betting they can keep borrowing such extraordinary sums at very low rates. But the markets may have other plans. Consider the evolution of this crisis. The crash happened because households consumed too much, sending their debts to the banks. The banks sent the debts to the government and, as we saw with Ireland, even governments might struggle to meet them. So they are sending their debts to the European Union. But to whom will the EU [European Union] send the bills when its credit card is maxed out?
>
> 'The problem with socialism,' Margaret Thatcher once said, 'is that eventually you run out of other people's money.' This time, it is worse: we are running out of our children's money, and our grandchildren's money. (Norberg, 2011, p. 16)

ISLAM AND PUBLIC DEBT

This last observation leads us very conveniently into Islamic attitudes to government budget deficits and public indebtedness. Iqbal and Lewis (2009) considered this subject in some detail, beginning with the basic principles and precedents that have a bearing on the issue of budget deficits. In terms of principles, in Islam, sovereignty belongs to Allah. Therefore, Islamic permissions and prohibitions apply equally to all: the state, legal persons, as well as individuals (Tahir, 1999).

Other than *zakah* transfers to the needy, justice requires that government not burden the general public for the provision of goods the benefits of which accrue only to a select group of people (Tahir, 1999). Public offices are to be construed as a trust. Embezzlement, corruption and waste of public funds are severely reprimanded.

Interest – that is, any stipulated excess (increase) on the principal amount in money lending – is prohibited. The ideal replacement is interest-free loans (*qard hasan*) for a charitable cause, and profit and loss sharing for commercial purposes. Buying and selling and commodity trading are considered different in essence from money lending. Although the determination of price in this activity is left to the mutual agreement of the buyer and seller, there is a difference of opinion on whether deferred payment sales agreed at a price higher than spot are permitted. As we saw above, contemporary Islamic banking legitimizes such activity, but there is at least some evidence that scholars of Maududi's (2002, Vol. 1, p. 251) stature considered such differential doubtful. See also Shaukat (2010) on this point.

In terms of precedents, Muslims look to the *sunna*, the sayings and doings of the Prophet Muhammad for an example. The Prophet borrowed in both cash and kind in his capacity as the leader of Muslim community for emergency needs and public purposes. At times, such borrowing was undertaken to repay maturing loans. The main purpose of borrowing was to fulfil the basic needs (livelihood) of those who sought help from Muhammad as well as to strengthen defence against aggression. There was no coercion involved in such borrowings. The borrowing was undertaken on an interest-free basis and there was no instance of repudiation of borrowing; debts incurred were always repaid. Also, Muhammad left no outstanding borrowings at the time of his death. There is also no indication that any of the borrowings that he took as the head of the Muslim community adversely influenced the political struggle of the community to live life in accordance with its conscience.

In view of the substantial improvement in public finances subsequent to Muhammad, there is no evidence of borrowing during the reign of the four rightly guided Caliphs (Siddiqi, 1996, pp. 77–96). Perhaps for this reason early Islamic writers on public finance such as Abu Yusuf and Abu Ubayd al-Qasim bin Sallam (774–838 CE) are silent on this issue (Islahi, 2005). The earliest writers to talk about borrowing by the state were Abu Yala al-Farra (990–1066 CE) and al-Mawardi (974–1058 CE), who saw it as a last resort in very rare circumstances. Their reasons seem to revolve around apprehension that the authorities may either fail to repay the loans or resort to extra taxation to do so (the burden of debt argument). Nevertheless, public borrowing was seen as permissible should regular income or payments to the *Bayt al-Mal* be temporarily delayed (Islahi, 2005). In this way the Prophet's 'urgent needs' motive was upheld. Because the *Bayt al-Mal* did not operate as a central bank, there was no concept of deficit financing by money creation, as can occur in the present era.

Despite these seemingly clear rules, contemporary *shari'ah* scholars have proven adept at using *ijtihad* (reasoning)[4] to come up with certain asset-based debt to finance public expenditure based on trading, leasing and partnership instruments. While it is not easy to provide outright support or condemnation of many of these instruments by direct reference to the Holy Qur'an or *sunna*, there can be little doubt that their innovation and use has revolutionized Islamic finance generally, and the financing of public expenditures in particular.

Has Islamic finance at last found a solution to the problem of *riba* in the financing of public sector deficits by the issue of government bonds (a practice that was almost universally condemned only two decades ago)? This is an issue that we take up in the next chapter. In the meantime, it can be safely inferred – although with some important qualifications noted from the historical heritage – that budget deficits are permitted in Islam subject to a prohibition upon fixed interest debt. The question at issue that we have deferred to later is the legitimacy in terms of *shari'ah* of the means used in recent innovations to circumvent the prohibition while allowing Islamic bonds (i.e. *sukuk*) to be issued on a regular basis.

Moreover, in addition to the question marks hanging over the *shari'ah* acceptability of some of the sales-based financing techniques and those of Islamic bonds, the intergenerational equity issues posed by the elevated borrowings and debt-to-GDP ratios of developed countries can be discerned in the Holy Qur'an, which places great score on trusteeship and guardianship. To these can be added the voices of Al-Ghazali (1937, 139–44) and Al-Shatibi (n.d., 8–25, 176–86), who listed the objectives of *shari'ah* that lie in protecting religion, life, freedom of conscience, family and property. To these concepts, we can further include the standard of duty and care specified in *shari'ah* in terms of an orphan's property.

The appeal to an orphan, while emotive, has some resonance since at the political decision-making level, the constituency of future generations does not receive the attention that it deserves. By *qiyas* (analogy), it can be said that the economic circumstances of future generations in relation to the current operations of government can be considered akin to the condition of an orphan's property in relation to the guardian or trustee of that property. On this point, one of the relevant injunctions from the Holy Qur'an on this issue is clear: 'Come not nigh to the orphan's property except to improve it until he attains the age of full strength; and fulfil (every) engagement for (every) engagement will be enquired into (on the Day of Reckoning)' (Al-Isrāa, 17:34).

As ordained, the prime task of a trustee is to improve an orphan's property, not detract from it. Only in the case of dire need is the trustee allowed to take even remuneration from the trust. What, it should be asked, are the equivalent circumstances of dire need in the case of a government?

If we recall the precedents of borrowing in the time of the Prophet Muhammad mentioned above, Ghazali and Shatibi's list of the objectives of *shari'ah* proves apposite. Muhammad borrowed to assist the poor or to defend against external aggression; in brief, to protect religion, life and freedom of conscience. In such action, too, the principle of interest-free finance was never compromised. Herein lies the *shari'ah* scope for using public borrowing.

Notably, the verses quoted above call not merely for retention but for an improvement in the orphan's property. To the extent that this obligation means improving living standards through public investment, as Lewis and Algaoud (2001, pp. 99–100, 227–31) contend, this end could be achieved by activating PLS through a variety of operational modes. Those authors suggest that it would seem most fitting to borrow only if the future debt (that is, tax) burden shifted to the future is accompanied by a commensurate benefit accruing to future generations, such as may come from infrastructure projects or public utilities or even defence procurement. These sorts of expenditures lend themselves readily to PLS techniques and other financing methods which are *shari'ah* compatible. One possibility is for the public sector to engage in public–private sector partnership arrangements for the provision of infrastructure (see Grimsey and Lewis, 1999, 2004, 2017). With projects so commercialized, they could conceivably be financed through PLS techniques. Another possibility is for public entities to be corporatized, with shares quoted on the stock market. Then there are other choices. PLS certificates could be floated to finance transport and communications activities, or 'revenue bonds' issued with returns a proportion of operating income. Leasing might also be used to purchase equipment. Goods required for the provision of government services (for example, for hospitals) could be acquired on a *murabaha* mark-up basis with deferred payments if necessary.

However, insofar as improvement through the route of deficit finance is concerned, the answer lies in reflecting on the history of Third World debt (for example, the debt crisis of the early 1980s), let alone the present predicament in the West, if not that of the role (or abuse) of sovereign debt in general in the history of mankind. It comes as no surprise therefore in the precedents of the classical caliphate, in whose time a broad tax system had become established, that we find no instance of borrowing. This is irrespective of the fact that Umar bin Khattab wished to build long-distance roads in compliance with Muhammad's developmental vision narrated in *Bukhari* (FN, p. 34), namely that the day is not far when a woman shall travel from Hirah (in Iraq) to Makkah – a distance of more than 1500 km – fearing none but Allah. It can safely be presumed that Umar was depending on taxes. In reaching this conclusion, Iqbal and Lewis (2009) are encouraged from the fact that many dams, canals and roads were completed during the early caliphate without need of debt financing.

THE UNEVEN PATH OF ISLAMIC FINANCING

Since we have been examining Islamic public debt and will be considering the legitimacy of Islamic finance in the next chapter, our comments relate to Islam. Muslims had an initial edge in developing various sophisticated financial instruments at least three to four centuries before medieval Europe. In later centuries, Muslims failed to maintain this pace. Why did Muslim trading practices remain unchanged as late as the sixteenth century, and why did they fail to evolve credit schemes or banking institutions as in Europe?

Udovitch (1975) pointed out that Muslims mostly confined their financial and trading transactions to personal interactions. There were no specialized banking institutions to support their commercial activities, since Muslim traders mostly served as their own bankers. Another contributing factor may have been that Islamic debt instruments were only negotiable or transferable at par value. Sale of debt at a discount or premium was not religiously permissible, which militates against a secondary market for the Islamic debt instruments.

Kuran (2005) explored why the Islamic world did not develop anything similar to the corporation. He argued that Islamic classical law only recognizes flesh-and-blood individuals as natural persons. The concept of an artificial person (that is, a corporation) was religiously objectionable to Muslim jurists even when its acceptability in the global economy was expanding. Partnership rules remained unchanged and partnerships were rendered null and void with either the withdrawal or the death of even a single partner. This vulnerability in partnerships discouraged long-lasting and large-scale business ventures. Reinforcing this factor, the inheritance system, as discussed before, discouraged the accumulation of wealth in Muslim societies. The result was small and short-term partnerships among Muslims. By contrast, in Europe families tended to have less children and Christian canon law did not standardize the inheritance system. This freedom made it relatively easy in Europe to keep properties and wealth intact as compared to the Muslim East.

Muslims, however, did eventually overcome their inheritance problems in the shape of the cash *waqf*, introduced under the Ottoman Empire in the sixteenth century. The cash *waqf* was a separate identity established for an infinite life span. Once created, it could not be dissolved and was considered as an alternative institution to partnerships, which dissolved at the death of any partner. Cash *waqf* were more like separate endowment funds in order to make investments and generate income distributed among its nominated families, or used for public welfare. *Waqf* were initially established to create income from physical assets. Cash *waqf* started a new debate among Islamic scholars as to whether cash collected under them could be invested in commercial ventures. Traders normally invested this money to finance their long-distance trade and tax farming (Pamuk, 2004).

Cash *waqf* was probably the only innovation introduced in Islamic partnerships over the centuries. During the Ottoman Empire the ability to shelter wealth from external forces made cash *waqf* popular, despite resistance from some religious corners. Lending operations under a cash *waqf* were confined among individuals or family members. Another shortfall of cash *waqf* was that it, unlike moneylenders, could not pool resources for larger investments or financings. These limitations eventually stopped cash *waqf* from transforming into an independent banking system. Kuran (2002) further explored the role of *kadis* (judges) who supervised the operations of *waqf* institutions and drew salaries for services. They supported the status quo, adding further resistance to converting *waqf* into proper commercial organizations.

As our earlier discussion makes clear, finance in the Muslim world is nowadays very different, with the revival of interest-free instruments under the aegis of Islamic banking. Public debt management has also changed, and some Muslim countries have started using *sukuk* (Islamic bonds) to finance budget deficits as an alternative to traditional interest-based bonds. For instance, the Central Bank of Bahrain sells state-owned assets to investors (Islamic banks) against up-front payment to the Treasury.

State-owned assets are transferred to investors after a period of three months, but immediately the Treasury buys back the same assets at a higher price, with the difference in sale and purchase price representing the return on investments to the Islamic banks. The Central Bank of Bahrain uses these contracts to absorb excess liquidity from the market. Importantly, these contracts are asset-backed and generally considered *shari'ah* (Islamic law) compliant (Wilson, 2008). However, many later *sukuk* are not asset-backed, but asset-based, raising issues of their true legitimacy (Radzi and Lewis, 2015). This is an issue taken up in the next chapter, along with other similar concerns about the legitimacy of Islamic debt-based instruments.

NOTES

1. The Ricciardi family of Lucca was among the prominent wool merchants during the thirteenth century. The English monarchs also officially appointed this family as royal banker during that period.
2. An exception to this is the *inan sharikat a'mal (abdan)* partnership where partners contribute labour. One partner can bind the others in undertaking to perform work for an employer, and each is entitled to claim the total salary due from the employer.
3. The Bank of England was founded in 1694 to act as the government's banker and debt manager (http://www.bankofengland.co.uk/about/pages/history/default.aspx).
4. The Holy Qur'an provides guidance, together with the *hadith*, the sayings and deeds of the Prophet. This guidance is eternal and unchanging, but over time, as societies and economies evolve, the interpretation and application of Islamic teaching may change. Through a process known as *ijtihad* or reasoning, Islamic scholars versed in *fiqh*, Islamic jurisprudence attempt to ascertain how Islamic teaching should apply in circumstances which are very different to those prevailing at the time of the Prophet (Wilson, 2014).

9. The future of interest-free financing

INTRODUCTION

At the time of writing (September 2018), the Banking Royal Commission is still under way in Australia (the Hayne Inquiry). So far (and there is no guarantee that more revelations will not unfold) the banks stand accused of – and have admitted to – mortgage fraud, bribery, false documentation, failure to verify borrowing customers' income, not assessing expenses, inadequacy of internal controls to remediate breaches of duty, and failures to report misconduct to the corporate regulator. As noted earlier, they also sold 'dud' insurance policies against which claims were delayed or denied, and rewarded mortgage brokers with generous up-front and trailing commissions. The banks' own loan officers were given cash rewards for writing loans, paid in white (rather than brown) envelopes. Then there were the multi-million-dollar bonuses and salaries paid to senior executives. After such a catalogue, it is easy to understand why usurers have been vilified over the centuries.

Yet, despite some protestations about bank and financial behaviour from both the general public and the Churches, it would seem that there is no turning back and the battle against usury (certainly) and usurious practices (probably) has been lost in the Christian West (although it is no longer predominantly practising Christian, except for the United States). And there are many, steeped in conventional economics, who would say that this result is not unwelcome. Echoing the views of Jeremy Bentham, they would argue that attempts to ban even excessive interest and lending charges would do more harm than good.

Judaism, for its part, has been able to use the 'Deuteronomic double standard' to charge interest to Gentiles. Indeed, some rabbinical scholars see it as the duty of Jews to do so in order to reinforce bonds within the Jewish community. In the case of loans made to fellow Jews, rabbis and sages have had to grapple with *avak ribbit*, literally 'the dust of interest', and for their solution to this matter rely on the formation of partnerships, and pseudo-interest, to legitimize lending which takes place effectively on a non-interest-free basis.

This leaves Islam. Amongst the Abrahamic religions, it remains the sole proponent of interest-free finance. Can it, going forward, sustain its prohibition upon interest? In fact, it can be argued – and has been by some Islamic scholars – that the prohibition has already been significantly undermined through the process of *ijtihad* by jurists keen to facilitate the ambitions of the Islamic banking and finance industry. Islam, in effect, also has its own sprinkling of the 'dust of interest' to deal with, and this issue will form the bulk of this final chapter.

Three questions will occupy us in the remainder of this chapter:

1. Why have interest-based financial transactions, such as in evidence today in conventional finance, proven so seductive and difficult to resist?
2. What problems have emerged in the application of Islamic financing principles, and what decisions have been taken to resolve these matters?
3. Where is Islamic financing heading; in particular, is it moving away from or toward an emphasis on interest?

WHY IS INTEREST-BASED FINANCING SO ATTRACTIVE?

Since neither of us are psychologists, we cannot with any authority evaluate what factors motivate decision-makers to prefer interest over non-interest financing. As economists, however, we can look to contract theory to suggest some answers to the question posed. An obvious factor is that interest-based finance dominates in the West and, as a consequence, in international financial markets. As a matter of common sense and practicality, it is generally less costly to borrow and lend in the largest financial markets, using well-established and thus interest-based transacting modes.

However, this explanation merely begs the question of why interest financing developed in the first place. In view of the punishments that faced usurers in medieval times, there must be compelling reasons as to why borrowers and lenders were drawn to this form of transacting. Here we turn to the theory of contract design. One result that has emerged from the contract design literature is that debt contracts are often optimal transacting vehicles because they minimize the costs associated with asymmetric information and/or unobserved actions. Three circumstances have been the subjects of examination, in terms of costly verification, moral hazard and adverse selection, that is, the information problems that beset financing.[1]

Information Issues

First, there are search costs. Potential transactors must search out, obtain information about, select, meet and negotiate with potential other parties to a contract. Second, there are verification costs. These arise from evaluating borrowing proposals when lenders are unable to assess the future prospects of a borrower accurately, particularly when some borrowers may have an incentive to paint an overly optimistic picture of the future. Adverse selection can occur when an asymmetry in information costs exists due to lenders' inability to observe the attributes of borrowers and the contingencies under which they operate. Third, monitoring costs are incurred when overseeing the actions of the borrower for consistency with the terms of the contract, and ensuring that any failure to meet the delivery promised is for genuine reasons. Moral hazard refers to the problems which may flow from the inability of lenders to ascertain and exercise control over the behaviour of borrowers, either with respect to the choice of investment project or the effort and diligence with which the business is managed. Fourth, enforcement costs arise should the borrower be unable to meet the commitments as promised, and a solution must be worked out between the borrower and lender or other aspects of the contract (for example, collateral) may need to be drawn upon. The nature of the contract influences these aspects.[2]

Verification

Verification is needed when there exists hidden information about the borrower's circumstances which must be uncovered by the lender, and/or information provided verified, and any changes in circumstances monitored, all of which is costly and time-consuming. Costly verification and/or monitoring points to the optimality of the 'standard debt contract', as it is known in the literature, in which the borrower pays the lender a fixed payment for good outcomes, when no verification or monitoring takes place, but must hand over the whole proceeds in the event of a bad outcome when the fixed repayment cannot be met and bankruptcy occurs. This result harks back to the pioneering analysis of Gale and Hellwig (1985).

Moral Hazard

Hidden actions or moral hazard point as well to the optimality of the same type of contract: a requirement to make debt payments independently of the state of the world may be a check against moral hazard. This issue has been analysed within the principal–agent framework. The principal–agent literature[3] is concerned with how a principal can design a contract which motivates another, his agent, to act in the principal's interests. A problem arises when there is imperfect information, concerning what action the agent has undertaken or should undertake. Obviously, in many situations, the actions are not easily observable. Should there be the possibility that output depends on the agent's hidden actions which the principal finds costly to monitor, then there is a moral hazard problem, identified by Kenneth Arrow (1964). The hidden action is usually the agent's choice of endeavour, and the moral hazard problem occurs if the agent reduces effort on the grounds that some (perhaps most) of any extra effort would accrue to the principal. If output is observable at no cost and the agent's wealth provides no binding constraint, Harris and Raviv (1979) show that moral hazard over an agent's level of effort in the face of costly monitoring leads to an optimal contract in which the agent makes a fixed payment in all states of nature. This contract form gives the entrepreneur the appropriate incentive to work by rewarding him with all of the marginal returns beyond the fixed repayment amount specified in the contract.

Verification costs and moral hazard both tend to encourage the parties involved to make debt contracts. Debt contracts are preferable under these conditions because they reduce the impact of hidden information (since it will often not matter *ex post* that the investor does not directly see the output) and also of moral hazard (since debt gives the entrepreneur a strong incentive to work hard and capture the residual returns).

Adverse Selection

Debt contracts may also be optimal, in certain circumstances, when there is the problem of adverse project selection: some important feature of the investor's project (or choice of project) is not observed by the investor. One such situation is where the investor does not observe the (appropriately defined) 'quality' of the project. In this case, debt contracts are still optimal over a wide range of circumstances (Innes, 1993; Dowd, 1996). The reason is that the entrepreneurs with better-quality projects would prefer debt contracts to maximise their residual profits, while the entrepreneurs with poor-quality projects would need to imitate them so as to avoid revealing themselves.

However, there can also be adverse selection relating to the riskiness of the investment project, and then debt contracts may no longer be optimal. In this situation, equity contracts involving profit and loss sharing (PLS) eliminate (or at least substantially reduce) the possibility that the entrepreneur could pass expected losses back to the investor. The investor now gets a given proportion of the net income from the project, and so the entrepreneur cannot manipulate the investor's expected profit or loss by choosing a more risky project. Since profits are shared, if the entrepreneur chooses a project to maximize his own expected profit, he also maximizes the investor's expected profit as well. The investor would then have no reason to object to the project choice even if he somehow got to find out what it was. The equity contract thus gets around the problem posed by adverse project selection and delivers the best result.

Note that this outcome depends on the output from the project being verifiable at negligible cost. If output is not verifiable at all, the entrepreneur could reduce the pay-off to the investor by declaring that output was lower than it actually was, and the investor would never be able to prove that he was lying. In fact, the entrepreneur would always want to declare that output was at its minimum possible level. Knowing that he had this incentive, the investor would presumably prefer to not invest, or at least, to invest elsewhere.

In such circumstances, contract choice may act as an important signalling device. When entrepreneurs know better than lenders of the riskiness of the projects they want to finance, one response of lenders envisaged in the literature is for them to offer contracts designed to encourage entrepreneurs to self-select appropriately. An additional consideration will be the extent of 'insider equity', signalling the degree to which proprietors are prepared to back their own ventures. Other things equal, the larger is inside equity, the safer is the venture to finance.

Collateral

In a similar vein, the extent and quality of collateral also acts as a screening device aimed at selecting the honest entrepreneur (profitable project) from the dishonest one. An entrepreneur who is convinced that the project is profitable will be prepared to offer collateral as security. Otherwise he will not risk his personal wealth, unless he chooses to engage in a strategic default, that is, the value of the collateral is lower than the expected extent of the default. Collateral thus has the potential of reducing the adverse selection problem, and by choosing the amount of collateral, a bank will be able to screen the riskiness of the entrepreneur, who is obliged to identify their risk attributes from the extent of collateral offered.

Other Factors

Of course, the real difficulty comes when all of the conditioning factors – costly verification, adverse selection, monitoring costs, moral hazard, enforcement costs, bankruptcy costs and risk aversion – are examined simultaneously (which is not and probably cannot be done theoretically). Bank contracting choice is complicated further by the fact that the institution must design contracts suited to both borrowers and depositors, and additional work in this field has attempted to identify the optimal form of the financial contract between lender (bank) and entrepreneur, and between depositor and bank simultaneously (Williamson, 1987 [1995]). For example, equity is a more flexible risk-sharing contract than debt, and the possibility of making the payment to the lender different in each state of the world reduces the borrowers' probability of bankruptcy. But depositors cannot observe directly the lending investments. Since the bank's pay-offs cannot be credibly revealed, depositors seem unlikely to accept claims which promise returns contingent on what is, in effect, private information. As before, a borrower's risk of bankruptcy may then be reduced by ensuring that repayments to the bank may be as unvarying as possible, subject to the borrower's ability to repay. Once again, the standard fixed (or predetermined) interest rate debt contract emerges as the optimal arrangement.

COMPARING DEBT AND EQUITY CONTRACTS

While many economists (e.g., Dowd, 1996) take comfort from the fact that debt contracts are defensible in theory, given that they figure so prominently in real-world financial arrangements and have done so for a very long time in conventional banking markets, the result is rather less than reassuring from the viewpoint of interest-free financing under Islamic banking. The standard debt (*riba*) contract, collateral requirements, loan covenants and enforced workouts – measures designed to ameliorate adverse selection and moral hazard – are all prohibited in Islam. Islamic banks go beyond pure financial intermediation of the traditional sort and have direct participation in business and investments with profit and loss sharing along equity lines as reflected, for example, in the *mudaraba* arrangement.

The contrast between this type of contract and the standard debt contract is sharp, and can be formalized as follows (Karsten, 1982). Let P_0 denote the amount of principal lent to the borrower in period t_0 and P_1 the agreed amount of capital that has to be returned in t_1. If $P_1 > P_0$, then the difference between P_1 and P_0 is the additional amount (*riba*), or interest in the orthodox Islamic sense:

$$r = P_1 - P_0 \qquad\qquad (9.1)$$

Profits and losses (*PL*) involve an element of uncertainty. Each partner in a *mudaraba* business is sharing an agreed proportion φ of the expected difference between total revenues *R* and total cost *C*. Expected profits (π) for a participant in a joint venture are consequently:

$$\pi = \phi \, E \, (R - C) = \phi \, E \, (PL) \qquad (9.2)$$

where *E* denotes expected value. Revenues can be shared on a pro rata basis among the various units of production after deducting incurred expenses. The distribution of profit shares is determined by a bargaining process between the investor (borrower) and the bank and, in turn, between the saver and the bank under a 'two-tiered' or 'triple' *mudaraba*. But, in comparison with interest, profit is not predetermined and fixed, but is uncertain and variable, and may even be negative.

Under what circumstances might this PLS contract be regarded as superior to the standard debt contract? This is the question address by W.M. Khan (1985, 1987). He sets out to compare the 'fixed return scheme' (FRS) of debt contracts with the 'variable return scheme' (VRS) of Islamic *mudaraba* partnerships. Initially he assumes that monitoring costs are zero, that is, both lender and entrepreneur can observe without cost the realized return on a project, and that the return is independent of the way the project is financed. Also assumed is the existence of a large number of mutually uncorrelated investment projects and the ability of lenders to put infinitely small amounts of money into each project. This allows lenders to diversify away all risk so that, if interest rates and profit-sharing ratios are set such that the expected returns in the FRS and VRS are equivalent, lenders will be indifferent between the two schemes. Borrowers' preferences then determine the choice between the two financing modes. For risk-neutral borrowers the choice does not matter; the standard Modigliani–Miller (1958) irrelevance theorem holds. However, if borrowers are risk-adverse (which, given mutually uncorrelated investment projects, is relevant because they are not allowed to diversify across projects), then the VRS is superior to the FRS and full equity is also superior to any combination of debt and equity, since equity spreads risk more optimally than debt. The VRS dominates the FRS because under the former the lender in effect shares some of the risk which under the latter is borne entirely by the entrepreneur.

Obviously, monitoring costs must be introduced into the analysis, and Khan then goes on to discuss extensions of some models, notably Stiglitz (1974), Jensen and Meckling (1976), and Grossman and Hart (1983) in which lenders can observe the outcome of investment projects only at a cost, and there is a trade-off between the incentive effects of debt and the benefits of risk-spreading under equity. These models are used to show that expected monitoring costs are in general lower under the FRS than the VRS. The intuitive explanation is that in the fixed return scheme only reported returns below the fixed interest rate are regarded as suspicious by the lenders. The choice of the FRS versus the VRS depends on the costs of less than optimal risk-sharing versus the benefits of less monitoring costs in the FRS. If the degree of risk-aversion is low, the FRS dominates.

In summary, the overall comparison between the two contract types involves a trade-off between lower monitoring costs under FRS conditions and better risk-sharing under VRS arrangements. The frequency of use of debt contracts in practice is presumably explained by supposing that the former often outweigh the latter (Ahmed, 1989). But, equally, there undoubtedly exist situations where this position is reversed, establishing at least a theoretical case for partnership-style Islamic banking practices for certain types of projects where monitoring and evaluation can be undertaken with relative ease. For this theoretical case to be realized in practice, however, clear contracting arrangements and monitoring procedures would need to be put in place. One way in which this might occur is through the development of *musharaka*, where the bank can bring in technical assistance in the form of preparing feasibility studies, planning, coordinating and managing project development. Another is by putting in place more sophisticated regulatory auditing procedures; for example, Khan's (1994) proposal for mandatory performance auditing.

The 'Religious Variable'

What may be termed the 'religious variable' may act as a counter to the incentive difficulties. Indeed, certain Muslim economists have argued that in a proper Islamic economic environment, incentive problems will not exist. In effect, Islamic religious ideology acts as its own enforcement mechanism to reduce the inefficiency that arises from the asymmetrical information and moral hazard. Their argument is twofold. On the one hand, the writers contend that an Islamic bank will overcome these problems by eliciting the right amount of information when a *mudaraba* contract is written so that it specifies the appropriate level of the actions of the entrepreneurs. The argument that an Islamic bank will induce full information in the contract is advanced, for example, by Nadeem Ul Haque and Abbas Mirakhor (1986). They argue that Islamic banking will overcome the problem of moral hazard by means of a profit-sharing contract:

> such that all relevant information is used to deduce the state that is realised when, in fact, it is realised. To this end an incentive compatibility constraint,

which is essentially like a truth-telling constraint, is utilised. Such a contract can be written to ensure that in each state the desired level of investment takes place. (Ibid., p. 12)

At the same time, these authors maintain that, in an Islamic society, the actions of the entrepreneur are shaped by the Islamic normative system, which will restrict him from acting contrary to what is socially acceptable. Thus, the argument given by Muslim scholars for the absence of incentive problems in Islamic banking is that the Islamic moral code will prevent Muslim entrepreneurs from behaving in ways that are ethically unsound. In effect, Islamic ideology will act in a way that minimizes the transaction costs arising from incentive issues, because a Muslim entrepreneur will always act honestly. As has been stated:

> to remain faithful to the terms specified in the contract, so much so that faithfulness to the terms of contracts is considered a distinguishing characteristic of a Muslim. The maxim that 'Muslims are bound by the stipulations' is recognised by all schools of Islamic thought. (Ibid., pp. 3–4)

Those of us who believe that the 'dark' side of human nature is not so easily overcome will likely remain sceptical about the universality of the religious variable. Precepts developed from a close-knit tribal society do not always carry over readily to an international context where transactors have no personal links and can ignore approbation.

In the absence of such mechanisms, an Islamic bank may be obliged to restrict the use of *mudaraba* and (to a lesser extent) *musharaka* contracts and instead provide funds by using other available financial instruments, where incentive problems are less serious and returns are more predictable and losses less likely. With *mudaraba* and *musharaka* downplayed as investment avenues, other financial instruments that can be used by the Islamic bank include mark-up (*murabaha*), and leasing and lease-purchase *ijara*, *ijara wa iqtina*). The characteristics of these instruments are much more similar to those provided by the traditional banking system, as we argue below. For Muslim investors another investment has opened up in the form of Islamic investment funds.

ISLAMIC INVESTMENT FUNDS

Islamic investment funds, like any investment pooling system, collect individual savings for investment and the sharing of benefits. Those subscribing capital to the pool receive documentation evidencing their subscription (certificates, units or shares), entitling them to a pro rata share of the profits (or losses) of the fund. Each fund consequently has its own idiosyncratic structure, capital, subscription, maturity and expected returns and risks.

There is some commonality, at least among the Islamic investment funds, for in order to be described as Islamic, the purpose of the investment must be to earn *halal* profits in conformity with the precepts of *shari'ah*, as interpreted by *fiqh*. While the funds may take many different forms, two essential conditions must be met. First, neither the principal amount nor the rate of return can be guaranteed. Instead, the units must carry a pro rata share of the actual profits earned by the fund and not a fixed return tied to the face value of the certificates. Second, the funds gathered in the pool must be invested in business and activities acceptable to Islamic principles. To this end the funds have a team of *shari'ah* advisors, either internal or external (outsourced via specialized consultancy firms), to advise on *shari'ah* compliance.

There are several types of Islamic investment funds including equity funds, *ijara* funds, commodity funds, real estate funds, *murabaha* funds, money market funds and mixed funds, embodying very different patterns of returns. Of the different types of Islamic investment funds, those involving equity investment are the single largest category and constitute 35 per cent of the total funds (Muhamed and Lewis, 2014). They take a variety of forms such as global funds, regional funds, sector funds, country funds, hedge funds and index funds, for example, the Dow Jones Islamic Market (DJIM) index fund. Whatever their form, however, they pose special issues.

Those wanting to invest in equities want access to the bigger and most liquid markets, and wish to hold the stock of the best companies. If such funds were confined to 'listed Islamic corporations', the number of funds would be a small fraction of those on offer. In order to gain a wide range of investments, necessary for diversification and liquidity, most investment has to take place through the major global and regional exchanges. However, the reality is that almost all the companies quoted on current stock markets are in some way engaged in an activity which violates the injunctions of *shari'ah*, and they cannot be expected to restructure their operations in order to suit Muslim investors (likely a small minority). If so, can it ever be acceptable to invest in them under *shari'ah* (Hasan, 1995)?

Quite clearly, dealing in the supply, manufacture or service of things prohibited by Islam (*haram*), such as *riba*, pork meat, alcohol, gambling and so on, cannot be condoned. Nevertheless, companies that are not involved directly in such *haram* activities could be considered acceptable. The main objection against them is that in their own internal accounting and financial dealings they lend and borrow from *riba* banks and other institutions, but the fact remains that their main business operations do not involve prohibited activities. Essentially, non-Muslim entities cannot be expected to work under the Islamic code of conduct, and in any case only a negligible amount of interest may be involved. Can such activities ever be considered 'Islamic'?

Such issues have led to an extensive debate amongst *shari'ah* experts (Usmani, 2001). Some said no, that it is not allowable for a Muslim to deal in the shares of such a company, even if its main business is *halal*. Their basic argument is that every shareholder of a company is a *sharik* (partner) of the company, and every *sharik*, according to Islamic jurisprudence, is an agent for the other partners in the matters of the joint business, and by implication would be giving consent to un-Islamic transactions. Other *shari'ah* scholars, who are in the majority, do not endorse this view. They contend that a joint stock company is basically different from a simple partnership. Being composed of a large number of shareholders, a company cannot give veto power to each shareholder, as would occur in a partnership. Consequently, if a company is engaged in a *halal* business, but also keeps its surplus money in an interest-bearing account, from which a small incidental interest income is received, this fact does not render all of the business of the company unlawful. In this case, where income from the interest-bearing activities and accounts is incorporated, the proportion of such income in the dividend paid to the Islamic shareholders must be given by them to charity. For example, if 5 per cent of the whole income of a company has come out of interest-bearing returns, 5 per cent of the dividend must be given in charity. This process is known as 'purification'. However, it must be preceded by 'screening' of the relevant company's business activities.

Screening takes place in two stages. First, the primary business of the company must be *halal* (permissible). Second, financial screens are then applied to screen out companies with unacceptable financial ratios:

- companies for which total debt divided by trailing 12-month average market capitalization is 33 per cent or more;
- companies for which cash plus interest-bearing securities divided by trailing 12-month average market capitalization is 33 per cent or more; and
- companies for which accounts receivables divided by 12-month average market capitalization is 33 per cent or more.

Next, there is reported a dividend cleansing/impure income figure. Here 'tainted dividend' receipts relate to the portion, if any, of a dividend paid by a constituent company that has been determined to be attributable to activities that are not in accordance with *shari'ah* principles and therefore

Religion and finance

should be donated to a proper charity or charities. Such cleansing cannot be counted as part of *zakat* obligations. In this and other matters, the index compilers are advised by *shari'ah* scholars.

Nonetheless, significant differences remain amongst the *shari'ah* scholars in two main respects. There are differences of opinion about 'purification'; in particular the scholars differ about whether the purification is necessary where the profits are made through capital gains (that is, by purchasing the shares at a lower price and selling them at a higher price). Some scholars are of the view that even in the case of capital gains, the process of purification is necessary, because the market price of the share may reflect an element of interest included in the assets of the company. The other view is that no purification is required if the share is sold, even if it results in a capital gain. The reason is that no specific amount of the price can be allocated for the interest received by the company (Usmani, 2001).

While there is general acceptance of these procedures, in our view they can still be questioned in two respects. First, our belief is that the *shari'ah* scholars have taken the easy way out, by focusing on what Muhamed and Lewis call the 'negatives', the four well-known prohibitions that apply to Islamic financing. These relate to:

- elements of interest (*riba*);
- uncertainty (*gharar*);
- gambling (*maysir*);
- prohibition of certain goods (such as alcohol and pork).

The 'screening' is based around excluding investments in which these activities are prominent.

Just as important, but less well publicized in comparison to the four well-known prohibitions, are the positive principles that ought to (and desirably, should) feature in Islamic economic and commercial activities. These are obligations both to humanity and society and also to humanity and the environment, along with decision-making rules. These are the 'positives', namely:

- promotion of justice (*adl*) and honesty and trust (*amanah*);
- involvement in decision-making and governance (*shura*);
- supervision, follow-up and monitoring (*hisba*);
- purification of wealth (*zakat*) and voluntary almsgiving (*sadaqah*);
- brotherhood and the advancement of the Islamic community (*umma*);
- protection of nature and the environment.

Lewis (2010) argued that Islamic investment fund managers should, in the words of the 1940s pop song, 'accentuate the positive'.[4] However, this is a hint that the funds have studiously ignored, in contrast to Western ethical investment funds that have pursued an activist, moral agenda.

A corollary of these positive elements is that Muslims cannot be disinterested investors, buying and selling shares and making investments without knowledge of the underlying business activities. By implication, since many individuals invest their savings through institutional investment vehicles, the fund managers must perform these roles on behalf of the capital providers by monitoring activities, engaging with investee companies, and contributing to the enhancement of social welfare and the environment. Some do, but regrettably most do not. Instead, they simply observe the negative stipulations regarding *riba*, *gharar*, *maysir* and *haram* activities.

A second criticism of Islamic investment funds comes from the different screening procedures being followed in the market. Muhamed and Lewis (2014) demonstrate that, in general, in terms of the screening of equity, Securities Commission Malaysia has been seen as utilizing the most lenient approach in the case of companies with mixed business, as compared to the Dow Jones indices that use a stricter approach. Securities Commission Malaysia from November 2013, for example, provides: (1) two different tolerance benchmarks for business activities: 5 per cent and 20 per cent on mixed activities of investee companies; and (2) one tolerance benchmark for financial ratios: 33 per cent on cash placed in conventional accounts and instruments over total assets, and 33 per cent on interest-bearing debt over total assets. A notable illustration is that, according to Securities Commission Malaysia, the alcohol-providing hotel industry when part of a mixed business is permissible based on their 20 per cent benchmark, for the reason that it provides *maslaha* (good deeds) to the public. Despite what may seem anomalies to some, it does seem more likely that a higher proportion of Malaysian companies operating in the Malaysian context will be *shari'ah*-compliant relative to companies that operate in Western markets. This expectation is supported by the numbers. As at 31 May 2013, 801 stocks in Malaysia (88 per cent of total listed stocks, accounting for more or less 64 per cent of market capitalization), were classified as *shari'ah*-compliant (Securities Commission Malaysia, 2013), giving perhaps a misleading impression of the extent of religious fervour amongst Malaysian companies.

ISSUES ABOUT ISLAMIC DEBT INSTRUMENTS

Conceptually the essence of Islamic finance is that loans should be made free of interest for charitable bodies, and on a PLS basis for commercial purposes. In practice, however, PLS instruments are in reality employed sparingly. Instead, a variety of debt or quasi-debt financing modes are used, designed to be based around trading activities, and involving a pre-agreed profit-sharing formula. These financing modes were developed once it was realized that partnership arrangements that arose in the context of a more simple, tribal community cannot be used, at least exclusively, when confronted by the peculiarities of a modern economy in which financing is separated both in distance and time, and transactors may not be known to each other. This posed a challenge to a system dedicated to making interest-free financing a reality, which was eventually met by adapting, for financing purposes, permissible trading contracts originally designed for the buying and selling of real goods.

Broadly speaking, as outlined in the previous chapter, the prevailing instruments of interest-free finance along these lines relevant for financing can be divided into three categories: the different buying-and-selling arrangements, most notably *murabaha*, adapted for credit financing through the process of *ijtihad* in the last three decades; leasing (rental) operations; and, more recently, Islamic bonds (*sukuk*). Islamic intellectuals, jurists and bankers have spent much effort examining the legitimacy of particular transactions and formalizing procedures. Nevertheless, we have some unease when the results are set out in the full light of day.

Murabaha

In the classical interpretation, this instrument was meant for engagement in the real business of buying and selling (Lewis, 2008), in which a seller discloses his cost of goods to a buyer and a mark-up is mutually agreed in lieu of profit for the seller. These concepts, combined and adapted for Islamic banking, allow a prospective trader or a potential real asset purchaser to approach a bank, specifying his need for a real good. The bank purchases the asset and on-sells it to him, adding its mark-up covering deferred payment and the risk that it takes in owning the goods between the original purchase and its on-selling to the customer. *Murabaha* and other mark-up instruments represent 86 per cent of financing in Islamic banks in the Middle East and North Africa, 70 per cent in East Asia, 92 per cent in South Asia, and 56 per cent in sub-Saharan Africa (Dusuki, 2007).

What makes the transaction Islamically legitimate in *fiqh* (Islamic jurisprudence) is that the bank first acquires the asset for resale at profit, so that a commodity is sold for money and the operation is not a mere exchange of money for money. In the process the bank assumes the risk of prices changing between purchase and resale and has to take responsibility for the goods before they are safely delivered to the client. Such services are regarded as different in kind from that of a pure loan.

The difficulty was that bankers, not being traders as such, felt themselves ill equipped to bear these risks, even though the sale transactions and the attendant risks actually legitimized their returns. The first step in converting the original *murabaha* into a vehicle for financing was to make the extension of credit an essential feature of the transaction, by having the *murabaha* concluded as deferred payment instead of cash settlement. The second step was to require that the sale contract be preceded by the customer's promise to buy the desired goods, upon acquisition by the financier.

To achieve these ends, the following actions have been found to be possible within the premises of Islamic law. The client can be appointed as the bank's agent to purchase the goods so that there is no risk of purchasing something that the client may not want, or that does not conform to the required specifications. As soon as goods are purchased, they are immediately sold without delay to the customer on a cost plus mark-up basis. Our concern is that, however this transaction is wrapped up, these actions reduce the bank's risk to a minimum and its return becomes effectively fixed and predetermined, as it might under an interest-based loan.

Ought this reality simply be conceded? In this respect, the following 'Man from Mars' observation is offered by Shamin Siddiqui (2014, p. 126) in his chapter in the *Handbook on Islam and Economic Life*. He writes:

From this author's experience of teaching Islamic economics for twenty years students in almost every class commented that they do not see any difference between buying a car through an Islamic bank on deferred sale with higher than cash price and buying a car after borrowing money on interest from a bank. Are they all like those who are prostrated by the devil's touch? Why don't we just take the most obvious meaning of the word trade (*bai*)? That is, buying something and selling it at a profit. One can make money through this trade or lending money on interest. The former is permitted in Islam and every other religion while the latter was once prohibited by all monotheistic religions and even in Hinduism. Does it make sense that on one hand Islam requires 0 per cent interest on cash loans but allows any rate of (effective) interest rate through deferred payment sale?

Leasing Operations (*ijara*)

With *ijara*, ownership and the responsibility that brings remains with the lessor, and its usufruct is transferred to the lessee for specified rental payments incorporating profit. Profits earned by the Islamic bank from the lease are permissible, despite the obvious similarity of the profit rate to an interest charge. According to jurists, *shari'ah* allows a fixed charge relating to tangible assets because the financier has assumed risks for which compensation is permissible and these risks legitimize the profits obtained. Conditions which attach to *ijara* clarify the risks to the lessor: first, the duty of repair is incumbent upon the lessor; second, the lessee is free to cancel the lease if the usufruct proves less beneficial than expected; and third, the price of the asset at the termination of the lease period cannot be fixed in advance (Warde, 2000, p. 135).

Again, by what appears as a process of 'dodging and weaving' the financier is able to ameliorate most risks. Responsibility for maintenance can be circumvented by the lessor appointing the lessee as its agent to undertake the maintenance, and by taking out insurance. Residual value risk can be handled by a lease period long enough for recovery of principal plus an appropriately benchmarked rate of return, with the asset transferred to the lessee at the end of the lease period, so generating a fixed return for the bank on its investment. Strictly speaking, rules on *gharar* prevent rental charges on a floating rate basis (pegged to the London Interbank Offered Rate, LIBOR, for example) since the *ijara* contract has to fix and define the terms of the lease. This requirement, however, can be bypassed by a non-binding 'gentleman's agreement' to renew the lease from time to time throughout its life at a new rate.

Once the banks adapted to – that is, avoided – the restrictions on Islamic leases in ways described above, the instrument emerged as a very flexible mode of finance, eminently applicable to different uses. It also solves the problem of collateral by generating its own specific to the asset. If it were not already obvious what has resulted, then the point is made clear by the fact that *ijara* contracts are now being standardized and the documentation merged with that for conventional leases (Tag El-Din and Abdullah, 2007).

Sukuk

Stretching *shari'ah* rules to the limit in order to mimic conventional financial instruments (in this case a traditional interest-bearing bond) is also a feature of the *sukuk* market. Radzi and Lewis (2015), in their critique of the workings of the industry, begin with the observation that, 'One of the unique aspects of *sukuk* (Islamic investment certificates or participation certificates) compared to conventional bonds is the use of an asset in structuring the *sukuk*' (p. 295).

In fact, it is the nature of the underlying asset in the *sukuk* structure that determines whether the *sukuk* is asset-based or asset-backed. A *sukuk* gives investors a share of an asset or business venture, along with the cash flows and risk commensurate with such ownership. But the distinction between asset-based and asset-backed is of crucial importance.

An asset-based *sukuk* is unsecured. The underlying asset used to structure the issuance remains on the balance sheet of the originator after the issuance of the *sukuk*. In this category, the originator only passes on the beneficial ownership of the asset to *sukuk* holders, while retaining legal ownership. In other words, from a legal perspective, there is no true sale in the asset-based structure since *sukuk* holders do not hold proprietary rights in the underlying asset (Rainey and Salah, 2011). As a consequence, the *sukuk* holders cannot sell the asset to a third party, in the case of default of the borrower. It also means the *sukuk* holders only have recourse to the entity originating the issuance.

However, by contrast, an asset-backed *sukuk* can be defined as an Islamic security issued pursuant to a securitization transaction. This is usually evidenced by an independent legal opinion stating that the rights to the underlying assets have been perfected through a 'true sale' transfer to the issuing special purpose vehicle (SPV), and thereafter the originator has limited or no access to such assets as part of its assets pool. If the borrower defaults, *sukuk* holders are able to exercise certain rights of ownership and control over such assets. In these respects, asset-backed *sukuk* are 'ideal' according to *shari'ah* (Islamic law) as this structure involves full transfer of the legal ownership of the underlying asset. However, in reality, much of the *sukuk* structure today is focused on replicating conventional bonds.

Significantly, asset-based *sukuk* are invariably attached with a purchase undertaking that replicates a conventional unsecured bond. Howladar (2009, p. 8) states that a purchase undertaking is the key in almost all asset-based structures. Likewise, IIFM (2009) reported that a purchase undertaking features in the structure of almost every *sukuk* that was issued between 2001 and 2009. This kind of credit enhancement gives the *sukuk* the fixed-income characteristics of a conventional unsecured bond. Since investors have no recourse to the assets, credit assessment of this transaction does not focus on assets but rather on the creditworthiness of the sponsors of the *sukuk*.

Certainly, there is no indication in the legal documents of asset-based *sukuk* that *sukuk* holders do, in fact, own the underlying asset. Only beneficial ownership is transferred and the underlying asset is simply used to facilitate the *shari'ah* requirements. In other words, no true sale transaction occurs in asset-based *sukuk*; the sale is made to comply with *shari'ah* in form but not in substance. While it is the case that all financial instruments must fulfil formal and substantial compliance in order to be labelled as *shari'ah*-compliant, some transactions are conforming to the letter of Islamic law, but failing to meet its substance and spirit. Hence, the clash of 'ideals' and 'realities' in the case of Islamic bonds, in the words of Radzi and Lewis (2015).

WHERE IS ISLAMIC BANKING HEADING?

How the System has Developed

In this, the final section of this chapter, we examine how the system has developed from its roots in Classical Islam and is in the process of evolving now, drawing on Lewis (2015a). In the formative years of Islamic banking, Muslim scholars expressed a preference for profit and loss sharing (PLS) over other modes of financing, and many scholars still do so. Interest-free banking in its purest form is based on the concepts of *shirkah* (or *sharika*, partnership) or *musharaka*, and *mudaraba* (profit-sharing). An Islamic bank is conceived as a financial intermediary mobilizing savings from the public on a *mudaraba* (trustee) basis and advancing capital to entrepreneurs on a PLS partnership basis. The two methods conform fully with Islamic principles, in that under both arrangements lenders share in the profits and losses of the enterprises for which funds are provided. The *musharaka* principle is invoked in the equity structure of Islamic banks. *Mudaraba* is used for investment accounts for depositors, and the Islamic bank manages the funds to generate profits subject to the rules of *mudaraba*. If the bank in turn invests the depositors' funds on a *mudaraba* basis, then the circle is closed in terms of the two-tiered or triple *mudaraba* system. This is the position illustrated in Table 9.1.

Obviously, if Islamic banking took this form it would be very different from conventional banking. The reality, however, is that neither *mudaraba* nor *musharaka* constitutes the main conduits for the outflow of funds from Islamic banks. In fact, both contribute little to the overall balance sheet investments of Islamic banks, except perhaps in the West where diminishing *musharaka* is a major method used for residential property financing. Those versed in finance literature would likely not be surprised by this result, for there would seem to be significant potential for adverse selection and moral hazard to come into play under PLS financing modes, with Islamic banks attracting the more risky ventures while being unable under *mudaraba* to exercise control over the borrowers' behaviour. That result, basically, is what happened.

In looking for a path forward, the system turned to Classical Islam. Monzer Kahf (2014) notes that classical writings on *shari'ah* endorse three essential sharing-based finance contracts, namely: equity-sharing (*musharaka*), equity-sharing with a sleeping partner (*mudaraba*) and crop-sharing (*muzara'a*). They also mention three sale-based finance contracts: deferred payment sale (*al bay' al 'ajil*), forward sale with cash advance (*salam*) and manufacturing finance sale (*istisnaa*). Classical writings also refer to leasing (*ijara*) as a form of financial contracting. Kahf goes on to point out that in all of these seven kinds of contract the finance provider owns assets or commodities – essential in Islamic finance. One significant feature is the deferred payment sale at a higher than the cash price because it gives a demarcation of interest vis-à-vis financing sale.

From this springboard, Islamic intellectuals, jurists and bankers have spent much effort through the process of *ijtihad* examining the legitimacy of particular transactions and formalizing procedures which have, with the help of some liberal interpretation noted above, enabled everyday banking, finance and commerce to be conducted on what is proclaimed as an interest-free basis.

The divergence of such mark-up financing from the ideal of PLS partnership financing (in which the profit-sharing is conditional upon the uncertain end-result or outcome of the project) has been, and continues to be, a source of disagreement between the practitioners on the one hand, and the scholars on the other. It has led some writers (e.g., Ahmed, 2011; Cizakca, 2011) to draw a distinction between a *shari'ah*-based approach (evolved from the original sources of Islam and built directly from the *shari'ah*) and a *shari'ah*-compliant approach (borrowed from the West after being made compliant to the *shari'ah*; that is, Islamically modified conventional banking).

Quite clearly, the first model (Table 9.1), the two-tiered or triple *mudaraba* model of which we have spoken, is *shari'ah*-based. Model 2 is the one-tier *mudaraba* model on the liabilities side with multiple investment

Table 9.1 Balance sheet of two-tier mudaraba *model*

Liabilities	Assets
Mudaraba investment accounts Demand deposits (*wadia* basis) Reserves Equity	*Mudaraba/musharaka* financing

Table 9.2   Balance sheet of one-tier mudaraba *and multiple investment avenues*

Liabilities	Assets
Mudaraba investment accounts	*Murabaha*
Demand deposits (*wadia*)	*Ijara*
Reserves	*Istisnaa*
Equity	*Mudaraba*/*musharaka*

Table 9.3   Balance sheets with fixed-income liabilities and related investment avenues

Liabilities	Assets
Fixed-income accounts (*tawarruq*)	*Tawarruq*
Demand deposits (*wadia*)	*Murabaha*
Reserves	*Ijara*
Equity	*Istisnaa*
	Sukuk

tools on the asset side, that is, PLS and sales-based financing (Table 9.2). Such a model is both *shari'ah*-based and *shari'ah*-compliant and typifies where the system was a decade ago. By contrast, Model 3 involves fixed-income liabilities with multiple related investment tools (Table 9.3). In this case, on the liabilities side there are fixed-income deposit investment accounts by means of commodity *murabaha* or organized *tawarruq*, while the asset side comprises only mark-up modes along with other fixed-income investments (*sukuk* and, again, *tawarruq*). This model is entirely *shari'ah*-compliant. Islamic banking has evolved from Model 1 to Model 2, and there is the perception that it may be moving in some locales, and to varying degrees, towards Model 3.

What can be said unequivocally is that Islamic banks go to considerable lengths to ensure that their returns follow benchmark conventional market interest rates, such as LIBOR, and that the loss-sharing option is not exercised, which is done by maintaining an investment risk reserve (IRR) and profit equalization reserve (PER) to mitigate displaced commercial risk (DCR), where the risk of losses facing investment account holders is displaced to shareholders (Archer et al., 2010). Islamic bankers know that, in a mixed system competing with conventional banks offering guaranteed deposits, they would be severely hampered, if not destroyed, if losses were passed through to depositors as they would be under true profit and loss sharing.

How Islamic Banking is Evolving

The advent of *tawarruq* marks a new development for Islamic banking. Where permitted, organized *tawarruq* or 'commodity *murabaha*' can operate on both the asset and liabilities side of the Islamic bank balance sheet. On the liabilities side, the technique can mobilize deposits as follows. First, the client buys a commodity on a spot basis from broker A. Second, the client sells the commodity to an Islamic bank using *murabaha* on a deferred basis (cost plus profit). Third, the Islamic bank sells the commodity to broker B on a spot basis and obtains the cash (actually the deposit of the client). Fourth, the Islamic bank makes the payment to the client of the deferred and higher price upon maturity. By such means, the Islamic bank receives cash (as deposit) and pays it back to the depositor with a mark-up. In the process, the liability side normally dominated by multiple *mudaraba* is transformed into fixed return-yielding conventional deposits (Cizakca, 2011, p. 148).

On the asset side, a *tawarruq* operates as follows. First, the Islamic bank buys a commodity (for example, metal) on the spot from broker A. Second, the bank sells this commodity to the client using *murabaha* on deferred basis (cost plus profit). Third, the client sells the metal to broker B on a spot basis and obtains the cash needed; or, alternatively, the bank sells the metal on behalf of the client to the broker, obtains the cash and passes it to the client. Fourth, the client makes periodic payments to the Islamic bank to cover the deferred price (Cizakca, 2011, p. 146).

While some Islamic banks practise *tawarruq*, the Islamic Fiqh Academy in 2009 declared organized *tawarruq* illegal as it entails elements of *riba* and does not conform to the true classical form of this technique (Ahmed, 2011, p. 50). Nevertheless, some *shari'ah* scholars regard it as being still preferable to 'conventional personal finance principles' (Housby, 2011, p. 68).

This last position can be disputed. What distinguishes *tawarruq* from the other sales-based financing techniques is that, as the examples above illustrate, *tawarruq* goods are purchased and sold only as a vehicle for obtaining cash. Goods do not end up with final users who actually employ them for their own industry or consumption (Kahf, 2014). As Volker Nienhaus observes:

Islamic banks provide unrestricted liquidity to their clients by using contractual arrangements in which neither the bank nor the client has any genuine interest in the underlying real asset (as in the case of *tawarruq* or commodity *murabahah* for liquidity purposes). Such contracts would allow the use of the same asset over and again in different transactions, and the result would be a detachment of finance from the real economy and also possibly an accumulation of Shari'ah compliant debt in the balance sheet of the client (i.e. leverage). (Nienhaus, 2014, p. 580)

This is a serious charge. One of the 'claims to fame' of the Islamic system, voiced in particular in the wake of the global financial crisis, is preventing excessive leverage and avoiding a build-up of debt divorced from the real sector. If this claim is diluted, what is left? Where is the system heading? Not so long ago, it was unthinkable to even talk about a tradeable Islamic bond that would guarantee a fixed return. Now they exist, with 'financially engineered' pay-off profiles used to generate returns that are, being derived from a 'cost plus' rate of profit – albeit from asset-based rather than asset-backed structures, and accompanied by purchase undertakings – as fixed and guaranteed as any interest-based instrument.

Are fixed return, negligible risk, Islamic securities, based on mark-up financing techniques pioneered by Islamic banks, needed if Islamic finance is to rival conventional finance? Or, do these instruments go too far? Is the Islamic financial system torn between the market success of emulating conventional structures on the one hand, and on the other hand developing modes that reflect its spiritual ethos (Agha, 2012)? These are, indeed, serious issues to ponder by those concerned about the future directions of the system.

NOTES

1. Since these terms recur, some definitions might be useful. First, 'asymmetric information' means that all economic transactors do not have the same information about all economic variables. Consider a market in which items of varying quality are exchanged and there exists asymmetric information in that only sellers can observe the quality of each unit sold. Without some device for buyers to identify good from bad, bad products will always be sold with the good products. Such a market illustrates the problem of adverse selection. This problem can be translated into what is known as the principal–agent model in which the principal delegates to the agent the responsibility for selecting and implementing an action. Adverse selection arises when the principal is not privy to some information which is relevant to the action, whereas the agent can make use of this information in selecting an action. By contrast, moral hazard occurs when the principal and agent share the same information up to the point at which the agent selects an action, but thereafter the principal cannot observe the action, only the outcome. An excellent survey is contained in Campbell (1995).
2. Surveys of the literature are given by Dowd (1992, 1996), Hester (1994), A. Lewis (1991), Lewis (1992) and Llewellyn (1994). The original references are cited in these surveys and are not referred to here in great detail. The present account draws upon Lewis (2014a).
3. The term 'principal–agent problem' is due to Ross (1973). Other early contributions to this literature include Mirrlees (1974, 1976) and Stiglitz (1974, 1975).

4. The title borrows from the 1944 song 'Accentuate the Positive' with lyrics by Johnny Mercer and popularized by the Andrews Sisters, which goes:

> You've got to accentuate the positive
> Eliminate the negative
> And latch on to the affirmative
> Don't mess with Mister In-Between.

Obviously, while not wanting to eliminate the negative, the theme of the paper is to accentuate the positive and latch on to the affirmative aspects of Islamic economic, financial and governance principles.

10. Conclusion

This book is concerned with religion and finance as it relates to the views of Judaism, Christianity and Islam, the three great Abrahamic religions. At their core, on this topic at least, all three have the same starting point. The prohibition of usury (interest) and an abhorrence of usurious behaviour (of which many examples in recent times have been given) lie at the heart of the attitudes of the three religions. And, not to put too fine a point on it, on this score, they can all be said to have failed.

Judaism, by virtue of what has been called the 'Deuteronomic double standard', has no qualms about charging interest to Gentiles. It also engages in pseudo-interest when lending to fellow Jews ('brothers' in Old Testament terms) via *hetter iska*, a practice which is considered by many to be tainted by the 'dust of interest' (*avak ribbit*).

Christianity, it can be said, deserves credit for its openness in explicitly abandoning the ban of interest, and in the end eschewing the legal fictions that developed to circumnavigate and so maintain the prohibition in name only. However, in its choice to substitute a ban on 'excessive' interest, in place of a ban on all interest, Christianity has failed miserably. Banks are able to levy establishment fees and other related charges to inflate the true interest rate well above any maximum rates mandated. Payday lenders can charge rates as astronomically high as 780 per cent per annum, seemingly with impunity (Lewis, 2015b). Conventional bankers, at least in the United States, United Kingdom and Australia, seem to have transgressed on almost every moral dimension of financial behaviour.

Islam has stuck to its guns in sustaining the prohibition on *riba* (usury, interest), but despite good intentions the actuality at times is at considerable variance with any such claim. Profit and loss sharing models are restricted to a minute fraction of Islamic banks' activities. Sales-based techniques have benefited from accommodating juristic rulings that have shifted risk and responsibilities from the banks to the borrowers, in apparent violation of *shari'ah* precepts. *Sukuk* are meant to be asset-backed but in practice are predominantly asset-based, with purchase undertakings and liquidity guarantees that make them indistinguishable (except in name) from conventional, fixed (or variable) interest rate bonds. The defence made of Islamic financing that, ultimately, it derives from real, trading transactions, not purely monetary ones, is violated by the growth of *tawarruq* on both sides of the balance sheet of Islamic financiers. In short, Islam would appear to have maintained the usury ban by opting for form over substance.

Consequently, when distilled down to the basics, the fact remains that on the core issue of the prohibition of usury, none of the three great religions have any claim to the moral high ground. Perhaps, in view of the transition from the relatively closed tribal societies of the Old Testament, New Testament and the Holy Qur'an, to the modern, open, pluralistic world, reliant on finance for international trade, development and poverty alleviation, this result is not unexpected and perhaps no bad thing.

However, it is important to emphasize that not all is lost from a religious viewpoint. All three religions stand for much more than the ban on interest, as we have documented in earlier chapters. They advocate zero-interest benevolent loans to the poor and needy, recommend laxity in enforcing credit repayments, and urge adherents to give generously of their wealth and good fortune in terms of tithes and *zakat* payments. The Abrahamic religions set out social and economic principles that should be followed in financial dealings and in the financial markets. These ethical precepts act as a 'light on the hill' to guide the consciences and behaviour of those working in the markets. Unfortunately, it pains us to say that there is scant evidence that the three religions will succeed in these aims while an ethos of greed, lack of shame and culture of arrogance rules and is far too evident in so much of the financial world. For their own good, as well as that of their customers and the overall economy, the 'moral compass' of bankers and financiers needs to be reset.

References

Abba, Raymond (1958), *The Nature and Authority of the Bible*, London: James Clarke & Co.

Abraham, I. (2011), 'Tensions in Christian Financial Ethics: An Historical Overview', in M. Ariff and M. Iqbal (eds), *The Foundations of Islamic Banking, Theory, Practice and Education*, Cheltenham, UK and Northampton, MA, USA: Edward Elgar Publishing, 235–54.

ABS Treasury (2017), 'Big Push for a New National Brand', *Australian*, 23 November, 2.

Abu Zahra, Muhammad (1970), *Buhuth fi al-Riba*, Kuwait: Dar al-Buhuth al-'Ilmiyya.

Accounting and Auditing Organization for Islamic Financial Institutions (AAOIFI) (2003), *Sharia Standard No. 17*, Bahrain: Accounting and Auditing Organization for Islamic Financial Institutions.

Agha, Oliver (2012), 'Is Islamic Finance a Failure? An Assessment', www. reuters.com/ article/2012/01/27islamicfrinance-future-idUSL5ECR0FV 20120127, accessed 31 January 2012.

Ahmad, A.U.F., M. Kabir Hassan and A.K.M. Shahed (2006), '*Zakah* and Re-Distributive Justice in Islam', *JMIFR*, 3 (1), 1–22.

Ahmad, Hadrat M.T. (2008), *Absolute Justice, Kindness and Kinship – The Three Creative Principles*, Tilford: Islam International Publications.

Ahmad, Ziauddin (1991), *Islam, Poverty and Income Distribution*, Leicester: Islamic Foundation.

Ahmed, Habib (2011), *Product Development in Islamic Banks*, Edinburgh: Edinburgh University Press.

Ahmed, N. (1997), 'Islamic Banking and its Mode of Investments', *New Horizon*, 67 (September), 3–7.

Ahmed, Shaghil (1989), 'Islamic Banking and Finance. A Review Essay', *Journal of Monetary Economics*, 24, 157–67.

Al-Ghazali, Abu Hamid (1356 AH/1937 CE), *al-Mustasfa min Ilm al-Usul*, 2 vols, Cairo: al-Maktabah al-Tijariyyah.

Al-Harran, S.A.S. (1993), *Islamic Finance – Partnership Financing*, Selangor Darul Ehsan, Malaysia: Pelanduk Publications.

Ali, Abdullah Yusuf (1938), *The Holy Qur'an: Text, Translation and Commentary*, Beirut: Dar Al Arabia.

Alias, Tunku Alina (2014), 'The Gift Economy: *Waqf* in the Islamic World Today', in M. Kabir Hassan and M.K. Lewis (eds), *Handbook on Islam and Economic Life*, Cheltenham UK and Northampton, MA, USA: Edward Elgar Publishing, 475–95.

Al-Qardawi, Allama Yusuf (1983), *Fiqhuz Zakah*, Vol. 1, 2nd edn, translated into Urdu by Sajidur Rahman Siddiqi, Lahore: Albadar Publications.

Al-Quduri al-Baghdadi, Abu al-Husayn Ahmad ibn Muhammad (n.d.), *Kitab al-Mukhtasar*, Cairo.

Al-Shatibi, Abu Ishaq Ibrahim (n.d.), *Al-Muwafiqat fi usul ak-Sharia'ah*, Vol. II, Cairo: Maktabah al-Tijariah al-Kubra.

Amis, Martin (2008), *The Second Plane*, London: Jonathan Cape.

Anwar, Muhammad (1987), *Modelling Interest-Free Economy: A Study in Macroeconomics and Development*, Herndon, VA: International Institute of Islamic Thought.

Aquinas, Thomas (1985), *Summa Theologiae*, Vol. 38, *Injustice (IIaiiae.63–79)*, trans. Marcus Lefébure, London: Eyre & Spottiswoode.

Archer, S., R.A.A. Karim and V. Sundararajan (2010), 'Supervisory, Regulatory, and Capital Adequacy Implications of Profit-Sharing Investment Accounts in Islamic Finance', *Journal of Islamic Accounting and Business Research*, **1** (1), 10–31.

Ariff, M. (1982), 'Monetary Policy in an Interest Free Islamic Economy: Nature and Scope', in M. Ariff (ed.), *Monetary and Fiscal Economics of Islam*, Jeddah: International Centre for Research in Islamic Economics, 287–310.

Ariff, Mohamed and Meysam Safari (2014), 'A Socio-Economic Profile of Muslim Countries', in M. Kabir Hassan and M.K. Lewis (eds), *Handbook on Islam and Economic Life*, Cheltenham UK and Northampton, MA, USA: Edward Elgar Publishing, 195–211.

Aristotle (2013), *Aristotle's Politics*, 2nd edn, transl. and with an Introduction, Notes and Glossary by Carnes Lord, Chicago, IL, USA and London, UK: University of Chicago Press.

Arrow, K.J. (1964), 'The Role of Securities in the Optimal Allocation of Risk-Bearing', *Review of Economic Studies*, **31** (2), 91–6.

Arrow, K.J. (1974), *The Limits of Organization*, New York, USA and London, UK: W.W. Norton.

Ashley, W.J. (1888, 1893 [1913]), *An Introduction to English Economic History and Theory*, 2 vols, London: Longman & Co. and New York: G.P. Putnam's Sons.

Asia News (2009), 'Pope: Greed, the Root of Global Economic Crisis', www.asianews.it/index.phpl=en&art=15052&size=A, accessed 20 November 2011.

Askari, H. and R. Taghavi (2005), 'The Principle Foundations of an Islamic Economy', *Banca Nazionale del Lavoro Quarterly Review*, **57** (235), 187–205.
Atiyah, E. (1955), *The Arabs*, Harmondsworth: Pelican.
Babylonian Talmud, Baba Mesi'a (1935), English translation, I. Epstein (ed.), A.M. Salis Daiches and H. Freedman (transl.), *The Babylonian Talmud, Seder NezikinIII, Baba Mezi'a*, London: Soncino Press.
Bagley, E.R.C. (1964), *Counsel for Kings*, trans. N. Al-Muluk, Oxford: Oxford University Press.
Baldwin, J.W. (1970), *Masters, Printers and Merchants*, 2 vols, Princeton, NJ: Princeton University Press.
Barrett, David B. (1990), *Dictionary of Christianity in America (Protestant)*, Downers Grove, IL: Intervarsity Press.
Barrett, D.B., G.T. Kurian and T.M. Johnson (eds) (2001), *World Christian Encylopedia: A Comparative Survey of Churches and Religions in the Modern World*, 2 vols, Oxford: Oxford University Press.
Barrett, P.M. and S. Lanman (2010), 'Thomas Hoenig is Fed Up', *Bloomberg Businessweek*, 27 September–3 October, 74–8.
Baumol, William (1969 [1995]), 'The Specialist: Operator of the Automatic Mechanism', in *The Stock Market and Economic Efficiency*, New York: Fordham University Press, 9–34; reprinted in M.K. Lewis (ed.) (1995), *Financial Intermediaries*, The International Library of Critical Writings in Economics, An Elgar Reference Collection, Cheltenham, UK and Northampton, MA, USA: Edward Elgar Publishing, 127–52.
Bekar, C. (2000), 'Income Sharing Amongst Medieval Peasants: Usury Prohibitions and the Non-Market Provision of Insurance', *International Institute of Economics and Trade, Conference Proceedings*, http://oregon state.edu/dept/iifet/2000/papers/bekar.pdf, accessed 12 January 2018.
Benedict XVI, Pope (2009), 'Encyclical Letter, *Caritas in Veritate*', 29 June, http://www.vatican.va/holy_father/benedict_xvi/encyclicals/documents/h f_ben-xvi_enc_20090629_caritas-in-veritate_en.html, accessed 2 August 2011.
Bentham, Jeremy (1787 [1818]), *Defence of Usury*, 4th edn, London: Payne and Foss, electronic facsimile Online Library of Liberty, http://oll. libertyfund.org/ToC/0167.php.
Berger, R. (1935), 'Usury in Installment Sales', *Law and Contemporary Problems*, **2** (2), 173–88.
Berman, H.J. (1983), 'Law and Revolution: The Formation of the Western Legal Tradition', *Valparaiso University Law Review*, **18** (3), 683–703.
Bernanke, Ben S. and Mark Gertler (1986), 'Agency Costs, Collateral and Business Fluctuations', National Bureau of Economic Research, Working Paper 2015, September.

Birnie, A. (1958), *The History and Ethics of Interest*, London: William Hodge.

Blackburn, Simon (2001), *Ethics: A Very Short Introduction*, Oxford: Oxford University Press.

Blaydes, Lisa and Eric Chaney (2013), 'The Feudal Revolution and Europe's Rise: Political Divergence of the Christian West and the Muslim World before 1500 CE', *American Political Science Review*, **107** (1), 16–34.

Bleich, J. David (2010), 'Hetter Iska, the Permissible Venture: A Device to Avoid the Prohibition Against Interest-Bearing Loans', in Aaron Levine (ed.), *The Oxford Handbook of Judaism and Economics*, New York: Oxford University Press, 197–220.

Boyce, James (2014), *Born Bad: Original Sin and the Making of the Western World*, Collingwood, VIC: Black Inc.

Brennan, S., A. Haldane and V. Madouros (2010), 'The Contribution of the Financial Sector, Miracle or Mirage?', *The Future of Finance: The LSE Report*, London School of Economics, http://www.bankofengland. co.uk/publications/speeches/2010/speech442. pdf, accessed 17 November 2010.

Brown, Gordon (2010), *Beyond the Crash: Overcoming the First Crisis of Globalization*, London: Simon & Schuster.

Broyde, Michael J. and Steven H. Resnicoff (1997), 'Jewish Law and Modern Business Structures: The Corporate Paradigm', *Wayne Law Review*, **43**, 1–78.

Buchanan, J.M. (1992), 'Public Debt', in P. Newman, M. Milgate and J. Eatwell (eds), *The New Palgrave Dictionary of Money and Finance*, Vol. 3, London: Macmillan, 228–32.

Burke, Joseph (2011), 'Usury Redux: Notes on the Scholastic Analysis of Usury by John T. Noonan', Working Paper no. 901, Department of Economics, Ave Maria University, Florida, http://mysite.avemaria.edu/ jburke/working-papers/WP0901-Burke-Usury-Redux-A.pdf, accessed 3 January 2018.

Callahan, D.J. (2004), 'Medieval Church Norms and Fiduciary Duties in Partnership', *Cardozo Law Review*, **26** (1), 215–85.

Callen, Jeffrey L. (2010), 'Risk and Incentives in the *Iska* Contract', in A. Levine (ed.), *The Oxford Handbook of Judaism and Economics*, New York: Oxford University Press, 91–106.

Campbell, D.E. (1995), *Incentives, Motivation and the Economics of Information*, Cambridge: Cambridge University Press.

Caruana, Jaime (2018), 'Opening remarks', Low for long or turning point? *BIS Papers*, No. 98, 1–2, July.

Cecchetti, S.G. and E. Kharroubi (2012), 'Reassessing the Impact of

Finance on Growth', BIS Working Papers, No. 381, Basel: Bank for International Settlements.

Chapra, M. Umer (2007), 'The Case Against Interest: Is it Compelling?', *Thunderbird International Business Review*, **49** (2), 161–86.

Chapra, Umer (1992), *Islam and the Economic Challenge*, Leicester: Islamic Foundation.

Chewning, Richard, John Eby and Shirley Roels (1990), *Business Through the Eyes of Faith*, San Francisco, CA: Harper & Row.

Cizakca, M. (1996), *A Comparative Evaluation of Business Partnerships; The Islamic World and Europe with Specific Reference to Ottoman Archives*, Leiden: E.J. Brill.

Cizakca, M. (2010), 'Was Shari'ah Indeed the Culprit?', MPRA Paper No. 22865, Kuala Lumpur: INCEIF, http://mpra.ub.uni-muenchen.de/22865/, accessed 15 February 2018.

Cizakca, Murat (2011), *Islamic Capitalism and Finance. Origins, Evolution and the Future*, Cheltenham, UK and Northampton, MA, USA: Edward Elgar Publishing.

Claessens, Stijn (2012), 'Shedding Debt', *Finance and Development*, **49** (2), 20–23.

Cline, W.R. (2010), *Financial Globalization, Economic Growth, and the Crisis of 2007–09*, Washington, DC: Peterson Institute for International Economics.

Cohn, H.H. (1971), S.v. 'Usury', *Encyclopedia Judaica*, Jerusalem: Keter Publishing House, 17–33.

Coogan, Michael (2008), *The Old Testament: A Very Short Introduction*, Oxford: Oxford University Press.

Council of Islamic Ideology (CII) (Pakistan) (1983), 'Elimination of Interest from the Economy', in Z. Ahmed, M. Iqbal and M.F. Khan (eds), *Money and Banking in Islam*, Jeddah: International Centre for Research in Islamic Economics; and Islamabad: Institute of Policy Studies, 103–211.

Coval, Joshua, Jakub Jurek and Erik Stafford (2009), 'The Economics of Structured Finance', *Journal of Economic Perspectives*, **23** (1), 3–25.

Das, Satyajit (2008), 'Voodoo Banking – Finance on Steroids', http://news.kontentkonsult.com/2008/12/voodoo-banking-finance-on-steroids.html, accessed 19 February 2009.

Das, Satyajit (2011), *Extreme Money: The Masters of the Universe and the Cult of Risk*, Camberwell, VIC: Penguin.

De Cecco, M. (1992), 'Genoese Exchange Fairs', in P. Newman, M. Milgate and J. Eatwell (eds), *The New Palgrave Dictionary of Money and Finance*, Vol. 3, London: Macmillan, 221–6.

Der Hovanesian, Mara (2006), 'Nightmare Mortgages', *Business Week*, 11 September, 70–81.

de Roover, R. (1942), 'Money, Banking and Credit in Medieval Bruges', *Journal of Economic History*, **2**, 52–65.

de Roover, Raymond (1948), *The Medici Bank: Its Organisation, Management, Operations, and Decline*, New York: New York University Press.

de Roover, Raymond (1954), 'New Interpretations of the History of Banking', *Journal of World History*, Paris: Librairie des Mieridiens, 38–76.

de Roover, Raymond (1963), *The Rise and Decline of the Medici Bank, 1397–1494*, Cambridge, MA: Harvard University Press.

de Roover, Raymond (1967), 'The Scholastics, Usury and Foreign Exchange', *Business History Review*, **43**, 257–71.

Dimbleby, Jonathan (2008), *Russia: A Journey to the Heart of a Land and its People*, London: BBC Books.

Divine, T.F. (1967), S.v. 'Usury', *New Catholic Encyclopedia*, New York: McGraw-Hill, 498–500.

Domb, Yoel (2010), 'Ethical Demands on Creditors in Jewish Tradition', in Aaron Levine (ed.), *The Oxford Handbook of Judaism and Economics*, New York: Oxford University Press, 221–38.

Doumani, B. (1998), 'Endowing Family: Waqf, Property Devolution, and Gender in Greater Syria, 1800 to 1860', *Comparative Studies in Society and History*, **40**, 3–41.

Dowd, K. (1992), 'Optimal Financial Contracts', *Oxford Economic Papers*, **44** (October), 672–93.

Dowd, K. (1996), *Competition and Finance: A Reinterpretation of Financial and Monetary Economics*, London: Macmillan.

Downs, A. (1961), 'In Defence of Majority Voting', *Journal of Political Economy*, **69** (April), 192–99.

Dusuki, A.W. (2007), 'The Ideal of Islamic Banking: A Survey of Stakeholders' Perceptions', *Review of Islamic Economics*, Special Issue, December, 11, 29–52.

East Asia Analytical Unit (1995), *Overseas Chinese Business Networks in Asia*, Commonwealth of Australia: Department of Foreign Affairs and Trade.

The Economist (2007), 'The Bible v the Koran: The Battle of the Books', *The Economist*, 22 December, 75–7.

The Economist (2009), 'The Banking Bonus Racket', *The Economist*, 31 January, p. 3.

The Economist (2012), 'Judaism and the Jews', Special Report, 28 July, 2–12.

The Economist (2014a), 'Who is a Jew?', *The Economist*, 11 January, 51–2.

The Economist (2014b), 'Bridges to Somewhere, Free Exchange', *The Economist*, 19 July, 65.

Einzig, P. (1962), *The History of Foreign Exchange*, London: Macmillan.

Ekelund, R.B., Jr, R.F. Hébert and R.D. Tollison (1989), 'An Economic Model of the Medieval Church: Usury as a Form of Rent Seeking', *Journal of Law, Economics and Organization*, **5** (2), 307–31.

Ekelund, R.B., Jr, R.F. Hébert and R.D. Tollison (2006), *The Marketplace of Christianity*, Cambridge, MA, USA and London, UK: MIT Press.

El Diwany, Tarek (2003), *The Problem with Interest*, London: Kreatoc.

El-Gamal, M.L. (2000), 'An Economic Explication of the Prohibition of Riba in Classical Islamic Jurisprudence', *Proceedings of the Third Harvard University Forum on Islamic Finance*, Cambridge, MA.

Elkin, Edward (2010), 'Full Faith and Credit: Jewish Views on Debt and Bankruptcy', *CCAR Journal: The Reform Jewish Quarterly*, **57** (2), 7–22.

Epstein, L.M. (1973), *The Jewish Marriage Contract*, New York: Arno Press.

Feldman, D.Z. (2010), 'The Jewish Prohibition of Interest: Themes, Scopes and Contemporary Applications', in Aaron Levine (ed.), *The Oxford Handbook of Judaism and Economics*, New York: Oxford University Press, 239–54.

Ferguson, Niall (2009), *The Ascent of Money: A Financial History of the World*, London: Penguin Books.

Fisher, Irving (1933), 'The Debt-Deflation Theory of Great Depressions', *Econometrica*, **1**, 337–57.

Fitzgerald, Frances (2017), *The Evangelicals: The Struggle to Shape America*, New York: Simon & Schuster.

Foster, J.B. (2007), 'The Financialization of Capitalism', *Monthly Review*, **58** (11), http:/www.monthlyreview.org/0407jbf.htm, accessed 20 November 2011.

Frankel, A.B. (2009), 'The Risk of Relying on Reputational Capital: A Case Study of the 2007 Failure of New Century Financial', BIS Working Papers No. 294, Basel: Bank for International Settlements.

Froud, J., S. Johal, A. Leaver and K. Williams (2006), *Financialization and Strategy: Narrative and Numbers*, London: Routledge, Taylor & Francis.

Fuller, G.E. (2010), *A World Without Islam*, New York and Boston, MA, USA; London, UK: Little, Brown & Company.

Gafoor, Abdul A.L.M. (1995), *Interest-Free Commercial Banking*, Groningen: Apptec Publications.

Galassi, F.L. (1992), 'Buying a Passport to Heaven: Usury, Restitution and the Merchants of Medieval Genoa', *Religion*, **22**, 313–26.

Gale, D. and M. Hellwig (1985), 'Incentive-Compatible Debt Contracts: The One-Period Problem', *Review of Economic Studies*, **52**, 647–63.

Gamoran, H. (1976), 'Talmudic Usury Laws and Business Loans', *Journal for the Study of Judaism*, **7** (2), 128–42.

Gamoran, H. (2008), *Jewish Law in Transition: How Economic Forces Overcame the Prohibition against Lending on Interest*, New York: Hebrew Union College, Jewish Institute of Religion.

Gätje, Helmut (1997), *The Qur'an and its Exegesis*, Oxford: Oneworld Publications.

Gellner, Ernest (1981), *Muslim Society*, Cambridge: Cambridge University Press.

Glaeser, E.L. and J.A. Scheinkman (1998), 'Neither a Borrower nor a Lender Be: An Economic Analysis of Interest Restrictions and Usury Laws', *Journal of Law and Economics*, **41** (1), 1–36.

Gluyas, R. (2012), 'Citigroup Chief Backs Volker Rule Principle', *Australian*, 27 July, 23.

Gonzales, Justo (1990), *Faith and Wealth: A History of Early Christian Ideas on the Origin, Significance and Use of Money*, New York: Harper & Row.

Goodhart, C.A.E. (2008), 'Lessons from the Crisis for Financial Regulation: What We Need and What We Do Not Need', *Review*, **78**, Financial Markets Group Research Centre, 3–4.

Goodhart, C.A.E. (2011), 'The Squam Lake Report: Commentary', *Journal of Economic Literature*, **49** (1), 114–19.

Goodin, Robert E. (1992), *Motivating Political Morality*, Oxford: Blackwell.

Gopal, M.H. (1935), *Mauryan Public Finance*, London: George Allen & Unwin.

Gordon, B. (1982), 'Lending at Interest: Some Jewish, Greek and Christian Approaches, 800 BC–AD100', *History of Political Economy*, **14** (3), 406–26.

Gorton, Gary (2009), 'The Subprime Panic', *European Financial Management*, **15** (1), 10–46.

Greenspan, Alan (2010), *The Crisis*, Encino, CA: Greenspan Associates.

Greif, Avner (1994), 'Cultural Beliefs and the Organization of Society: A Historical and Theoretical Reflection on Collectivist and Individualist Societies', *Journal of Political Economy*, **102** (5), 912–50.

Grimsey, D. and M.K. Lewis (1999), 'Evaluating the Risks of Public Private Partnership for Infrastructure Projects', *The Third International Stockholm Seminar on Risk Behaviour and Risk Management, June 14–16*, School of Business, Stockholm: University of Stockholm.

Grimsey, D. and M.K. Lewis (2004), *Public Private Partnerships: The Worldwide Revolution in Infrastructure Provision and Project Finance*, Cheltenham, UK and Northampton, MA, USA: Edward Elgar Publishing.

Grimsey, D. and M.K. Lewis (2017), *Global Developments in Public Infrastructure Procurement: Evaluating Public Private Partnerships and other Procurement Options*, Cheltenham UK and Northampton, MA, USA: Edward Elgar Publishing.

Grossman, S.S. and O.P. Hart (1983), 'An Analysis of the Principal–Agent Problem', *Econometrica*, **51** (1), 7–45.

Hamid, A. (1992), 'Addendum on Recent Developments', in R.C. Effros (ed.), *Current Legal Issues Affecting Central Banking*, Vol. 1, Washington, DC: International Monetary Fund.

Hamilton, E.J. (1947), 'Origin and Growth of the National Debt in Western Europe', *American Economic Review*, **37** (2), 118–30.

Haque, Nadeem Ul and A. Mirakhor (1986), 'Optimal Profit-Sharing Contracts and Investment in an Interest-Free Islamic Economy', IMF Working Paper No. 12, Washington, DC: International Monetary Fund.

Harris, M. and A. Raviv (1979), 'Optimal Incentive Contracts with Imperfect Information', *Journal of Economic Theory*, **20** (2), 231–59.

Hasan, S.U. (1995), 'Islamic Unit Trusts', *Encyclopaedia of Islamic Banking*, London: Institute of Islamic Banking and Insurance, 159–63.

Hasan, Samiul (2007), *Philanthropy and Social Justice in Islam: Principles, Prospects and Practices*, Kuala Lumpur: A.S. Noordeen.

Hasan, Zubair (2002), 'Maximisation Postulates and their Efficacy for Islamic Economics', *American Journal of Islamic Social Sciences*, **19** (1), 95–118.

Hassan, M. Kabir and M.K. Lewis (2014), 'Islam, the Economy and Economic Life', in M. Kabir Hassan and M.K. Lewis (eds), *Handbook on Islam and Economic Life*, Cheltenham, UK and Northampton, MA, USA: Edward Elgar Publishing, 1–17.

Hawtrey, Sir Ralph (1932), *The Art of Central Banking*, London: Longmans, Green & Co.

Hawtrey, Sir Ralph (1950), *Currency and Credit*, 4th edn, London: Longmans, Green & Co.

Hay, Donald (1989), *Economics Today: A Christian Critique*, Leicester: Apollis, Inter-Varsity Press.

Hayek, F.A. (1944), *The Road to Serfdom*, London: Routledge & Kegan Paul.

Hayek, F.A. (1960), *The Constitution of Liberty*, Chicago, IL: Chicago University Press.

Hennigan, P.C. (2004), *The Birth of a Legal Institution: The Formation of the Waqf in the Third-Century A.H. Hanafi Legal Discourse*, Leiden, Netherlands and Boston, MA, USA: Brill.

Henning, J. (2007), 'The Mediaeval Contractum Trinius and the Law of Partnership', *Fundamina*, **13** (2), 33–49.

Hester, Donald D. (1994), 'On the Theory of Financial Intermediation', *De Economist*, **142** (2), 133–49.

Hoover, C.B. (1926), 'The Sea Loan in Genoa in the Twelfth Century', *Quarterly Journal of Economics*, **40** (3), 495–529.

Hoshi, Takeo (2011), 'Financial Regulation: Lessons from the Recent Financial Crises', *Journal of Economic Literature*, **49** (1), 120–28.

Houkes, J.M. (2004), *An Annotated Bibliography on the History of Usury and Interest from the Earliest Times through the Eighteenth Century*, Lewiston, NY: Edwin Mellen Press.

Housby, E. (2011), *Islamic Financial Services in the United Kingdom*, Edinburgh: Edinburgh University Press.

Howladar, K. (2009), '*Shari'ah, Sukuk* and Credit Risk: A Moody's Primer', *Abana Review*, **24** (1), 18–21.

Hussain, Jamila (1999), *Islamic Law and Society: An Introduction*, Sydney: Federation Press.

Hussain, Z. (2008), 'Theory of Profit from Islamic Perspectiv', MPRA Paper No. 8129, http://mpra.ub.uni-muenchen.de/8129/, accessed 15 January 2018.

Iannaccone, L.R. (1998), 'Introduction to the Economics of Religion', *Journal of Economic Literature*, **36** (3), 1465–95.

Iannaconne, L.R. and R. Finke (1996), 'Religion, Science and Rationality', *American Economic Review. Papers and Proceedings*, **86** (2), 433–7.

Ibn Taymiyyah (1976 [1982]), *al-Hisbah fi'l-Islam*, Cairo: Dar al-Sha'b; English transl. by Muhtar Holland (1982), *Public Duties in Islam: The Institution of the Hisbah*, Leicester: Islamic Foundation.

Iley, Richard A. and M.K. Lewis (2011a), 'Has the Global Financial Crisis Produced a New World Order?', *Accounting Forum*, **35**, 90–103.

Iley, Richard A. and M.K. Lewis (2011b), 'The Post-Crisis World: Can Asia's Outperformance be Sustained?', *Taylors' Business Review*, **1** (1), 25–43.

Iley, Richard A. and M.K. Lewis (2013), *Global Finance After the Crisis: The United States, China and the New World Order*, Cheltenham, UK and Northampton, MA, USA: Edward Elgar Publishing.

Innes, R. (1993), 'Financial Contracting Under Risk Neutrality, Limited Liability and *Ex Ante* Asymmetric Information', *Economica*, **60** (237), 27–40.

International Islamic Financial Market (IIFM) (2009), *Sukuk Report*, 1st edn, Manama, Bahrain: IIFM.

Iqbal, Zafar and M.K. Lewis (2009), *An Islamic Perspective on Governance*, Cheltenham, UK and Northampton, MA, USA: Edward Elgar Publishing.

Iqbal, Zafar and M.K. Lewis (2014), '*Zakat* and the Economy', in M. Kabir Hassan and M.K. Lewis (eds), *Handbook on Islam and*

Economic Life, Cheltenham, UK and Northampton, MA, USA: Edward Elgar Publishing, 453–74.

Islahi, A.A. (2005), *Contributions of Muslim Scholars to Economic Thought and Analysis* (11-905 AH/632-1500 AD), Jeddah: Scientific Publishing Centre, King Abdulaziz University.

Iyer, Sriya (2016), 'The New Economics of Religion', *Journal of Economic Literature*, **54** (2), 395–441.

Jain, L.C. (1929), *Indigenous Banking in India*, London: Macmillan.

Jensen, M. and W. Meckling (1976), 'Theory of the Firm: Managerial Behaviour, Agency Costs and Ownership Structure', *Journal of Financial Economics*, **3**, 305–60.

Joas, Hans (2000), *The Genesis of Values*, transl. Gregory Moore, Oxford: Polity Press and Blackwell Publishers.

Johnson, L.T. (2010), *The New Testament: A Very Short Introduction*, Oxford: Oxford University Press.

Jones, N. (1989), *God and the Moneylenders*, Oxford: Basil Blackwell.

Kahf, Monzer (1997), 'Potential Effects of Zakat on Government Budget', *IIUM Journal of Economics and Management*, **5** (1), 67–85.

Kahf, Monzer (2003), 'The Role of Waqf in Improving the Ummah Welfare', Paper presented in an international seminar on 'Waqf as a Private Legal Body', organized by Islamic University of North Sumatra, Medan, Indonesia, 6–7 January.

Kahf, Monzer (2014), '*Riba* in Islamic Economics and Finance', in M. Kabir Hassan and M.K. Lewis (eds), *Handbook on Islam and Economic Life*, Cheltenham, UK and Northampton, MA, USA: Edward Elgar Publishing, 132–52.

Kaleem, A. and S. Ahmad (2009), 'The Quran and Poverty Alleviation: A Theoretical Model for Charity Based Islamic Microfinance Institutions', *Non-Profit and Voluntary Sector Quarterly*, **39** (3), 409–28.

Kaleem, A. and M.K. Lewis (2014), 'Non-Interest Financing Arrangements in Three Abrahamic Religions', in M.K. Lewis, M. Ariff and M. Shamsher (eds), *Risk and Regulation of Islamic Banking*, Cheltenham, UK and Northampton, MA, USA: Edward Elgar Publishing, 155–67.

Kant, I. (1940), *Fundamental Principles of the Metaphysics of Morals*, ed. T.K. Abbott, London: Longmans Green.

Karsten, I. (1982), 'Islam and Financial Intermediation', *IMF Staff Papers*, **29** (1), 108–42.

Kaufman, Eric (2010), *Shall the Religious Inherit the Earth? Demography and Politics in the Twenty-First Century*, London: Profile Books.

Kerridge, Eric (2002), *Usury, Interest and the Reformation*, Aldershot: Ashgate.

Keynes, John Maynard (1930), *Economic Possibilities for our Grandchildren*, http://www.econ.yale.edu/smith/econ116a/keynes1.pdf, accessed 22 February 2018.

Khan, M.A. (1994), *Rural Development Through Islamic Banks*, Leicester: Islamic Foundation.

Khan, M.S. and A. Mirakhor (1992), 'Islamic Banking', in P. Newman, M. Milgate and J. Eatwell (eds), *New Palgrave Dictionary of Money and Finance*, Vol. 2, London: Macmillan, 531–3.

Khan, W.M. (1985), *Towards an Interest-Free Islamic Economic System*, Leicester: Islamic Foundation.

Khan, W.M. (1987), 'Towards an Interest-Free Islamic Economic System', in M.S. Khan and A. Mirakhor (eds), *Theoretical Studies in Islamic Banking and Finance*, Houston, TX: Institute for Research and Islamic Studies.

Kindleberger, Charles (1984), *A Financial History of Western Europe*, London, UK and Boston, MA, USA: Allen & Unwin.

King, Ian (2009), '351 words lit the fuse of the financial crisis', *The Times*, reprinted in *The Australian*, 4 March, 28.

King, Mervyn (2010), 'Banking: From Bagehot to Basel, and Back Again', Buttonwood Gathering, New York City, 25 October.

Kodres, Laura and Aditya Narain (2012), 'Fixing the System', *Finance and Development*, **49** (2), 14–16.

Kohn, M. (1999), 'Merchant Banking in the Medieval and Early Modern Economy', Working Paper No. 99-05, Department of Economics, Dartmouth College, Hanover, NH.

Krauss, S.E., A. Hamzah and F. Idris (2007), 'Adaption of a Muslim religiosity scale for use with four different faith communities in Malaysia', https://www.researchgate.net/publication/224910957_Adaption_of_a_Muslim_religiosity_scale_for_use_with_four_different_faith_communities_in_Malaysia, accessed 15 January 2017.

Kulikovsky, A. (2007), 'Justice and the Bible', Paper presented at Summit Australia Conference, http://hermeneutics.kulikovskyonline.net/hermeneutics/JusticeAndBible.pdf.

Kuran, Timur (1997), 'The Genesis of Islamic Economics: A Chapter in the Politics of Muslim Identity', *Social Research*, **64** (1), 301–38.

Kuran, Timur (2001), 'The Provision of Public Goods under Islamic Law: Origins, Impact, and Limitations of the Waqf System', *Law and Society Review*, **35**, 841–97.

Kuran, Timur (2002), 'The Islamic Commercial Crisis: Institutional Roots of Economic Underdevelopment in the Middle East', Research Paper No. C01-12, University of Southern California, Center for Law, Economics and Organization, Los Angeles, CA.

Kuran, Timur (2003), 'The Islamic Commercial Crisis: Institutional

Roots of Economic Underdevelopment in the Middle East', *Journal of Economic History*, **63** (2), 414–46.

Kuran, Timur (2005), 'The Absence of the Corporation in Islamic Law: Origins and Persistence', *American Journal of Comparative Law*, **53** (4), 785–834.

Kuran, Timur (2011), *The Long Divergence: How Islamic Law Held Back the Middle East*, Princeton, NJ: Princeton University Press.

Lagarde, Christine (2016), 'Decisive Action to Secure Durable Growth', Lecture hosted by the Bundesbank and Goethe University, Frankfurt, 5 April, https://www.imf.org/ external/np/speeches/2016/040516.htm, accessed 3 December 2016.

Lal, Deepak (1999), *Unintended Consequences*, Cambridge, MA: MIT Press.

Langholm, O. (1984), *The Aristotelian Analysis of Usury*, Bergen: Bergen Universitetsforiaget; distributed in the USA by Columbia University Press, New York.

Lara, G.Y. (2002), 'Institutions for Contract Enforcement and Risk-sharing: from Debt to Equity in Late Medieval Venice', *European Review of Economic History*, **6** (2), 257–62.

Le Goff, Jacques (1979), 'The Usurer and Purgatory', *The Dawn of Modern Banking*, Los Angeles: Center for Medieval and Renaissance Studies, University of California, 25–52.

Le Goff, Jacques (1984), *The Birth of Purgatory*, trans. A. Goldhammer, Chicago, IL: University of Chicago Press.

Levine, Aaron (1987), *Economics and Jewish Law: Halakhic Perspective*, Hoboken, NJ: Ktav and Yeshiva University Press.

Levine, Aaron (ed.) (2010a), *Oxford Handbook of Judaism and Economics*, Oxford, UK and New York, USA: Oxford University Press.

Levine, Aaron (2010b), 'Introduction', in Aaron Levine (ed.), *The Oxford Handbook of Judaism and Economics*, Oxford, UK and New York, USA: Oxford University Press, 3–24.

Levine, Aaron (2010c), 'The Global Recession of 2007–2009: The Moral Factor and Jewish Law', in Aaron Levine (ed.), *The Oxford Handbook of Judaism and Economics*, Oxford, UK and New York, USA: Oxford University Press, 404–28.

Lewis, A. (1991), *Law of Banking Services*, Wirral: Tudor Business Publishing.

Lewis, C.S. (1947), *The Abolition of Man*, New York: Macmillan.

Lewis, M.K. (1992), 'Modern Banking in Theory and Practice', *Revue Economiqué*, **43** (2), 203–77.

Lewis, M.K. (1994), 'Banking on Real Estate', in D.E. Fair and R. Raymond (eds), *The Competitiveness of Financial Institutions and*

Centres in Europe, on behalf of the Société Universitaire Européenne de Recherches Financières, Dordrecht: Kluwer Academic Press, 47–71.

Lewis, M.K. (1999a), 'The Cross and The Crescent: Comparing Islamic and Christian Attitudes to Usury', *IQTISAD, Journal of Islamic Economics*, **1** (1), 1–23.

Lewis, M.K. (1999b), 'Corporate Governance and Corporate Financing in Different Cultures', in Z. Sevic (ed.), *Banking Reform in South East European Transitional Economies*, London: Balkan Centre for Public Policy and Related Studies, Humanities Research Centre, University of Greenwich, 33–66.

Lewis, M.K. (2007), 'Comparing Islamic and Christian Attitudes to Usury', in M. Kabir Hassan and M.K. Lewis (eds), *Handbook of Islamic Banking*, Cheltenham UK and Northampton, MA, USA: Edward Elgar Publishing, 64–81.

Lewis, M.K. (2008), 'In what Ways does Islamic Banking Differ from Conventional Finance?', *Journal of Islamic Economics, Banking and Finance*, **4** (3), 9–24.

Lewis, M.K. (2009), 'The Origins of the Sub-prime Crisis: Inappropriate Policies, Regulations, or Both?', *Accounting Forum*, **33** (2), 114–26.

Lewis, M.K. (2010), 'An Islamic Economic Perspective on the Global Financial Crisis', in Steve Kates (ed.), *Macroeconomic Economic Theory and its Failings: Alternative Perspectives on the Global Financial Crisis*, Cheltenham, UK and Northampton, MA, USA: Edward Elgar Publishing, 159–83.

Lewis, M.K. (2011a), 'Ethical Principles in Islamic Business and Banking Transactions', in Mohamed Ariff and Munawar Iqbal (eds), *The Foundations of Islamic Banking: Theory, Practice and Education*, Cheltenham UK and Northampton, MA, USA: Edward Elgar Publishing, 39–50.

Lewis, M.K. (2011b), 'Monetary Policies during the Financial Crisis: An Appraisal', in Steve Kates (ed.), *The Global Financial Crisis: What Have We Learnt?*, Cheltenham, UK and Northampton, MA, USA: Edward Elgar Publishing, 138–53.

Lewis, M.K (2014a), 'A Theoretical Perspective on Islamic Banking and Financial Intermediation', in M.K. Lewis, M. Ariff and M. Shamsher (eds), *Risk and Regulation of Islamic Banking*, Cheltenham, UK and Northampton, MA, USA: Edward Elgar Publishing, 11–42.

Lewis, M.K. (2014b), 'An Islamic Perspective on the Global Financial Crisis and its Aftermath', in M. Kabir Hassan and M.K. Lewis (eds), *Handbook on Islam and Economic Life*, Cheltenham, UK and Northampton, MA, USA: Edward Elgar Publishing, 636–57.

Lewis, M.K. (2015a), 'Models of Islamic Banking: The Role of Debt and Equity Contracts', *Journal of King Abdulaziz University. Islamic Economics*, **28** (1), 163–77.

Lewis, M.K. (2015b), *Understanding Ponzi Schemes: Can Better Financial Regulation Prevent Investors from Being Defrauded?*, Cheltenham, UK and Northampton, MA, USA: Edward Elgar Publishing.

Lewis, M.K. and L.M. Algaoud (2001), *Islamic Banking*, Cheltenham, UK and Northampton, MA, USA: Edward Elgar Publishing.

Lewis, M.K., Mohamed Ariff and Mohamad Shamsher (eds) (2014), *Risk and Regulation of Islamic Banking*, Cheltenham, UK and Northampton, MA, USA: Edward Elgar Publishing.

Lewis, M.K. and K.T. Davis (1987), *Domestic and International Banking*, Oxford: Philip Allan.

Lewis, M.K. and P.D. Mizen (2000), *Monetary Economics*, Oxford: Oxford University Press.

Leys, Simon (1997), *The Analects of Confucius*, translation, New York: W.W. Norton.

Lindholm, C. (1996), *The Islamic Middle East: An Historical Anthropology*, Oxford: Blackwell.

Lister, R.J. (2006), 'The Composition of Interest: The Judaic Prohibition', *Accounting, Business and Financial History*, **16** (1), 121–7.

Litan, Robert (ed.) (2011), *The World in Crisis: Insights from Six Shadow Financial Regulatory Committees From Around the World*, Philadelphia, PA: FIC Press.

Llewellyn, D.T. (1994), *The New Economics of Banking*, Société Universitaire Européenne de Recherches Financières Studies No. 5, Amsterdam: Société Universitaire Européenne de Recherches Financières.

Long, D. Stephen (2010), *Christian Ethics: A Very Short Introduction*, Oxford: Oxford University Press.

Lopez, R.S. (1948), 'Italian Leadership in the Medieval Business World', *Journal of Economic History*, **8** (1), 63–8.

Lopez, R.S. (1979), 'The Dawn of Medieval Banking', *The Dawn of Modern Banking*, Los Angeles, CA: Los Angeles Center for Medieval & Renaissance Studies, University of California, 1–24.

Lopez, R.S. and I.W. Raymond (1955), *Medieval Trade in Mediterranean World*, New York: Columbia University Press.

Luther, Martin (1524 [1915]), *On Trading and Usury*, translation from *Works of Martin Luther*, Philadelphia: A. Holman Company, 1915, Vol. 4.

Lutheran World Federation and the Catholic Church (1999), Joint Declaration on the Doctrine of Justification, http://www.vatican.va/roman_curia/pontifical_councils/chrstuni/documents/rc_pc_chrstuni_d oc31101999_cath-luth-joint-declaration_en.html, accessed 9 September 2017.

MailOnline (2008), 'Pope Brands Global Financial System as "Self-Centred, Short-Sighted and Lacking Concern for the Poor"', http://www.dailymail. co.uk/news/worldnews/article-1093914/Pope-brands-global-financial-self -centred-short-sighted-lacking-concern-poor.html, accessed 21 August 2011.

Maimonides, Moses (1956), *The Guide for the Perplexed*, New York: Dover Publications.

Martin, R. (2002), *Financialization of Daily Life*, Philadelphia, PA: Temple University Press.

Maududi, S. Abul A'ala (1994), *Economic System of Islam*, transl. into English by Riaz Husain, ed. K. Ahmad, 2nd edn, Lahore: Islamic Publications.

Maududi, Sayyid Abu al-A'la (2002), *Rasa'il-o Masa'il*, 4 vols, Lahore: Islamic Publications.

McChesney, R.C. (2004), 'Islamic Philanthropy', in D. Burlingame (ed.), *Philanthropy in America: A Comprehensive Historical Encyclopedia*, Santa Barbara, CA: ABC-CLIO.

McCleary, R.M. (2011), *The Oxford Handbook of The Economics of Religion*, Oxford: Oxford University Press.

McCleary, R.M. and R.J. Barro (2006), 'Religion and Economy', *Journal of Economic Perspectives*, **20** (2), 49–72.

McDonald, L.G. and P. Robinson (2009), *A Colossal Failure of Common Sense*, New York: Crown Business.

McMillen, Michael J.T. (2007), 'Islamic Project Finance', in M. Kabir Hassan and M.K. Lewis (eds), *The Handbook of Islamic Banking*, Cheltenham, UK and Northampton, MA, USA: Edward Elgar Publishing, 200–239.

Mews, C. and A. Walsh (2011), 'Usury and its Critics: From the Middle Ages to Modernity', in M. Ariff and M. Iqbal (eds), *The Foundations of Islamic Banking: Theory, Practice and Education*, Cheltenham, UK and Northampton, MA, USA: Edward Elgar Publishing, 211–21.

Mirrlees, J. (1974), 'Notes on Welfare Economies, Information, and Uncertainty', in M.S. Balch, D.L. McFadden and S.Y. Wu (eds), *Contributions to Economic Analysis*, Amsterdam: North-Holland, https:// www.researchgate.net/publication/ 246981257_Notes_on_Welfare_Eco- nomics_Information_and_Uncertainty, accessed 2 September 2017.

Mirrlees, J. (1976), 'The Optimal Structure of Incentives and Authority within an Organisation', *Bell Journal of Economics*, **7** (1), 105–31.

Modigliani, F. and M.H. Miller (1958), 'The Cost of Capital, Corporation Finance and the Theory of Investment', *American Economic Review*, **48** (3), 261–97.

Moynihan, Robert (2009), 'Vatican Perspective: The Global Financial Crisis. Papal Encyclical Coming', http://www.globalresearch.ca/PrintArticle.php?articleId=12527, accessed 21 August 2011.

Muhamed, Nurul Aini bt and M.K. Lewis (2014), 'Globalizing Islamic Investment Funds', in M. Kabir Hassan and M.K. Lewis (eds), *Handbook on Islam and Economic Life*, Cheltenham, UK and Northampton, MA, USA: Edward Elgar Publishing, 370–93.

Muller, Jerry Z. (2010), *Capitalism and the Jews*, Princeton, NJ: Princeton University Press.

Munn, G.G., F.L. Garcia and C.J. Woelfel (1991), *Encyclopedia of Banking and Finance*, 9th edn, London: McGraw-Hill.

Munro, J.H. (2003), 'The Medieval Origins of the Financial Revolution: Usury, Rentes, and Negotiability', *The International History Review*, **25** (3), 505–62.

Munro, J.H. (2006), 'Entrepreneurship in Early-Modern Europe (1450–1750): An Exploration of Some Unfashionable Themes in Economic History', Working Paper No. 30, online version, http://repec.economics.utoronto.ca/files/tecipa-257-1.pdf, accessed 15 January 2018.

Mustafa, M.O.A., M.H.S. Mohamad and M.A. Addan (2013), 'Antecedents of *Zakat* Payers' Trust in an Emerging *Zakat* Sector: An Exploratory Study', *Journal of Islamic Accounting and Business Research*, **4** (1), 4–25.

Naqvi, Sayed Nawab Haider (1994), *Islam, Economics and Society*, London: Kegan Paul International.

Nelson, Benjamin (1949), *The Idea of Usury: From Tribal Brotherhood to Universal Otherhood*, Princeton, NJ: Princeton University Press.

Neusner, Jacob (1990a), *The Economics of the Mishnah*, Chicago, IL: University of Chicago Press.

Neusner, Jacob (trans.) (1990b), *The Talmud of Babylonia: An American Translation*, Atlanta, GA: Scholar's Press.

Nienhaus, Volker (2014), 'Religion and Development', in M. Kabir Hassan and M.K. Lewis (eds), *Handbook on Islam and Economic Life*, Cheltenham, UK and Northampton, MA, USA: Edward Elgar Publishing, 567–92.

Noonan, John T., Jr (1957), *The Scholastic Analysis of Usury*, Cambridge, MA: Harvard University Press.

Noonan, John T., Jr (1993), 'Development in Moral Doctrine', *Theological Studies*, **54** (4), 662–77.

Norberg, J. (2011), 'The Binge to End Them All', *Weekend Australian*, 1–2 January, 16.

Normani, F. and A. Rehnema (1995), *Islamic Economic Systems*, Malaysia: S. Abdul Majeed & Co.

Novak, Michael (1982), *The Spirit of Democratic Capitalism*, Lanham, MD, USA: Madison Books; and London, UK: Institute of Economic Affairs.

Nyazee, Imran Ahsan Khan (1994), *Theories of Islamic Law*, Islamabad: International Institute of Islamic Thought and Islamic Research Institute.

Nyberg, Lars, M. Persson and M.W. Johansson (2008), 'The Financial Market Turmoil – Causes and Consequences', *Sveriges Riksbank Economic Review*, **1**, 38–48.

Nyazee, Imran Ahsan Khan (1995), *The Concept of Riba and Islamic Banking*, Islamabad: Niazi Publishing House.

Nyazee, Imran Ahsan Khan (1999), *Islamic Law of Business Organisation: Partnerships*, New Delhi: Kitab Bhamn.

Obaidullah, Mohammed (2007), 'Securitization in Islam', in M. Kabir Hassan and M.K. Lewis (eds), *The Handbook of Islamic Banking*, Cheltenham, UK and Northampton, MA, USA: Edward Elgar Publishing, 191–9.

Obstfeld, M. (2011), 'Gross Financial Flows, Global Imbalances, and Crises', Twelfth L.K. Jha Memorial Lecture, Reserve Bank of India, Mumbai, 13 December.

Ohrenstein, R.A. (1970), 'Economic Self Interest and Social Progress in *Talmudic* Literature: A Further Study of Ancient Economic Thought and its Modern Significance', *American Journal of Economics and Sociology*, **29** (1), 59–70.

Pamuk, Sevket (2004), 'The Evaluation of Financial Institutions in the Ottoman Empire, 1600–1914', *Financial History Review*, **11** (1), 7–32.

Paris, D. (1998), 'An Economic look at the Old Testament', in S.T. Lowry and B. Gorden (eds), *Ancient and Medieval Economic Ideas and Concept of Social Justice*, Leiden: Brill, 39–104.

Patinkin, D. (1968), 'Interest', in David I. Stills (ed.), *International Encyclopedia of the Social Sciences*, Vol. VII, London: Macmillan, 471–85.

Pava, M.L. (1998), 'The Substance of Jewish Business Ethics', *Journal of Business Ethics*, **17** (6), 603–17.

Pew Research Center (2016), '5 facts about the Muslim population in Europe', http://www.pewresearch.org/fact-tank/2016/07/19/5-facts-about-the-muslim-population-in-europe/, 19 July, accessed 17 November 2017.

Pinker, S. (2018), *Enlightenment Now: The Case for Reason, Science, Humanism, and Progress*, New York: Viking.

Pipes, Richard (1997), *Russia under the Old Regime*, London: Penguin.

Poliakov, Léon (1977), *Jewish Bankers and the Holy See: From the Thirteenth to the Seventeenth Century*, London: Routledge & Kegan Paul.

Presley, John and John Sessions (1994), 'Islamic Economics: The Emergence of a New Paradigm', *Economic Journal*, **104** (May), 584–96.

Pryor, John H. (1977), 'The Origins of the Commenda Contract', *Speculu*, **52** (1), 5–37.

Rabinovich, L. (1993), 'Introduction to Secured Transactions in *Halakha* and Common Law', *Tradition*, **27** (3), 36–50.

Radzi, Rafisah Mat and M.K. Lewis (2015), 'Religion and the Clash of "Ideals" and "Realities" in Business: The Case of Islamic Bonds (*Sukuk*)', *Thunderbird International Business Review*, **57** (4), 295–310.

Rae, N.D. (1997), 'The Medieval Islamic System of Credit and Banking: Legal and Historical Consideration', *Arab Law Quarterly*, **12** (1), 43–90.

Rahman, Fazlur G. (1958), 'A Study of Commercial Interest in Islam', *Islamic Thought*, **5** (4/5), 24–46.

Rahman, Fazlur G. (1964), 'Riba and Interest', *Islamic Studies*, **3** (1), 1–43.

Rahman, Y.A. (1994), *Interest Free Islamic Banking*, Kuala Lumpur: Al-Hilal Publishing.

Rahman, Y.A. (1999), 'Islamic Instruments for Managing Liquidity', *International Journal of Islamic Financial Services*, **1** (April–June), 21–7.

Rainey, M. and O. Salah (2011), 'Why Does Categorisation of *Sukuk* Structures Matter?', *ISRA International Journal of Islamic Finance*, **3** (20), 113–31.

Rangaswami, K. (1927), *Aspects of Ancient Indian Economic Thought*, Mylapore: Madras Law Journal Press.

Rapp, D. (2010), 'The Employee Free Choice Act, Unions and Unionizing in Jewish Law', in A. Levine (ed.), *The Oxford Handbook of Judaism and Economics*, New York: Oxford University Press, 429–44.

Rayner, S.E. (1991), *The Theory of Contracts in Islamic Law*, London: Graham & Trotman.

Razi, Muhammad Fakr al-Din (1872 [1938]), *Mafatih al-Ghayb*, known as *al-Tafsir al-Kabir*, Bulaq Cairo: Dar Ibya al-Kutub al-Bahiyya.

Reinhart, C.M. and K.S. Rogoff (2009), *This Time is Different: Eight Centuries of Financial Folly*, Princeton, NJ: Princeton University Press.

Reinhart, C.M. and K.S. Rogoff (2011), 'A Decade of Debt', NBER Working Paper Series, Working Paper 16827, http://www.nber.org/papers/w16827.pdf?new _window=1, accessed 12 February 2018.

Rida, Muhammad Rashid (1959), *Al-Riba wa al-Mu'amalat fi al-Islam*, Cairo: Maktabat al-Qahira.

Rippin, A. (1993), *Muslims: Their Religious Beliefs and Practices. Volume 2: The Contemporary Period*, London: Routledge.

Rivlin, Yoef (2010), 'Economics and Law as Reflected in Hebrew Contracts', in Aaron Levine (ed.), *The Oxford Handbook of Judaism and Economics*, New York: Oxford University Press, 584–604.

Robinson, Joan (1962), *Economic Philosophy*, Harmondsworth: Penguin Books.

Roll, Sir Eric (1953), *A History of Economic Thought*, London: George Allen & Unwin.

Ross, S. (1973), 'The Economic Theory of Agency: The Principal's Problem', *American Economic Review*, **63** (2), May, 134–9.

Rubin, Jared (2014), 'Islamic Institutions and Underdevelopment', in M. Kabir Hassan and M.K. Lewis (eds), *Handbook on Islam and Economic Life*, Cheltenham, UK and Northampton, MA, USA: Edward Elgar Publishing, 593–609.

Russell, Bertrand (1923 [1959]), *The Prospects of Industrial Civilization*, London: George Allen & Unwin.

Russell, Bertrand (1946), *History of Western Philosophy*, London: George Allen & Unwin.

Saeed, A. (1996), *Islamic Banking and Interest*, Leiden: E.J. Brill.

Sahnun, 'Abd al-Salam ibn Sa'id ibn Habib al-Tanukhi (1905), *Al-Mudawwanah al-Kubra*, Cairo: Matba'at al-Sa'adah.

Salin, E. (1948), 'Usury', in *Encyclopaedia of the Social Sciences*, Vol. 15, London: Macmillan.

Salt, Bernard (2016), 'Cashing In on Rise of China's Big Cities', *Australian*, 21 April, 28.

Sapori, A. (1948), 'Review Article of *Italian Leadership in the Medieval Business World*, by Robert Lopez', *Journal of Economic History*, **8** (1), 63–8.

Schacht, J. (1964), *An Introduction to Islamic Law*, Oxford: Oxford University Press.

Securities Commission Malaysia (2013), '2013 List of Shariah-Compliant Securities by SC's Shariah Advisory Council', Kuala Lumpur: Securities Commission.

Shah, Syed Yaqub (1967), *Chand Mu'ashi Masa'il aur Islam* (Islam and some Economic Problems), Lahore: Idara Thaqafat-e-Islamia.

Shaukat, M. (2010), 'Sale of Goods and Sale of Debt: A Comparative Analysis', INCEIF Working Paper Series, http://arzim.blogspot.com.au/2010/01/sale-of-goods-and-sale-of-debts.html, accessed 5 January 2018.

Shin, H.S. (2011), 'Global Banking Glut and Loan Risk Premium', Paper presented at 12th Jacques Polak Annual Research Conference, IMF Washington, 10–11 November.

Shirazi, Nasim Shah (1996), *System of Zakat in Pakistan*, Islamabad: International Institute of Islamic Economics.

Siddiqi, Muhammad Nejatullah (1996), *Role of the State in the Economy: An Islamic Perspective*, Leicester: Islamic Foundation.

Siddiqui, Shamin A. (2014), '*Riba*, Time Value of Money and Discounting', in M. Kabir Hassan and M.K. Lewis (eds), *Handbook on Islam and Economic Life*, Cheltenham, UK and Northampton, MA, USA: Edward Elgar Publishing, 113–31.

Smith, Adam (1776 [1937]), *The Wealth of Nations*, Reprint, Edwin Cannan (ed.), New York: Modern Library.

Solomon, Norman (2014), *Judaism: A Very Short Introduction*, Oxford: Oxford University Press.

Sombart, Werner (1911 [1951]), *The Jews and Modern Capitalism*, transl. M. Epstein, Glencoe, IL: Free Press.

Spiegel, H.W. (1992), 'Usury', in P. Newman, M. Milgate and J. Eatwell (eds), *The New Palgrave Dictionary of Money and Finance*, Vol. 3, London: Macmillan, 743–5.

Stigler, G.J. (1964 [1975]), 'Public Regulation of the Securities Markets', *Journal of Business*, **37** (March), 117–32; reprinted in G.J. Stigler, *The Citizen and the State: Essays on Regulation*, Chicago, IL: University of Chicago Press.

Stigler, G.J. (1971), 'The Theory of Economic Regulation', *Bell Journal of Economics and Management*, **2** (1), 1–21.

Stigler, G.J. and C. Friedland (1962 [1975]), 'What can Regulators Regulate? The Case of Electricity', *Journal of Law and Economics*, October; reprinted in G.J. Stigler, *The Citizen and the State: Essays on Regulation*, Chicago, IL: University of Chicago Press.

Stiglitz, J.E. (1974), 'Risk Sharing and Incentives in Sharecropping', *Review of Economic Studies*, **61**, 219–55.

Stiglitz, J.E. (1975), 'Incentives, Risk and Information: Notes Towards a Theory of Hierarchy', *Bell Journal of Economics*, **6** (2), 552–79.

Stockhammer, E. (2004), 'Financialization and the Slowdown of Accumulation', *Cambridge Journal of Economics*, **28** (5), 719–41.

Summers, Lawrence H. (2016), 'The Age of Secular Stagnation: What It Is and What to Do About It', *Foreign Affairs*, **95** (2), https://www.foreignaffairs.com/articles/united-states/2016-02-15/age-secular-stagnation, accessed 20 April 2016.

Swidler, L.J. (1976), *Women in Judaism: The Status of Women in Formative Judaism*, Metuchen, NJ: Scarecrow Press.

Tag El-Din, S.I. and N.I. Abdullah (2007), 'Issues of Implementing Islamic Hire-Purchase in Dual Banking System: Malaysian Experience', *Thunderbird International Business Review*, **49** (2), 225–49.

Tahir, Sayyid (1999), *IIE's Blueprint of Islamic Financial System including*

Strategy for Elimination of Riba, Islamabad: International Institute of Islamic Economics.

Tamari, Meir (1987), *With All Your Possessions: Jewish Ethics and Economic Life*, New York: Free Press, Macmillan.

Tawney, R.H. (1926), *Religion and the Rise of Capitalism*, London, UK and New York, USA: Harcourt Brace.

Taylor, Arthur J. (1972), *Laissez-faire and State Intervention in Nineteenth Century Britain*, Economic History Society, London: Macmillan.

Taylor, Bryan (2012), 'Paying off Government Debt: Two Centuries of Global Experience', *Global Financial Data*, accessed 23 November 2012. http://www.globalfinancialdata.com/news/articles/government_debt.pdf.

Taylor, Charles (1989), *Sources of the Self: The Making of the Modern Identity*, Cambridge, MA: Harvard University Press.

Taylor, T.W. and J.W. Evans (1987), 'Islamic Banking and the Prohibition of Usury in Western Economic Thought', *National Westminster Bank Quarterly Review*, November, 15–27.

Thomson, J.A.K. (1953), *The Ethics of Aristotle*, Harmondsworth: Penguin.

Tinker, Tony (2004), 'The Enlightenment and its Discontents: Antinomies of Christianity, Islam and the Calculative Sciences', *Accounting, Auditing and Accountability Journal*, **17** (3), 442–75.

Trever, Albert (1916), *Greek Economic Thought*, Chicago, IL: University of Chicago Press.

Tully, Shawn (2008), 'What's Wrong with Wall Street – and How to Fix It', *Fortune*, **157** (7), 42–6.

Udovitch, A.L. (1962), 'At the Origins of the Western Commenda: Islam, Israel, Byzantium?', *Speculum*, **37** (2), 198–207.

Udovitch, A.L. (1970), 'Theory and Practice of Islamic Law: Some Evidence from the Geniza', *Studia Islamica*, **32**, 289–303.

Udovitch, A.L. (1975), 'Reflections on the Institutions of Credits and Banking in the Medieval Islamic Near East', *Studia Islamica*, **41**, 5–21.

Usher, A.P. (1943), *The Early History of Deposit Banking in Mediterranean Europe*, Vol. 1, Cambridge, MA: Harvard University Press.

Usmani, I.A (2002), *Meezan Bank's Guide to Islamic Banking*, Karachi: Darul Ishaat, Urdu Bazar.

Usmani, Maulana Taqi (2001), 'Principles of Shari'ah Governing Islamic Investment Funds', http://www.witness-pioneer.org/vil/Articles/economics/principles_of_shariah.htm, accessed 10 May 2009.

Van Biema, David (2008), 'The Financial Crisis: What Would the Talmud Do?', http://www.cosy.org.au/indarch.php?article=214, accessed 27 April 2011.

Veatch, Henry B. (1971), *For an Ontology of Morals: A Critique of Contemporary Ethical Theory*, Evanston, IL: Northwestern University Press.

Visser, W.A.M. and A. McIntosh (1998), 'A Short Review of the Historical Critique of Usury', *Accounting, Business and Financial History*, **8** (2), 175–89.

Wall Street Journal Custom Studios (2016), 'Smaller Cities Offer an Easier Gateway into Middle Kingdom', produced in association with ANZ Institutional Bank, *Australian*, 15 December, 29.

Wallis, J. (1990), *The Soul of Politics: Beyond 'Religious Right' and 'Secular Left*, London: Harcourt Brace & Company.

Watt, W.M. (1996), *A Short History of Islam*, Oxford: One World.

Warde, Ibrahim (2000), *Islamic Finance in the Global Economy*, Edinburgh: Edinburgh University Press.

Weber, A.A. (2008), 'Financial Market Stability', *Review, Financial Markets Group Research Centre*, 1–2.

Weber, Max (1904–05 [1930]), *Die protestantische Ethik und der Geist des Kapitalismus*, In *Gesammelte Aufsäzte zur Religionssoziologic*, I. Originally appeared (1904–1905) in *Archiv für Sozialwissenschaft und Sozialpolitik*, xx–xxi. English transl. Talcott Parsons, Foreword by R.H. Tawney, *The Protestant Ethic and the Spirit of Capitalism*, London: Collins.

Wessel, David (2008), 'Big Banks Model is Broken and Must be Fixed in a Hurry', *Australian*, 11 January, 22.

Williamson, S.D. (1987 [1995]), 'Recent Developments in Modeling Financial Intermediation', *Federal Reserve Bank of Minneapolis Quarterly Review*, Summer, 19–29; reprinted in M.K. Lewis (ed.) (1995), *Financial Intermediaries*, The International Library of Critical Writings in Economics, 43, Aldershot, UK and Brookfield, USA: Edward Elgar Publishing, 286–96.

Wilson, Rodney (1983), *Banking and Finance in the Arab Middle East*, London: Macmillan.

Wilson, Rodney (1997), *Economics, Ethics and Religion: Jewish, Christian and Muslim Economic Thought*, New York: New York University Press.

Wilson, Rodney (2008), 'Islamic Economics and Finance', *World Economics*, **9** (1), 177–95.

Wilson, Rodney (2014), 'Economics and Morality from an Islamic Perspective', in M. Kabir Hassan and M.K. Lewis (eds), *Handbook on Islam and Economic Life*, Cheltenham, UK and Northampton, MA, USA: Edward Elgar Publishing, 268–82.

Wogman, J. Philip (1986), *Economics and Ethics: A Christian Enquiry*, London: SCM Press.

Wong, P. (2016), 'China's Belt and Road is Here for the Long Haul', *Australian*, 29 December, 19.

Woodhead, Linda (2014), *Christianity: A Very Short Introduction*, Oxford: Oxford University Press.

Wright, C.J.H. (1990), *God's People in God's Land*, Grand Rapids, MI: Eerdmans.

Yasin, Norhashimah Mohd. (1997), 'Shariah Contracts Used by Islamic Banks', *Al-Nahdah*, **17**, 5–11.

Yasseri, A. (1999), 'The Experience of the Islamic Republic of Iran in Musharakah Financing', *Arab Law Quarterly*, **14** (3), 231–44.

Zaman, Asad (2014), 'Islam versus Economics', in M. Kabir Hassan and M.K. Lewis (eds), *Handbook on Islam and Economic Life*, Cheltenham UK and Northampton, MA, USA: Edward Elgar Publishing, 45–70.

Zarqa, Muhammad Anas (1995), 'Islamic Distributive Schemes', in IDB (ed.), *Readings in Public Finance in Islam*, Jeddah: Islamic Research and Training Institute, IDB, 181–227.

Index